THE KILLING GAME

THE KILLING GAME

MARTYRDOM, MURDER AND THE LURE OF ISIS

MARK BOURRIE

JAICO PUBLISHING HOUSE

Ahmedabad Bangalore Bhopal Bhubaneswar Chennai
Delhi Hyderabad Kolkata Lucknow Mumbai

Published by Jaico Publishing House
A-2 Jash Chambers, 7-A Sir Phirozshah Mehta Road
Fort, Mumbai - 400 001
jaicopub@jaicobooks.com
www.jaicobooks.com

Published in arrangement with
HarperCollins*PublishersLtd*
Toronto, Canada

To be sold only in India, Bangladesh, Bhutan,
Pakistan, Nepal, Sri Lanka and the Maldives.

THE KILLING GAME
ISBN 978-81-8495-903-1

First Jaico Impression: 2016

Printed by
Replika Press Pvt. Ltd.

Hence that chip on your shoulder. And since your first thought about me ran to "orphan," that's what I'd say you are. Oh, you are? I like this poker thing. And that makes perfect sense! Since MI6 looks for maladjusted young men, who give little thought to sacrificing others in order to protect queen and country.

—Vesper Lynd, *Casino Royale* (film)

CONTENTS

A Note on Terminology

There's been some controversy over the name of the organization that is trying to establish a caliphate in northern Syria and Iraq. Members of the organization, and much of the Western media, prefer "Islamic State." Several other countries, however, claim to be Islamic states or Islamic republics. To suggest that this is *the* Islamic state is to make an assumption that I would not want to have to defend. "Islamic State of Iraq and the Levant" seems not only dated but also, in a geographic sense, inaccurate, since much of the actual Levant region of the eastern Mediterranean is, so far, out of its grasp. "ISIS" seems to work best, since it captures both "Islamic State in Iraq and Syria" and "Islamic State in Syria and el-Sham." I will call the organization ISIS in this book, unless another term is used in a quote.

Terrorism is a word that means many things to many people. I see it as a form of warfare. I try to use the term without judging the merits of the cause that uses it. I follow this definition crafted by Paul Wilkinson, an expert in the field:

It is premeditated and designed to create a climate of extreme fear;
It is directed at a wider target than the immediate victims;

> *It inherently involves attacks on random or symbolic targets, including civilians;*
>
> *It is considered by the society in which it occurs as "extra normal," in the literal sense that it violates the norms regulating disputes, protests and dissent;*
>
> *It is used primarily, though not exclusively, to influence the political behaviour of governments, communities or specific social groups.*[1]

"Jihadi terrorism" and "jihad" are, admittedly, contentious words. For millions of Muslims, jihad is a personal struggle to fulfill themselves spiritually through actions that cause no harm to others. However, in this book the term is used in its second meaning, one that is used by ISIS and other Muslim fighters, as a descriptor for violence motivated by extreme interpretations of Islam. It does not revolve around any single conflict or campaign.[2]

Caliphate is a regime that claims its leader is the successor to the Prophet Mohammed and the spiritual leader of all Islam, with the responsibility to push the frontiers of Islam. Historically, caliphates involved governance under Islamic law, with the leadership elected according to Sunni practice and selected from a group of imams under Shia traditions. The rulers of the Ottoman (Turkish) Empire claimed the title of caliph until they were deposed after the First World War.[3]

CHAPTER 1

A Canadian Boy in Syria

Kill one—frighten ten thousands.
—Sun Tzu[1]

THE CAREFULLY SHOT VIDEO STARTS WITH A WIRY young man with long, stringy hair and a thin beard, clad in a loose black robe, walking along the edge of a ruin somewhere in the Middle East. He's wearing a brown ammunition vest and carrying an AK-47. An ISIS logo flashes, then, after a short invocation to Allah, John Maguire—former Canadian college boy, former punk rock musician—begins to speak to the folks back home.

> *O people of Canada. You are said to be an educated people, so what is preventing you from being able to put two and two together and understanding that operations such as that of brother Ahmad Rouleau (Martin Couture-Rouleau), of Montreal, and the storming of Parliament Hill in Ottawa are carried out in direct response to your participation in the coalition of nations waging war against the Muslim people?*
>
> *Your leaders, those men and women that you have elected to represent yourselves in the running of your country's affairs, have gone far out*

of their way to involve themselves in the global war against the Islamic State. Your representatives and your leaders have voluntarily chosen to join the coalition of countries waging war against the Muslims. So it should not surprise you when operations by the Muslims are executed where it hurts you the most—on your very own soil—in retaliation to your unprovoked acts of aggression towards our people.

You have absolutely no right to live in a state of safety and security when your country is carrying out atrocities on our people. The more bombs you drop on our people, the more Muslims will realize and understand that today waging jihad against the West and its allies around the world is beyond a shadow of a doubt a religious obligation binding upon every Muslim.

The video is a well-made digital production. It's edited to show different, and very flattering, angles of John Maguire's face. The background was chosen carefully. There's a bullet-pocked building with an upper floor blown apart—perhaps by an air strike by Canadian pilots or those of one of the other Western nations that bombs ISIS. A big black ISIS flag flutters in front of a lovely, undamaged mosque.

Maguire's threats continue:

And the more Muslims living amongst you whom you oppress by imprisoning them, and spying on them and preventing them from migrating to the Islamic State, the more they will be inspired to punish your citizens with the likes of that which you are inflicting on our citizens. Your people will be indiscriminately targeted, as you indiscriminately target our people. I warn you of punishment in this life by the mujahedeen and I would also like to warn you of a greater punishment. And that is the eternal punishment of hellfire promised for those who die having not submitted as Muslims to the one true God of all that exists.

Then Maguire tries to connect with Canadians and explain how a fairly ordinary kid from a small Ontario town ended up in front of an ISIS propaganda crew without a knife to his throat. At the same time, he tries to paint himself as a healthy young man who made a free, intelligent choice, rather than one of the duped emotional cripples that Western media says join ISIS:

> *I was one of you. I was a typical Canadian. I grew up on the hockey rink and spent my teenage years on stage playing guitar.*
>
> *I had no criminal record. I was a bright student and maintained a strong GPA in university. So how could one of your people end up in my place? And why is it that your own people are the ones turning against you at home? The answer is that we have accepted the true call of the prophets and the messengers of God.*

After a short lecture on theology, an ISIS logo flashes briefly, then Maguire is back on, flashing from profile to face-on with the camera. He turns his attention to Canada's Islamic minority, who must put up with the horrors committed in the name of their religion while at the same time trying to make a new start in an unfamiliar land.

> *To the Muslims living in Canada, I say to you, "How can you remain living among the disbelievers, under their unjust, man-made laws, which are slowly but surely eliminating the rights of the Muslims, especially now that the caliphate has been established? And furthermore, how can you stand to live amongst them peacefully, when their leaders, who represent the masses, are waging a crusade against your Muslim brothers and sisters at this very moment? According to Islamic principles, you are living in a land of war, a land that is relentlessly oppressing and constantly in support of the oppression of Muslims all around the world. A Muslim has*

> *absolutely no place living in a land such as Canada, or America or Europe today, except to carry out his duty of fighting in Allah's cause. Do not be deceived by Western leaders telling you that they have nothing against Islam and Muslims and that they are only fighting terrorism. The results of their carpet bomb air strikes speak for themselves. They are attacking the Muslim people as a whole. Have you forgotten that Allah tells us how the disbelievers will act towards the believers?"*

After a while, Maguire says Muslims in the West have a clear choice.

> Hijrah *[migration] or jihad. You either pack your bags or you prepare your explosive devices. You either purchase your airline ticket or you sharpen your knife. You either come to the Islamic State and live under the laws of Allah or follow the example of Brother Ahmad Rouleau and do not fear the blame of the blamers.*

The video ends with an ISIS flag superimposed over a soft-focus shot of John Maguire walking away. It's a professional piece of propaganda and advertising. A Canadian musician would have to pay serious money for a six-minute video shot and edited with that level of quality.

Canadian politicians and media took the video very seriously. It was posted to YouTube on December 8, 2014, just a few weeks after Martin Couture-Rouleau, another Muslim convert, killed a soldier walking on a road near Montreal. At the same time, another young man who had rediscovered the Muslim faith of his childhood gunned down Nathan Cirillo, an unarmed sentry at the National War Memorial. Then he hijacked a car and stormed into the Centre Block of the Parliament Buildings.

Some Muslims in Canada were not as impressed by Maguire's

video. Muhammad Robert Heft, a Toronto Muslim leader and outspoken critic of extremism, said he doubted the YouTube clip would inspire more attacks in Canada or more John Maguires to join ISIS. "[Maguire is] so delusional and arrogant that he actually thinks his message is resonating with Muslims in Canada and worldwide. It probably hurts their cause more than it helps their cause because it shows how uneducated they are. He says he is supporting Syrians, but isn't he killing the Syrians if they don't submit to his group? It's not difficult to deconstruct his theology."

It turned out to be Maguire's one flirtation with fame. A few weeks later, according to ISIS, he was killed fighting Kurds in a battle for a town that most Canadians have never heard of. Muslims who oppose ISIS's terror tactics said they expected Maguire to end up dead. Hammad Raza, a University of Ottawa engineering student who met Maguire in the university prayer room and had become his friend, had stopped talking to Maguire when he realized his friend had embraced a "disgusting ideology."

"There are so many people that he may have killed before getting killed. It's really unfortunate that this happened. These people are like walking time bombs. They could go off any time."

HOW DID A COLLEGE BOY FROM CANADA END UP AS THE star of an ISIS propaganda video? What would motivate someone leading a seemingly normal life—playing in a band, fussing about his grades, spending a bit of time on the hockey rink—to leave his family and friends, get rid of his belongings, and scrape up the money to travel to one of the most dangerous parts of the world to join an organization that crucifies and beheads its enemies? And why are so many young people, those raised as Muslims and those who were not, making the same journey to join ISIS?

Leaving home to become a fighter for ISIS has become so common that *Saturday Night Live* did a spoof video of Dakota Johnson, star of *Fifty Shades of Grey*, being dropped off at an airport by her father, a band of gun-wielding ISIS fighters waiting for her.

ISIS video star and soon-to-be-casualty John Maguire was raised in Kemptville, a small town between Ottawa and the St. Lawrence River. Kemptville has about 3,500 people, enough to support a small main street and a few churches and schools. It was home to an agricultural college and is connected to the Rideau Canal, one of the more popular recreation areas in the region. There's a bridge over the St. Lawrence River to upstate New York, just a twenty-minute drive away. Kemptville is a nice little place, one of dozens of small towns in southern Ontario that attract people who like the outdoors or detest city life.

His childhood was a mess. John's father, Peter, was a mechanic. He was also a motorcycle enthusiast and played in a garage band in his off-hours. Peter had some unconventional ideas about politics and current events. Friends told reporters Peter Maguire believed 9/11 was an inside job, and the story of the Holocaust is a hoax. He and John's mother, Patricia Earl, began to fight when John was a small boy. In 2003, when John was twelve, the family broke up and John went to live with his father. That seemed to work out all right. Peter didn't have much money, but he was able to fit John out with hockey equipment and, later, a motocross bike.

In high school, John's friends had called him "JMag" and he had dressed as a city street kid (as interpreted through the cultural lens of Kemptville teens). Maguire played in punk rock and hip-hop bands, and could also play classic rock and pop (one of his favourite bands was Marky Mark and the Funky Bunch, a bubblegum group that was big before Maguire was born). He'd stayed away from booze and drugs, even when he was playing with his bands. His bandmates were also pretty straight. Evan Massey, a member of Maguire's band The Shackles, became a Christian pastor in Kemptville. He says his friend had questions about faith but his beliefs were simplistic, shallow and ill-formed. "He definitely did not know anything about God." Nor did he open up to Massey about his home life, which was becoming unglued. "He kept to himself about a lot of things that were either important or things that bugged him."

Massey and Maguire got into a bit of trouble in school, little transgressions that got them kicked out of a few classes. But mostly people remembered him for having a fast wit that often generated self-deprecating jokes. The punk rock act was a bit of a put-on, and Maguire sometimes joked about it. "The really punk thing to say was 'Anarchy, maaaan,'" Evan Massey remembered. "He would make fun of that almost on the daily."

Maguire was an extrovert. There were the bands, and Maguire also volunteered to read the morning announcements on his high school's intercom. He would lace them with jokes and mock the principal for not standing during the national anthem. He put a lot of energy into everything he did, pulling down good grades and gaining the reputation of an intense young man who was quite likely to succeed in life. Another student later called him "strong willed intellectually" and "an out of the box thinker," adding, "Maybe it does kind of make sense that if he fell into that world [of ISIS], he'd go full blast into it."

When the ISIS video came out, friends, especially from his Kemptville years, didn't recognize the Maguire they had grown up with. One friend said, "Everything that I hear about him now is honestly nothing like the JMag we knew, and from the time we spent jammin' in high school, or hanging out on the weekend, I never noticed any behaviour that would foster that kind of hatred towards any religious or social groups . . . I was saddened to hear about his recent inclinations toward radical extremism. There are tons of things I could sit down and say, but I don't know if he'll get out [of Syria] alive."[2]

Whatever the motivation for Maguire's conversion to a fringe group within Islam, it was not something done in haste. Rather, he spent months learning about the religion, reading the Qur'an and talking face-to-face and online with people who took Islam very seriously.

Luke Lavictoire, a friend of Maguire's, said Maguire liked to research things intensely. "He definitely asks a lot of questions. He's not a dumb kid, and for someone to misguide him or mislead him—he wouldn't say yes to anything. He would make sure he had all of the answers before doing something drastic." Maguire was "ambitious" and believed he was born for a purpose. "He wanted to do something with his life." Other classmates expected him to do "great things."

Because of his intensity and his habit of completely throwing himself into anything he did, some women did find him a bit strange. A former classmate at Kemptville's North Grenville High School said she noticed he had "never had a girlfriend. He hung out with punk rockers in my grade. I used to get weird vibes from him. Just a very difficult person to be around."

In the early years of high school, Maguire's life still included hockey as well as music. Maguire was not National Hockey League material, but he was fast and tough. All in all, he seemed, at a cursory glance, like a normal small-town Canadian kid who appeared to be getting about as much as could be hoped for out of childhood and adolescence. Whatever was happening inside, he kept to himself.

Things started to go badly when Maguire was seventeen. He

hadn't seen much of his mother, partly because his father worked hard to drive a wedge between mother and son. But suddenly his father, Peter, decided he was going to remarry and move to Russia to teach English. John didn't want to go. For a short time, he tried to live with his mother, but that didn't work out, so he moved to Ottawa to stay with his grandmother. His father disappeared from his life.

Once he realized he couldn't live with his mother, Maguire left Kemptville in a hurry. "He just got rid of everyone on Facebook and kinda disappeared. He never told us why," a friend said after Maguire gained notoriety as an ISIS propagandist.

One woman who worked with him at a neighbourhood grocery store, The Independent, while Maguire lived nearby with his grandmother, remembers the changes in the young man.

"He was shy but he was always vying for attention," she remembers. "He was also really sweet and really kind. I don't see him having bad intentions. There were a couple of guys who were weirdos, but not him. He was kind, shy, wanting friends, wanting to be accepted.

"I found he was like a child. If I wasn't giving him attention, he would just make sure he got it. In many instances, he would arrive after I started talking to someone else and jump into the conversation. It was his way of wanting to be told that he was a friend. That's the way I remember him: always wanting to be accepted by someone."

The co-worker, who grew up Muslim, was surprised to hear Maguire had converted to Islam. "Someone came up to me in a coffee shop and told me that he had converted. I sent him a Facebook message and asked why. He told me [someone he worked with] had introduced him to Islam. He had been curious about it. He wanted to know about the prayers, the fasting."

It's not clear whether Maguire was recruited by the people who converted him, or if he was recruited by the much larger group of ISIS propagandists who scour the Internet looking for prospects. Each of the clusters of Canadians who are known to have left the country to fight for ISIS have had at least one recruiter who drew them together. These men, however, were not ISIS agents per se. They were men who had made strong connections online to people in the Middle East. But within a couple of years, Maguire was a true believer in ISIS's cause and was, himself, a recruiter, looking for potential ISIS fighters among Muslims—born and converts—in Montreal and Ottawa.

Maguire's coworker saw him again when she was close to finishing university. They both went to the University of Ottawa, but the woman was not in the same year of school, and she hadn't seen him around campus. She soon found out he had converted to Islam just as he finished high school.

"The University of Ottawa was having Islam Awareness Week. They do it every March. He was at a booth explaining Islam to people who came by. He asked me why I wasn't helping out in the booth. He told me he changed a lot after his conversion. He believed he had become a better person. But he was afraid to tell his grandparents. When he started growing a beard, he told his grandmother that Jesus had one. When she made pork, he found some reason not to have dinner. It was a struggle for him to hide his Islam."

Friends, even those who were Muslim converts, found him very distant and even secretive when he came back from California, where he studied business for a year. He had immersed himself in the online speeches of Anwar al-Awlaki, a U.S.-born Muslim cleric who amassed a large following among English-speaking converts by peddling an extremist form of Islam in simple, entertaining English. Al-Awlaki became a propagandist for al-Qaeda and other jihadi groups while hiding out in Yemen. Al-Awlaki was killed in a U.S. drone strike—the first American to be targeted for that kind of assassination, which was personally approved by President Barack Obama—but his message inspired many North American terrorists, including the Tsarnaev brothers, who bombed the Boston Marathon in 2013. Maj. Nidal Hasan, who murdered thirteen people at Fort Hood, Texas, in 2009, was also a fan, as were the so-called Toronto 18 terror cell and several of the Canadians who have gone to the Middle East to fight for ISIS and its jihadi competitor, al-Nusra.

Stephane Pressault, an acquaintance who used to pray with him at the University of Ottawa, said Maguire didn't let people get close: "People had very superficial relationships with him." The two had a bitter falling out after Maguire went to Syria. Pressault, who had no interest in extremism, wrote an opinion piece in a local newspaper about what he called the "tragedy" of the death of Damian Clairmont, a Canadian convert from Calgary who was killed while fighting alongside jihadis in Syria.

Adam Gilani, a former president of the University of Ottawa Muslim Students Association, said no one in his organization knew Maguire well. He didn't tell any of his friends in the university's Muslim group of his plans to join ISIS or talk to them about his circle of extremist friends. Like almost everyone else, the Muslim students at the University of Ottawa found out about Maguire's decision to join ISIS when the video was posted to YouTube.

He seemed to be able to hide the damage caused by his troubled childhood and the plans he was making to fight for Islamic extremists. "There were no clues and no red flags. And for us that is the most concerning thing," Gilani says. "He was isolated and not looking for answers in the right places. We [Muslims] have a responsibility to make sure we reach out to these isolated individuals."[3]

ISIS deliberately set out to attract foreigner fighters. And its campaign has been very successful. The best comparison in recent history would be Republican Spain in the late 1930s, when the leftist government of that country recruited young men from the rest of Europe and from North America to try to put down an army revolt backed by Hitler and Mussolini. The fascists under Francisco Franco won that war, but the trade union activists, working men and students who fought for the leftist Republicans were immortalized as martyrs and heroes.

The self-styled Islamic State, which has now elevated itself to a new caliphate, needs people. ISIS needs men to fight and govern its territory. It also recruits young women to encourage and marry its fighters, settle in ISIS territory and have children. All of the foreign fighters are useful for propaganda and psychological warfare. ISIS can point to them as evidence that its version of Islam is more desirable than the West's material culture. ISIS is not a homegrown insurgency in Iraq and Syria, even though most of its fighters are from the region. Rather, ISIS is an amalgam of jihadis from the Middle East, Afghanistan, Pakistan, the former Soviet Union, the Balkans, the West and North Africa that seeks to impose its rule and its values on as much territory as it can seize, no matter what the local people believe about religion and politics. It must expand to survive. Colonization is a part of ISIS ideology. So are rape, slavery, torture and genocide.

ESTIMATES OF THE NUMBER OF CANADIANS FIGHTING in ISIS's army vary between about 60 and 150. Academics, journalists and members of Canada's intelligence agencies try to track the Canadians among the twenty thousand to thirty thousand foreigners fighting in Syria and northern Iraq—about half of ISIS's army. Some, like Maguire, have no qualms about showing their faces in videos and engaging in conversations with journalists and professors on Twitter. Many more have gone to ISIS's territory quietly. There's a good chance they will never come back. ISIS's foreign fighters, especially those from Western countries, tend to die very quickly.

Unless ISIS faked his death, something Interpol hasn't discounted completely, John Maguire was one of the ISIS fighters who didn't live long.

In December 2012, Maguire left Canada for Syria. He was able to get out of Canada and make it to the Middle East, even though the Canadian government had cancelled his passport.[4] Maguire probably got into the country through its porous border with Turkey, a country that has a complex relationship with ISIS. Both entities are enemies of the Kurds, whose homeland straddles northern Syria, southern Turkey, northern Iraq and a corner of Iran.

Access to the war zone used to be easier back then. The prewar economies of northern Syria and southern Turkey were tightly integrated and the border had always been porous. Turkey was also keen to remove, or at least destabilize, Syria's Assad regime, which sought to be a regional power. However, the growing strength of the Kurds has frightened Turkey, and it has tried to establish complete dominance in its southern provinces. It's assumed that Maguire was able to get out of Turkey by paying a small bribe to its border police.

He hadn't left on his own. Police believe Maguire was part of a cluster of Ottawa-based extremists. Its members included Awso Peshdary, an Algonquin College student and campus Muslim leader who, the Royal Canadian Mounted Police believe, gave Maguire his travel money.

Maguire remade himself again, joining ISIS's army under the *nom de guerre* Yahya. Years before, he had left Kemptville in a hurry and had severed ties with his friends, but this time he kept in touch with people back home. He was a frequent poster on social media like Twitter and Facebook, and was well known to the small number of bright reporters in Canada and other Western countries who analyze ISIS's Internet postings. On Facebook, Maguire wrote, "Evil is very prominent in Canadian culture, homosexuality, fornication and adultery are generally accepted, drugs and alcohol are easily accessible and widely accepted as being 'normal,' women and men are often not properly covered, music is widespread in public places."

National Post reporter Stewart Bell, who has written extensively on terrorism and tracks Canadian jihadis, communicated with Maguire on social media in the summer of 2014. He located the former university student just as ISIS's atrocities and conquests began to capture space in Western media. Bell says Maguire called Canada "evil" and said Christians must convert "or face the sword." Bell asked him if he was with the Islamic State. Maguire replied: "There is nothing called ISIS. But there is an Islamic caliphate."

Maguire told Bell that Canada is a country Muslims should "hate for the sake of Allah." It has given "support for the enemies of Islam," specifically the United States and Israel, and waged "war against the Muslims in Afghanistan."

Maguire said he hadn't tried to get support from his parents to go to Syria. In fact, he hadn't told his grandparents either. They got the bad news when they found a note in his empty bedroom. Jihad was "obligatory" and "in this situation the son is to go for jihad regardless of what his parents say." To please God "one should sacrifice what he has in the West and make *hijrah* to a land of jihad."[5]

After Maguire's video was posted on YouTube, his Facebook

page was closed down, but he continued to be fairly easy to contact. ISIS had deliberately put him forward as one of its army of social media propagandists.

Maguire wasn't the only "jihadi" to star in videos threatening Canada, nor was ISIS the only organization making them. Nasser bin Ali al-Ansi, a leader of the Yemeni-based al-Qaeda in the Arabian Peninsula, posted a video urging his supporters to launch their own "lone wolf" terrorist attacks in Canada. He named the country as one of the "Western countries that fight Islam" in a "Crusader campaign."[6] And he wasn't the only Canadian fighting alongside—or against—ISIS. One of the senior commanders in the ISIS-held city of Raqqa called himself Abu Mohammed al-Kanadi, which translates into "Mohammed's father, the Canadian." Local people said he was "one of the princes, the emirs" of the region. In one ISIS video, a jihadi from Quebec burns his Canadian passport in front of a camera. Then he puts a few bullets into it.

In the last months of 2014, Maguire was with the ISIS army that was fighting for the Kurdish town of Kobani. The town, in northern Syria, had been torn apart by months of fighting. ISIS had captured the villages in the surrounding countryside in the fall of 2014, then attacked Kobani, the main city in the region, in October. Some 400,000 people, mostly Kurds, fled Kobani and the surrounding villages into Turkey. The city itself, along with the towns around it, were turned into piles of rubble by artillery, bombs dropped from airplanes, and suicide bombers. The civilians who fled the region were treated horribly. A *Vice* journalist who covered the fighting described Kobani as a "modern-day Stalingrad." ISIS tried to overrun the Kurdish town during a four-month siege in the fall and winter of 2014–2015, managing to grab parts of the city but never able to take the whole thing. Each time a major ISIS attack failed, the Islamists were able to deflect world attention by posting horrendous atrocity videos on the Internet. Through the winter of 2015, ISIS was driven from the countryside around Kobani, but in the early summer, it launched yet another attack on the city and drove out more refugees. Kobani and the surrounding countryside were flattened and stripped clean, and its people were dead or on the road as refugees. Aylan Kurdi was one of those people who were forced out of the city. The three-year-old boy drowned, along with his mother and older brother, while trying to reach the Greek island of Kos. A photo of the little boy in red shorts, a T-shirt and sneakers, lying dead in the sand of a Turkish beach, shocked the world in the summer of 2015.[7]

Despite the awful destruction and slaughter, Maguire never seemed to doubt the cause that he'd adopted. The *Toronto Star*'s Michelle Shephard, one of Canada's best foreign affairs correspondents, tracked down a man who knew Maguire in the Middle East. Ahmed, a twenty-two-year-old working for ISIS's media wing, met Maguire in Raqqa, Syria, fourteen months after Maguire left Canada. Ahmed was trying to get out of ISIS while Maguire was trying to get in. Ahmed felt ISIS had tried to brainwash him and Ahmed worried he'd end up like two of his friends who had been accused of spying and killed by ISIS. "He was a happy guy all the time. He would carry the kids around, joking with them," Ahmed said. And he wasn't a complete stooge for ISIS. Once, Maguire had caught Ahmed smoking a cigarette but did not report it.[8]

In the spring of 2014, Maguire got engaged to a young woman named Hedeal. He invited his mother to the wedding, but she couldn't make the complicated travel arrangements. She, too, had remarried, and John had warned his stepfather, "The fire will last forever when you go to Hell."[9]

Then, after making his video threatening Canada and praising an attack on Canada's Parliament Building, Maguire went back to the killing grounds of Kobani. According to an ISIS-affiliated Twitter account, Maguire was killed in battle in January 2015. Coalition air strikes softened up ISIS's dugouts and ravaged its supply lines. The Kurdish Popular Protection Units (YPG), made up of men and women fighters, along with Free Syrian Army forces, attacked Kobani and drove ISIS from the ground it had taken. Maguire was killed in that counterattack.

Chapter 2

Other Moms' Kids, Other Men's Armies

THERE WAS A TIME WHEN FOREIGN FIGHTERS WERE THE norm. In the Middle Ages, sociopaths and thrill-killers could easily find work in the small armies that fought the interminable, ugly little wars in Europe. The ferocity of mercenaries in the pre-gunpowder age was shared, during the Wars of Religion, by Jesuits, with their vow to obey every instruction of the Pope of Rome "even if this should take us among the Turks or any other infidels . . . even unto the realm that is called the Indies or among heretics and unbelievers of any kind as soldiers of Christ."[1]

Whether fighting for money, for Christ, or for some other god or cause, people have found struggle and war to be a way of finding a comfortable place in the world.

Adolf Hitler was living an aimless life on the streets when he found meaning for his life in the anti-Semitism of Hapsburg Vienna. After a few years in the trenches of Flanders during the First World War, the simple prejudice crystalized into a driving hatred. He found comradeship among the rage-filled men who loitered in the streets and beer halls after Germany's defeat. He was able to craft a movement that would be a powerful draw to young men. Current events worked in Hitler's favour. The revolution that overthrew the Kaiser exposed the rift between extreme right and extreme left in Germany. Attempted coups, runaway inflation and a desperate economic depression undermined Germans' sense of economic and social security and killed the hopes of the generation that had fought in the trenches and the men who came of age in the decade after the war. Hitler was able to redirect the postwar grief, frustration and class hatred toward racism and scapegoating.

He was able to attract followers who otherwise felt they had no reason to live. Joseph Goebbels, who crafted one of the most powerful propaganda machines in history, was one of those men. Before finding Hitler, Goebbels had no life to speak of. After, he became so enthralled with the Nazi project that he could not stand the idea of outliving it, and ended up killing himself and his wife after they murdered their six young children.

There was no room for cripples in the Germany of a century ago. Goebbels, a bright boy from a small German town, was born with a deformed foot that may have been made worse by a botched operation during his childhood. For the rest of his life, he walked with a noticeable limp, even when he wore a leg brace. And standing just over five feet tall made life even worse in a culture that so valued appearance and athleticism.

Even at its most desperate, the German army had no use for Goebbels during the First World War. The stigma of being called unfit to fight haunted him all his life—Goebbels was one of the very few men at the top of the Nazi movement who had not seen some kind of wartime service. In the early 1920s, even though he had finished a doctorate, he was working as a junior bank clerk, making almost no money. He was so depressed that he twice tried to kill himself. He was isolated from his family, he had problems with women, and he saw himself as a man whose future was somehow being stolen.[2]

Then, in early 1924, Goebbels began following the treason trial of Adolf Hitler, who had tried to pull off a coup in Munich a few months before. Goebbels was soon put in charge of developing the Nazi movement in Berlin, a job that he would hold, along with his propaganda duties, until the Soviets crushed the capital in the spring of 1945. Goebbels's propaganda would immortalize another aimless, troubled young man, Horst Wessel. Goebbels and the rest of the Nazis created many rumours about Wessel, but the bare-bone facts of his life are simple. He was born in 1907 the son of a Lutheran minister. The family lived in a small town, but the elder Wessel was promoted to be a pastor of a larger church in Berlin, located in a Jewish quarter of the city. When Horst was about eight years old, his father left the family to serve as the personal pastor of Field Marshal Paul von Hindenburg. Horst Wessel was eleven years old when his father, a determined conservative monarchist, returned from the defeated army. As he went into his teenage years, Horst made it clear to his parents that he would not follow his father and grandfathers into the ministry. He seems to have had no other plan. Germany was being wrenched through the postwar years. The leftist government that emerged in defeat and revolution was barely hanging on. The economy was shattered, and the country was forced by the victorious Allies to accept the financial and moral blame for the war.

Wessel finished high school and was accepted into the University of Berlin's law program. But he really spent most of his time on the street, in various thug groups run by right-wing political parties. By 1926, he had been kicked out of them all for being too violent.

He may have impressed his street thug friends, but Wessel was a barely-functioning young adult. He shared dirty apartments in the grim, overcrowded working-class sections of downtown Berlin. He was able to pay the rent by working as a labourer and chauffeur. His neighbours were the Communist workers whom he fought in the streets at night. A strange truce existed inside the apartment blocks, and, after a night of brawling, Communists and Nazis lived side-by-side in relative peace.

Wessel finished his law degree but despised the legal system and did nothing toward building a practice. He had been a member of two university fraternities but, after he got to know their members, had nothing to do with them. The Nazi Brownshirts, which Wessel joined in 1926, were the only group of young men that he got along with. The Nazis offered a complete way of life: an ideology, mentorship, adventure, comradeship, even clothing. In 1926, the Nazis were just one of the many politically motivated gangs fighting it out on the streets. It wasn't clear they would win, but they were growing all the time.[3] In 1929, Wessel wrote a simple set of lyrics to an old tune to create a marching song to compete with those that were sung by Berlin's Communist gangs. Goebbels published the lyrics in Berlin's Nazi newspaper a few months before Wessel was gunned down by Communists, possibly because of a dispute over the rent, in an apartment that he shared with a prostitute.

Goebbels had been looking for a hero. With a little work, Wessel fit the bill. In Berlin, the murder had broken the unspoken truce that allowed Nazis and Communists to feel safe inside their homes. The city was on the verge of a new wave of extreme violence. Goebbels edited Wessel's past to remove the unsavoury characters. His song, the "Horst Wessel Lied," became a sort of Nazi, then national, anthem, and both Wessel, with his "Aryan" features, and his simple little song was an important part of the aesthetics that still attract young men to Nazism.

Hitler was a mediocre artist. (History might have been far different if he had had a bit more talent, or had worked harder at his trade.) He did, however, have a grasp of aesthetics, as did many of the early Nazis. Their use of imagery, art, architecture, logos, music, film, radio—even the stylings of high-fashion designers to create dashing uniforms—were hooks that caught many recruits. The Nazis were years ahead of the rest of the world in developing the new medium of television. Spectacle was vital to the Nazi movement, and it awed even the most cynical people. French diplomat André François-Poncet described one of the giant annual Nuremberg rallies as so hypnotic that "many returned home seduced and conquered, ready to collaborate, failing to perceive the sinister reality hidden behind the false pomp." Philip Johnson, the first curator of the architectural department at New York's Museum of Modern Art, went to the 1938 rally and came out smitten by the show, though, fortunately, not by the message. "Like the *Ring* [of the Nibelung], even if you were at first indifferent, you were at last overcome, and if you were a believer to begin with, the effect was even more staggering. Even the Americans who were there—no special friends of the Nazis—were carried away by it all."[4]

Much of Europe was drawn to Hitler's movement. After the war, the entire continent would claim to be his victim, but the startling fact is that by the end of the war, about a million people in the German army and SS units were foreigners, and thousands of people throughout Europe had volunteered to work for the Third Reich in their home countries and in Germany. The Wehrmacht had Irish, English, American, Chinese, Swiss, Portuguese and Swedish members, along with hundreds of thousands of volunteers from the countries that had been overrun by the Nazis. Canadians found themselves facing Russian soldiers in the Scheldt Estuary downstream from Antwerp, Belgium, and picked up Indian soldiers dressed in Wehrmacht uniforms on the coast of Holland. Some of these men, especially the Russians, were either conscripts or prisoners of war who had joined the German military to survive, but the bulk of them—and all of the ones from neutral countries—were true believers in the prosperous, united, orderly and simple Europe that Hitler offered.

Nazi recruiters scoured prisoner of war camps to find men from Britain and the Empire to join the Legion of St. George, an SS unit that was probably designed as a propaganda tool. Only three Canadians signed up. German generals thought the whole project dubious, and worried about the legality of brainwashing POWs protected by the Geneva Convention (the Soviet Union was not a signatory, so the Germans had no compunction about brutalizing and killing its soldiers). Only a very few committed British anti-Communists saw action, but they were among the last soldiers to fight to the death in the fall of Berlin.

The Canadians who adopted Hitler's cause stayed in Canada. Hate campaigns against Jews and other "foreigners" began in this country well before Hitler took power. The Roman Catholic Church in Quebec, with its mass-market publications and its trade unions, loudly supported Mussolini's fascist project in Italy. By the early years of the Depression, three papers in Montreal pumped out nothing but anti-Semitism, and Jew-baiting was common in the more mainstream papers like *Le Devoir*. When Hitler took power in 1933, there was already a small but busy grassroots fascist movement based in Quebec, though certainly not limited to that province. And organizations like the Ku Klux Klan and the Loyal Orange Lodge were strong in some parts of the country, especially in the west and Ontario respectively. Ontario's Swastika Clubs, which, rather bizarrely, existed before the Nazis, adopted fascist ideology. In the west, the Nationalist Party was eventually replaced by the Canadian Union of Fascists. All of these groups attracted people who believed the economic and social problems plaguing the world after the Great War could not be solved by democratic governments.

Adrien Arcand, a tall, thin man who aped Hitler's speaking style, was the leader of the country's main fascist party, the National Union Party of Canada. He was a failed journalist who had been driven out of the mainstream Quebec newspaper business for being obnoxious and ended up as a tool of renegade publisher Joseph Ménard. Despite being on the fringe of media and politics, Ménard and Arcand were funnelled money by wealthier, more respectable sympathizers, in the same way Hitler was in his early years. By 1929, they had already started the nationalist group Ordre Patriotique des Goglus. A year later, Arcand's publications pushed Montreal's twenty-two thousand Italian-Canadian voters to support his choice of candidates for city council, stressing the candidates' sympathy for Mussolini. At that point, Mussolini was strongly supported by the Papacy, and the Church was still the bedrock of intellectual life in Quebec. (Camillien Houde, Arcand's choice for mayor of Montreal, would go on to oppose Quebec's participation in the Second World War and end up spending most of it in internment camps.)

At one point, Arcand claimed to have seventy thousand followers in Montreal alone. That number seems very high, but he was able to fill very large halls in the city and wield some political clout, especially at the city council level. The priests connected to the movement were among its best organizers. When the Italians invaded Ethiopia in 1935, the priests, helped by Italian diplomats, ran a campaign to convince ethnic Italian women in Montreal to donate their wedding rings to Mussolini. Outside of the Church, most of the fascist leaders were men who were somehow thwarted in life. Typically, they were victims of Quebec's chronic underemployment and the poverty of the 1930s. Even those who seemed successful, like Gabriel Lambert, nursed some kind of grievance. In Dr. Lambert's case, it was rage against the medical profession, which had laughed at him for his claim that the eye was the body's mirror, and that all diseases could be found and diagnosed by examining a patient's retina. Lambert wrote some of the Quebec fascist movement's most vicious propaganda. Much of the rest came straight from Germany.

There were other losers who became propagandists, like failed doctor P.E. Lalanne, and Jean Tissot, the police chief of the backwater of Rouyn, Quebec. Tissot ended up in the frontier after being fired from the Ottawa police force for libelling A.J. Freiman, owner of a downtown department store. Like the Nazis, the Quebec fascists organized boycotts of Jewish-owned businesses, although without the violence of Hitler's street thugs.

There was no real opportunity for Canadian fascists to go abroad. Spain's rebel movement, led by fascist Francisco Franco and backed by Hitler and Mussolini, did not actively seek soldiers, especially from the ranks of untrained and untested Canadian sympathizers. Forced by circumstance and geography to stay at home, Arcand and his followers set to work to try to make a Nazi state in Canada. They also tried to shut down rallies for the leftist Spanish Republicans who visited Montreal to raise money and gather recruits. In Toronto, police sympathized when Canadian fascists fought street brawls with Stalinists and Trotskyites, just as they had when thugs attacked Jews in the Christie Pits Riot in 1933.

Arcand's men and fascists in English Canada wore the full fascist uniform of brown and black shirts. They carried flags emblazoned with the swastika wreathed in maple leaves surmounted by a beaver. Arcand's newspaper, *Le Fasciste Canadien,* went from being a mimeographed sheet to a somewhat slick magazine. But as fascism hung on in Quebec, it withered in much of the rest of the country as Hitler's regime showed its fangs in Czechoslovakia and Poland. In Quebec, the movement started to collapse when Hitler and the Catholic Church had their falling out in 1938. Arcand, now somewhat, though not completely, isolated, defended Hitler when the Führer made a deal with Stalin and launched his attack on Poland. A year later, Canada appeared to be losing the war and the government started rounding up "fifth columnists," including Arcand and many of his henchmen. The gutter and mainstream press, though, still carried wild rants about Jews and supported the collaborationist Vichy regime in France to the bitter end. The fascist elements of Quebec nationalism were stripped away after the war, although the racism that underlay the movement still surfaces.[5]

Communism, too, attracted young men. As soon as they took power in Russia, the Soviets opened their border to immigrants, mainly for their propaganda value. Most of the early immigrants were drawn by illusions, rather than any real knowledge of the situation in Russia. The Communists, at first, hoped to develop a group of foreign organizers who could go back to their home countries and start their own revolutions. The doors were also open to anyone who claimed religious or political persecution. Thousands of Marxists took the Soviets up on their offer, but few of them were happy. Russia's civil war was brutal, and many of the foreigners, while dedicated Communists, avoided military service. The Soviets tried to draw them into the fight by offering them citizenship but, within three years of the revolution, they realized foreigners were a burden, rather than an asset. By the early 1920s, as the postwar depression bit hard throughout the world, and the Soviet Union staggered from one near-disaster to another, the doors were closed.

Westerners would have to stay in their own countries. Throughout the 1920s, domestic Communist groups attracted hundreds of Canadians, most of them unassimilated immigrants. They often had much more loyalty to the Soviet Union than they did to Canada, and the Soviets put the most trustworthy of them to work as spies. Through the 1920s, membership of the Canadian Communist Party grew to about three thousand members. Canada had diplomatic relations with the Soviet Union, and the country's diplomats acted as recruiters and spy handlers. They found converts in the union halls and social clubs that were set up in Canadian logging and mining villages. The towns that are now part of the city of Thunder Bay, with their large community of exploited Finnish bush workers, were fertile ground. So was Winnipeg, which erupted into a violent general strike in the spring of 1919. Communists were shadowed by American intelligence agents, who set up listening posts in Winnipeg and other cities. The Americans filed reports to Washington on the young men who were invited to the Soviet Union. Canadian police shut down Communist newspapers starting in the 1920s and banned them all during the Second World War, even though the Soviets were Canada's allies against Hitler.[6]

CANADIANS ARE NOT EAGER WARRIORS UNLESS THEY'RE provoked. A small group of Canadians were always willing to travel to war, even if the enemy posed no threat to them or their homes. In colonial times, a few volunteered to fight in the American Civil War, usually on the Union side. Although slavery persisted in Canada into the 1800s, most Canadians had no use for it, and were eager to see the North win. There was the added bonus, for French Canadians, that the British government supported the

Confederacy. And there was also the fairly generous cash bonus paid to recruits.

Adventurous mixed-race and First Nations voyageurs left unemployed by the death of the fur trade paddled the Nile to relieve Khartoum from the forces led by Muhammad Ahmad bin Abd Allah, self-proclaimed Mahdi, or Muslim messiah, in 1884–1885. Canadian college boys signed up to fight the Boers in South Africa at the end of the nineteenth century, partly because they believed the British Empire's propaganda, partly because it was the right thing to do in a very militarized society in which service as an officer could propel a man into a higher social class. And in Montreal, McGill University students found supporting the Boer War had the added attraction of provoking the young men in French-Canadian colleges.

During the Great Depression, some twelve hundred Canadian men went to Spain to fight on the side of its socialist Republican government. (Just two Canadians joined Francisco Franco's fascist legions, and both of them quickly deserted.) More than four hundred Canadians were killed in the Spanish Civil War, which ended just a few months before the outbreak of the Second World War. The average Canadian volunteer in the Spanish Republican army was thirty-two years old, about five years older than the typical American who went to Spain. Economic deprivation shaped most of their lives. Many of them had known nothing but hard times. This was a generation that rarely got a chance to work at its potential or get a higher education. Many young men looked left and, more rarely in English Canada, to fascism for solutions to their personal problems and the economic messes in their home countries. The Spanish Republicans even accepted people with criminal records. Usually the offences admitted to by the Canadians had to do with Communist protests, violence on picket lines and the kind of charges police laid against the very poor—vagrancy, soliciting money without a permit and hopping freight trains. Real hard-core criminals found sanctuary in the French Foreign Legion. About 215 of the Canadians who fought in Spain, mainly older ones, had military training and were veterans of the First World War or the conflicts that followed.

One striking fact is that the vast majority of the Canadian volunteers who fought in Spain were born outside Canada. This was also the case for early volunteers in the First World War, who were almost all new arrivals from Britain. Some 78 per cent of the Spanish volunteers arrived as children or young men in the last years of the 1920s.[7] The Canadian contingent was entirely male, although they did fight alongside Spanish women who had joined the Republican forces. A large number were homeless and had already made a big geographic move at least once in their lives, so packing up and going to Spain may not have seemed like an outrageous decision. They saw ads in big city newspapers offering free travel and adventure. For smart young men like Jules Pavio, a Young Communist and committed anti-fascist, Spain offered the chance to turn talk into action.[8] And many of them, in years when democratic governments were trying to appease Hitler, realized the danger posed by fascist dictators, believed war was coming and decided they might as well get at it.

What attracted the foreign fighters to Spain? Partly, it was the vast, often violent clash between the world visions of the far left and far right, which manifested itself in fights on the streets of many European capitals. German and Italian leftists hoped to start an armed movement that would eventually end in the streets of Berlin and Rome. Some, including members of the teams stranded at the Workers' Olympics in Barcelona when the war broke out, were simply in the wrong place at the wrong time. But most wanted to be there because they believed in the cause. Many were dedicated Communists—men swayed on factory floors, in lumber camps and in universities. Others were men who wanted to do something good with their lives.

TODAY, ISIS IS THE MOST FAMOUS FOREIGN RECRUITER, but it's not the only faction in Iraq and Syria that has outsiders among it. All of the Islamic militant groups look for foreigners. So, in 2014, did the Kurdish militias. They realized they needed the fighting skills of men trained in foreign armies. They also saw the propaganda value of putting foreigners in their front lines—especially if some of them died. And all sides are working hard to get support of foreign governments. Russia and Iran are backing the Assad regime. A coalition led by the French and Americans is bombing ISIS, presumably on behalf of the Iraqi regime. Western countries, including Canada, have sent "advisers" to the Iraqis and Kurds, who are engaged in combat with ISIS.

Carleton Place is a short drive from John Maguire's hometown of Kemptville. It, too, is a small town in the orbit of a bigger city, Ottawa. A four-lane highway recently connected it with Canada's capital and it has started to become a bedroom community, but it still retains that feeling of being a backwater. A mural of Capt. Roy Brown shooting down the Red Baron dominates the Victorian main street. Nearby, a plaque in front of a farmhouse commemorates the childhood home of James Naismith, the inventor of basketball.

Dillon Hillier was born in Carleton Place in 1988. He, too, made a choice to go to the Middle East to fight, but on the side of the Kurdish Peshmerga. "Peshmerga" means "one who confronts death," and it is the fighting force of the mainstream Kurdish leadership.

Hillier is, in many ways, different from Maguire. His father, Randy, is an electrician by trade. The Hillier family seems tight-knit. Dillon's parents didn't split up, and even now Dillon's brothers have given him more than just verbal support for his adventures.

But the Hilliers are not a typical Ottawa Valley family either. During Dillon's childhood, Randy Hillier moved the family farther away from Ottawa, to the town of Perth, where his wife, Jane, had found a secluded 150-year-old stone farmhouse. Perth is part of the backbone of old Tory Ontario. Randy Hillier represents a great swath of that countryside in the Ontario legislature.

Dillon joined the Princess Patricia's Canadian Light Infantry in 2010 and did most of his training at Shiloh, Manitoba. He spent a few years on bases in Canada, then was posted to Afghanistan. Eventually, he was flown to Kandahar, site of Osama bin Laden's old command centre and one of the toughest, most Taliban-friendly towns in the country.

But the real fighting was over. Previously, Canadians headquartered in a fortified base at the Kandahar airport waged search-and-destroy warfare against Taliban units in the surrounding countryside. By the time Hillier arrived in 2013, the mission had changed to training Afghan government soldiers and police. When that tour was over, Hillier retired from the Canadian army in March 2014, with the rank of corporal. Soon afterward, he was recruited by a Kurdish militia, the Peshmerga.

Hillier found the Peshmerga through Facebook. A U.S. army ranger referred him to a woman named Kerry Dragon, who put him in touch with someone named Ali. The Peshmerga recruiter didn't do much screening. "I'm a Canadian vet," Hillier told Ali.

"Yea, OK," Ali wrote back. "I looked at your Facebook pictures and I know that you were in Afghanistan so that's good enough."

Hillier, just about the same age as John Maguire, became the first former Canadian Forces member to join the Peshmerga. Almost all of the handful of other former Canadian Forces soldiers who have joined the Kurds were members of the Patricias, and all of them did tours in Afghanistan after Canada stopped active combat missions.

Hillier was vocal about his reasons for going.[9] "Some people don't do their homework. I researched. My motivation was mainly in response to the attacks in Ottawa and Quebec. My thinking was—I am trained for this. And if there are ninety Canadians fighting with ISIS, then I am in a position to balance that number out one notch by fighting against them," said Hillier.

"I did it entirely on my dime. I did not take a salary from the Kurds. There was zero religion involved, for me at least. I was fighting alongside Kurdish Muslims. But eventually, you could tell we were being held back. Things changed and they didn't want foreigners in maximum risk. When that happened, it was time to come home."

In mid-November 2014, less than a month after Michael Zehaf-Bibeau shot up the Canadian Parliament Building, Hillier left Canada for Kurdish territory. Hillier didn't tell his parents that he planned to join the Peshmerga. Just as he was about to get on the plane in Calgary, he sent an email to his father saying he was leaving for Iraq, but he wanted his mother to be told he was on vacation in Thailand. Randy Hillier wouldn't lie. He did tell his wife and he "made many phone calls" to try to stop Dillon. Dillon flew to London and then to Qatar. From there, he got a flight to Sulaymaniyah, in northern Iraq, and found his way into the ranks of the Kurdish forces, seeing intense action at a battlefront that he compares to the trenches of the First World War.

Much of Hillier's adventure was recorded and published on the Internet. Hillier took battlefield video with his GoPro and still pictures of himself helping to bandage wounds, posing with Kurdish and American soldiers, and documenting life among the Peshmerga. His Facebook page was filled with shots of the countryside that was being fought over by ISIS and the Peshmerga.

The ground in front of the old stone Hillier family home was still covered with snow when Dillion Hillier arrived home. He had planned to stay six months, but left after just two. His parents, who had been worried the whole time, were glad to have him back.

"I went there planning on a much longer trip. And the political climate did not allow me to stay any longer." In the end, Hillier says, it was the Americans who forced him out of the region. By the end of 2014, U.S. military advisers had started exerting more control over the Kurds. They wanted the foreign fighters, who they believed would be difficult to control, out of the lines. Hillier might have been able to stay on in a support job or working behind the lines as a security guard but, he says, that was not the kind of work that had lured him to the Peshmerga. So he came home.

BRANDON GLOSSOP ARRIVED IN KURDISH TERRITORY in the wake of the publicity that followed Hillier. Glossop, like Hillier, was twenty-six when he went to the Middle East, and was an Afghanistan veteran of the Princess Patricia's Canadian Light Infantry and a worker in Alberta's oil fields. He left Edmonton at the beginning of 2015 to join the Kurds, Britons and Americans who comprise the Peshmerga group Lions of Rojava, in Syria. Glossop stayed there for three months and returned in mid-May 2015, with an ISIS battle flag as a souvenir. Customs agents seemed to have no objections to him bringing it into the country, if they noticed it at all. Pictures of Glossop and his flag quickly ended up on social and mainstream media.

"There's still a need for people to fight over there," he told the *National Post*'s Stewart Bell. "Going over there, we definitely did contribute. ISIS is just such a massive step backwards in humanity. They're fucking crazy . . . It should be an obligation for us to intervene if we can, when we can."

Glossop said he was motivated to fight with the Kurds by watching videos of ISIS throwing homosexuals off rooftops. Glossop, whose brother is gay, believes ISIS members are modern-day Nazis. He finally gave in to the urge to go to Syria after he saw the video of "that fucking prick" John Maguire urging attacks on Canada.

So, on the advice of online contacts, he made his way to Syria. He says it's easy, once you connect to the pipeline. International pressure on the Peshmerga—the same as the arm-twisting described by Dillon Hillier—had swayed that group to stop accepting Western recruits, so he joined the Lions of Rojava. First, Glossop flew to Munich, where he met a Romanian volunteer who acted as a guide. They travelled to northern Syria, where Glossop was handed off to Don Mealy, a British ex-serviceman. Glossop was given an M-16 rifle and sent to a Lions camp.

During his sojourn in Syria, Glossop met British, French, Spanish and American soldiers, and another Canadian. Glossop said the Kurds were grateful for foreign help, and honoured dead foreign fighters with banners put up throughout their territory. As well, the group posts pictures of its dead fighters on a Facebook page, which also keeps a steady stream of pictures and propaganda flowing to its twenty-one thousand followers.

What motivated Glossop? Certainly, there was a strong desire to help the Kurds. He was also inspired by Ernest Hemingway's novels. He kept notes of his trip, started a blog and posted many pictures of himself with his war buddies. Like Hemingway, he had some close calls, like the time he was stopped at an Iraqi checkpoint and caught with an ISIS book, which he'd kept as a souvenir. But it would be the flag, he hoped, that would be more valuable. In mid-2015, he said he hoped to sell it to raise money to go back to the front lines in Syria.[10]

CANADIAN-ISRAELI GILL ROSENBERG WAS THE FIRST foreign woman to join the Peshmerga. The Kurdish militia is proud of its all-woman units, which are deployed at the front lines. Rosenberg says she volunteered because she needed to "turn her life around" after being jailed in the United States for an international phone scam. Before that, Rosenberg had done her obligatory service in the Israeli Defense Forces, where she had trained to be part of a search-and-rescue unit.

The all-woman units have seen some very tough combat. Their very existence shakes up ISIS soldiers, who are trying to build a world in which women don't go around bare-headed, in army fatigues, ready for combat. (ISIS may have a female military unit, but it gets no publicity. It is probably—if it exists at all—a support unit.) In an interview with Israel's Army Radio, Rosenberg said she had taken part in "some pretty major firefights" with ISIS fighters.

Things changed, though, in the spring and early summer of 2015. Rosenberg says she saw much more evidence that the war in northern Iraq and Syria was becoming a struggle between Shiites and Sunnis. Iran, which has used the instability to assert itself as a regional power and protector of the Shiites, has been shipping arms and soldiers to the conflict.

In the mind-splitting web of Middle East alliances and hatreds, that put Rosenberg in a bad spot. Iran backs both the Assad regime and the fiercely anti-Israeli Hezbollah in southern Lebanon. It also refuses to recognize the existence of the Jewish state.

"In the past few weeks I think a lot of the dynamics have changed there, in terms of what's going on in the war," she said to the Israeli radio reporter. "The Iranian involvement is a lot more pronounced. Things changed enough that I felt that it was time to come home." She urged Israel to help the Kurds by sending advisers to train Peshmerga soldiers.

Rosenberg, who turned thirty-one in 2015, holds dual citizenship with Israel. She had emigrated there after a rough life in Canada. "I think we as Jews, we say 'never again' for the Shoah, and I take it to mean not just for Jewish people but for anyone, for any human being, especially a helpless woman or child in Syria or Iraq," she told Army Radio the day after she arrived back in Israel in mid-July 2015. In that same flurry of media interviews, she said she was also motivated to fight ISIS because of its murderous attacks on Iraq's Yazidi minority. "For me, that was the difference between a regular war and genocide," she said.[11]

She had become something of a celebrity in Israel, especially after media reports mistakenly said that she had been captured by ISIS. For several days, media in the West had speculated about her fate, but Rosenberg put the rumours to rest with a Facebook post.

She told another journalist that she needed to atone for being part of a phone scam run out of Israel that fleeced elderly Americans out of thousands of dollars. She was arrested in 2009 after the FBI tracked her down. Israeli authorities extradited her to the United States. When she joined the Peshmerga, she was still on parole.

"I was young and stupid and, you know, did something I shouldn't have . . . and, you know, spent four and half years in jail for it, and wanted to turn my life around and do something good for a change," she told Israel's Channel Two television. "For me, it was kind of like seeking redemption, or something, for my past."

The Canadian government warned her, along with Hillier and Glossop, that there was almost nothing Ottawa could do to help them. She still risked being charged for breach of probation and breaking Israeli laws against travelling to Iraq and Syria, but her celebrity status may have dampened the enthusiasm of prosecutors.[12]

The Canadians who have gone to Iraq and Syria, like the people attracted to Nazism and Communism, and even groups like the Jesuits, were outliers. All of them felt a need to fight for a cause, even one that had no real implications for their country. People will fight for money and they'll fight when they're drafted and forced to, but they will also go to war or put themselves in danger when they find a cause—political or religious—that makes them feel valued, important and wanted. Ideology, in the sense of traditional left-right constructs, isn't the motivator it used to be—though Dillon Hillier was drawn to the Kurds by it. Islamic radicalism has become the most dynamic challenge to Western secularism and capitalism. For people who feel disenchanted by Western materialism, directionless and lonely, groups like ISIS offer the whole package: jobs, acceptance, dignity and a sense of belonging to a winning side.

Chapter 3

The Mind of a Child

It's actually quite fun. It's really, really fun. It's better than that game Call of Duty. It's like that but it's in 3D where everything is happening in front of you.
—tweet by Abu Sumayyah al-Britani, a British fighter with ISIS[1]

In 2015, the Canadian military launched a video ad campaign to drum up men for front-line combat infantry. The target audience was young, male and aggressive. The ads mimicked the video games that are so popular with that audience. They depict guerrilla warfare with flash explosions, leaping paratroopers and thumping sound effects.

"The ads were generally considered thought-provoking, emotional, realistic and attractive despite the unsettling nature of the combat scenes," focus group testers who pre-screened the ads reported to Canada's Department of National Defence. "[One] ad's high energy creatively communicated by the music, rapidly changing images and unusual work environments grabbed viewers' attention and reminded many of a video game."

They were meant to. Just as ISIS propaganda is meant to. The ads and ISIS's propaganda are directed at the same group of people—military-age men—so they use the extreme, graphic violence that is part of the new language of young men raised on video games and CGI. They appeal to cravings for action, not to patriotism or to public service. Many of the men in the target audience don't have much going for them. The chance to breathe life into their fantasies, a world in which war is fun and they are heroes, is seductive.

"The tone was described as 'aggressive,' 'dark,' 'extreme,' 'high energy,' 'positive,' 'exciting,' 'adventurous,' 'dynamic,' 'harsh,' 'exhilarating' and 'rough,'" the focus group monitors said of the ads. But the message failed to click with what the testers oddly described as "niche audiences including women, visible minorities and Aboriginal peoples."

The makers of the ad called Ready When You Are knew their audience. The title suggests it was directed at potential recruits who were just a bit too young to sign up but who might be willing to embrace soldiering when they were old enough. The focus group organizers thought the military had hit the mark. "The intensity of the creative approach implies that the message is directed at a young, adventurous and predominantly male audience. The ads' creative approach was reminiscent of a video game or movie trailer." There were great sound effects: lots of heavy breathing, helicopter rotors and gunfire.

So where do you put an ad that's supposed to resonate with idle hands connected to bored, testosterone-drenched bodies? The focus group monitors told the military something it already knew. "To reach the perceived intended audience of young, adventurous, predominantly male individuals, the campaign should be featured on television channels with sports, news, the outdoors, comedy or music videos."

Those were good suggestions. But the military decided to do what ISIS does. It bypassed the TV networks, at least temporarily, and put Ready When You Are on YouTube. The ad drew 156,000 views in six months.

And the target audience liked the ad. In fact, they liked it a lot.

Here are some of the comments that were posted under its YouTube page: "Do you have to be a graduate in order to join?" "I want to join right out of high school." "I love this commercial and I definitely love our homeland." "You are preaching to the converted; I just need to graduate from high school first."[2]

THAT'S NOT TO SAY THAT TODAY'S YOUNG PEOPLE ARE more violent or evil than people brought up before the Internet, and television, and rock music, and all the things that were supposedly invented to skew young minds. Urban terrorism, especially in Europe and North America, has been a threat for centuries, while guerilla fighters fighting for homelands have vexed colonizers and empire-builders all over the world.

Nor are Western cities less safe than ever. In fact, the opposite is true. The mass murder of office workers and airline passengers on September 11, 2001, was in a league of its own, but cities have been targeted by bombers since at least 1567, when aristocratic conspirators blew up Henry Stuart, Lord Darnley, the estranged husband of Mary, Queen of Scots. The one child of that marriage, James I of England, was targeted by Robert Catesby, Guy Fawkes and their friends, who plotted to blow up the state opening of Parliament in 1605. Five years later, the king of France was assassinated after two earlier attempts failed. The 1600s and 1700s had enough gore for anyone who wanted it. Religious wars tore countries apart, and for three generations there wasn't a safe city in Europe. Riots continued in major cities through the next hundred years, with at least eleven people killed near London in one clash with soldiers in 1768. The rioting spread into the city, where dockworkers destroyed the rigging on ships and labourers attacked their own factories.[3] Two years later, British soldiers again fired into a crowd, this time in Boston, touching off the American Revolution, which in turn inspired the French to take to the streets and destroy their government.

Bombers and assassins kept at it. In 1812, Spencer Perceval, the prime minister of Great Britain, was gunned down on his way to Parliament.[4] In colonial Canada, people we would now call terrorists blew up the monument to War of 1812 hero Gen. Isaac Brock in 1840 and targeted the Welland Canal the next year, temporarily wrecking it. But those were the gunpowder days, when you needed barrels of the stuff to make an impression. In 1867, Alfred Nobel patented dynamite, and almost immediately, frustrated, angry and sociopathic people went to work making bombs with this much more potent explosive.

The Irish nationalist Fenians were on the cutting edge of the new technology. Their "Dynamite Campaign" began in 1867 with the Clerkenwell Outrage, the bungled attempt to free Irish nationalist prisoners from Clerkenwell Prison in London. None of the prisoners got away, but twelve people who lived in houses near the jail died in the blast. Michael Barrett was executed for the bombing at the last public hanging in England. There was a lull in the campaign for fourteen years. Beginning in 1881, the Irish Republican Brotherhood planted bombs in Liverpool, Chester and Manchester. In 1882, they set off a bomb at Mansion House, home of the Lord Mayor of London. In 1883, they planted bombs in Westminster and at the office of *The Times* of London. They also bombed a gasworks in Glasgow. Bombs were set off in the London Underground at Paddington and Westminster Bridge stations.

The next year, the now-renamed IRA set off a bomb in London's Victoria Station when the building was closed, and bombs were defused the same night at three other railway stations. On May 30, 1884, bombs went off at the Criminal Investigation Division, the office of the Metropolitan Police Department's Special Irish Branch, the Carleton Club (a rookery for Conservative MPs), and outside the home of Conservative MP Sir Watkin Williams-Wynn, injuring some pedestrians. Police defused a fourth bomb planted at the foot of Nelson's Column. At the end of that year, three members of the Irish Republican Brotherhood, led by American Civil War veteran William Lomasney, were blown up while assembling a bomb on London Bridge. Less than a month later, another dynamite bomb exploded at the Gower Street underground station. And in the same month, bombs were set off in the House of Commons, Westminster Hall, and the Tower of London.

People were afraid of enemies that moved among them. Back then, they were called anarchists and nihilists, and conventional wisdom, usually wrong, blamed Jews and foreigners (no matter where they lived). Many young people, most of them alienated from their own society, believed they could bring down the social and political system through terror and assassination. They learned to be quite good at it, even without the Internet to provide technical advice and link them up with like-minded radicals. In Russia, people mourned Tsar Alexander II, who was killed in 1881 when one of his legs was blown off by a bomb thrown by a member of the revolutionary group Land and Freedom. He wasn't the only leader killed by anarchists and nihilists in the *belle époque*. In 1898, Italian drifter Luigi Lucheni stabbed Empress Elisabeth of Austria to death at a Lake Geneva resort with a sharpened file. He was sentenced to life in prison in solitary confinement. Umberto I ("The Good"), who had survived a stabbing attack in 1879, was finally done in by Giovanni Passanante, who returned from New Jersey to Italy in 1900 to put a bullet into the king.

Few terrorist attacks of this era created the kind of revulsion that swept Britain in 1882 when Chief Secretary for Ireland Lord Frederick Cavendish (brother of the Duke of Devonshire and a relative of Queen Elizabeth II) and under-secretary Thomas Henry Burke were assassinated. They were walking in Dublin's Phoenix Park when they were attacked from behind and stabbed to death by five members of an Irish splinter group called the Irish National Invincibles just hours after Cavendish arrived in Ireland. The killers were caught and hanged. Cavendish was buried in his family plot, with three hundred members of Parliament and thirty thousand mourners following the coffin. The bombs kept going off. On May 4, 1886, someone blew up a labour rally in Chicago's Haymarket Square. A police officer was killed in the blast. His colleagues opened fire into the smoke and dust, killing seven of their own men and at least four protesters. Four men were hanged for the bombing after a trial that was, then and now, considered a sham.

But France took the brunt of the violence. On December 8, 1893, Auguste Vaillant planted bombs in the French Chamber of Deputies, injuring twenty people. He would have killed many more, but his arm snagged on a woman's dress as he threw the homemade bomb, which was cobbled together from explosives and scraps of metal that Vaillant had scrimped and saved to buy. When Vaillant was guillotined, Emile Henry took revenge by tossing a bomb into the popular Café Terminus and shot at a police officer who chased him. He later told the court that condemned him: "I wanted to demonstrate to the bourgeoisie that from now on it would no longer enjoy the delights of a bliss too perfect, that its arrogant triumphs would be troubled, that its golden calf would be violently shaken on its pedestal until the final push would topple it in mud and blood." Bomber François Ravachol, who tried to blow up the judge and prosecutor in an 1892 anarchist trial, dug up the corpse of the Comtesse de la Rochetaillée, hoping to steal whatever jewellery was on the body so that he could afford to continue his terror campaign. When he was caught, Matthew Carr wrote in his 2006 book *The Infernal Machine*, "the accordion-playing sociopath proved surprisingly popular with some of the French middle-class intellectuals who gravitated towards anarchism in the Belle Epoque, who variously compared him to Socrates and Jesus Christ."

But the radical chic urbane crowd was hardly safe. The same year that Vaillant tried to remake the French political landscape, anarchist and shoemaker Léon-Jules Léauthier had dinner in a fine restaurant, then lashed out with a knife at the people closest to him and killed the Serbian ambassador. Léauthier then walked out, found a police officer and said he had "just stabbed a bourgeois and eaten a fine meal." The mayhem died down a bit after French president Sadi Carnot was assassinated in 1894 in retaliation for Vaillant's execution. But the French anarchy briefly surfaced in London, where a bomb went off at the Greenwich Observatory, killing no one but the French anarchist who planted the explosives.

The anarchist violence, aimed at the burgeoning middle class, spread to Spain, where, in 1893, someone bombed the Liceu Opera House in Barcelona, killing twenty-two people in the audience. Five years later, someone threw a bomb into the Corpus Christi procession in Barcelona, killing fourteen people. Spanish authorities launched a wave of repression and torture. It ended with the execution of five of the four hundred people arrested after the attack. The following year, in retaliation for the Barcelona executions, Italian anarchist Michele Angiolillo shot Spanish prime minister Antonio Cánovas dead outside a health spa. Angiolillo was garroted.

North America wasn't safe. William McKinley, the president of the United States, was killed in Buffalo by anarchist Leon Czolglosz in 1901. In 1910, a bomb set off in the *Los Angeles Times* building by a union activist killed twenty-one people, and another hundred were seriously hurt. Beginning in 1914, bombings blamed on the followers of the Italian anarchist Luigi Galleani took place in New York, Boston, San Francisco and Washington, DC. In 1916, ten people were killed in a bomb attack at a Preparedness Day rally in San Francisco. The bombers were never caught and no one took responsibility. In Milwaukee, a bomb killed nine policemen and a civilian woman at a police station in November 1917. That one may have been set off by a German saboteur. And the jury is still out on whether the fire that destroyed the Canadian Parliament Building in 1916 was an accident.

Certainly, there were German agents operating in Canada and the United States during the First World War, supervised by Franz von Papen (who was later to play a key role in Hitler's rise to power and was one of the few people acquitted at the Nuremberg war crimes trials). Most of their bombs were set off in industrial plants in the New York City area, but there was also an abortive plot to blow up the Welland Canal. In July 1915, Prof. Eric Muenter set off a bomb in the reception room of the U.S. senate. He fled Capitol Hill and the next day tried to murder financier J.P. Morgan Jr., and was caught. He killed himself in jail four days later.

There was a wave of anarchist bombings in Europe and the United States after the First World War, which culminated on September 16, 1920, with an attack on Wall Street that killed between thirty-three and thirty-eight people and wounded three hundred others. It was the first recorded use of a car bomb (in this case, a horse and hay cart), detonated by someone who was never caught. The blast obliterated the horse, ripped apart ground-floor brokerage firms and flung cars down the street. But cleaners got to work, the stock market reopened the next day, and the Constitution Day event held the day after the attack was attended by thousands of New Yorkers.

People have forgotten that the IRA was waging a bomb campaign in England for almost a year before the outbreak of the Second World War and kept at it until Nazi bombing raids made the attacks rather redundant. And since the war, we've had bomb attacks by European communists; ethnic fighters like the IRA, the Basque group ETA and the Front de libération du Québec; socialist radicals like the Weathermen in the United States in the 1970s, the Baader-Meinhof gang in Germany and the Red Brigades in Italy. As the century came to an end, Europe and North America were targeted by neo-fascists and survivalists like Timothy McVeigh and his friends, who blew up the federal building in Oklahoma City, killing 168 people.

Urban violence, inspired for political or religious reasons, has always attracted enough discontented people to keep fear alive. There are always people who are willing to give up whatever comfort they have to fight in other people's wars, for Communists in Russia and for socialists and democrats in Spain during their civil wars, and in the Muslim world now. What's changed today is the ability of recruiters to get their foot in the door of every home, and into every phone that has access to new media (and, sometimes, meet potential recruits face-to-face in the troubled Muslim ghettos in the suburbs of Paris and in mosques run by extremists).

The U.S. State Department says that more than 9,700 terrorist incidents in ninety-three countries were reported in 2013. More than 18,000 people died in these attacks. Another 30,000 people were injured and almost 3,000 were kidnapped and held hostage. Nearly 60 per cent of these attacks happened in Afghanistan and Pakistan. That percentage was certain to change when ISIS ramped up its attacks in 2014.[5] If publicity is the lifeblood of terrorism—and terrorist leaders like Osama bin Laden have argued that it is—those numbers make for very tough competition for money and volunteers. Newcomers have to come up with ways to stand out from the crowd. ISIS has proven itself to be a master of that.

PEOPLE OF ALL AGES NOW LIVE IN A MEDIA MATRIX that engulfs and entraps them. For many of us, backing away from computer-transmitted messaging is simply too difficult. New media provides an addictive level of brain stimulus. It kills time for the bored. It makes the unimportant seem important and connects individuals into communities that are very real. About 93 per cent of American young people are frequent Internet users, with more than 80 per cent having wireless access. The poorer the people and the more impoverished the country, the more likely that the connection to the Internet will be wireless. Most Middle Eastern countries rely on cellular systems because the infrastructure is much cheaper—and harder to steal—than copper wire. In the United States, Black people, per capita, are the heaviest users of wireless.

In 2010, academics in eighteen universities started an experiment to test the addictiveness of the Internet, cell phones and other media. They called it Unplugged: 24 Hours without Media. The experiment was led by Prof. Susan Moeller of the University of Maryland, working through the Fourth Salzburg Academy on Media and Global Change. As part of the experiment, professors at Bournemouth University in England asked 189 students in the Journalism & Communications and the Corporate Marketing Communications programs to let go of all types of media, including mobile phones and smart phones, tablets and MP3 players, TV, newspapers, radio and the Internet, for twenty-four hours. About one-third of the students wouldn't even try. The rest of the students found the experiment almost impossible to complete.[6] To succeed, one of the students said, she had to live "like a hermit and keep to my room." The experiment "taught [her] that the media is inescapable, anything short of setting up camping in a field and you are pretty much guaranteed face to face with some kind of media." Like the rest of the students, she was allowed to read books, but they didn't scratch the itch. So she did laundry "and . . . got a little too transfixed by watching it go around in the tumble dryer."[7]

Physically, teenagers have the deck stacked against them, at least when it comes to resisting stimulus. The pleasure centre of the brain that's stimulated by the Internet is the same as the one stimulated by drugs.[8] The brain craves dopamine, which is a chemical compound that is released as a sort of reward. The same chemical forces that lock people into drug addictions are also at work on heavy Internet users. The brain releases more dopamine in response to increased stimulation, and that neurotransmitter's reception in the rest of the brain is enhanced. The quest for dopamine encourages people to seek pleasure.

As many parents come to realize, the teenage brain is wired differently from the adult's. Teenage brains get a stronger sense of reward from the dopamine that is synthesized and released. The parts of the brain that deal with risk-taking are not completely formed. So, in the fight between pleasure-seeking and risk-aversion, pleasure has a very good chance of winning.

The frontal lobes, which exert cognitive control, are still in the process of being hard-wired into the rest of the brain. The anterior cingulate cortex—the part of the brain that helps a person learn from mistakes—is also underdeveloped in teenagers, so that even if they realize they made a mistake, they may not necessarily learn from it.[9]

This is the first generation of young people to be raised with computers and smart phones integrated into their lives and minds. They have been given control over devices that can instantaneously bring them information, pornography, companionship, laughter and fantasy. That gives them the power to decide how much dopamine is created and used by the brain, since the brain produces dopamine when it feels pleasure or reward. As Dr. Frances Jensen, an expert on the teenage brain, recently wrote: "In some ways, technology *is* a drug." Hours spent on the Internet damage the brain, making it more difficult for people to store and recall information.[10]

Another study showed that the brains of teenagers who self-identified as Internet addicts had brains that were changed significantly. Structures deep in the brain were rewired, while surface-level brain matter seemed to shrink over time. "I'd be surprised if playing online video games for ten to twelve hours a day didn't change the brain," neuroscientist Nora Volkow of the U.S. National Institute on Drug Abuse told *Scientific American*.

China has a startlingly high rate of Internet addiction. About 14 per cent of urban youth—some 24 million people—are serious Internet addicts, according to the China Youth Internet Organization, whereas in the United States, the figure is about 5 to 10 per cent. Internet cafés are ubiquitous in Chinese cities, and teens immerse themselves in games like World of Warcraft.

China also leads the world in studying the impact of Internet addiction. Researchers have found voluntary, excessive online use leads to depression, increased irritability and more impulsiveness to go online (which makes quitting even harder). The Chinese researchers also found physical changes to the brain that affect speech, memory, motor control, emotion and the senses. They found online addicts' brains shrunk by as much as 20 per cent, with more tissue loss occurring in people with the longest and most serious addictions.[11]

Many of the students who are drawn to the Internet for companionship and feelings of reward are the kind of people who question authority and want to change the system but feel frustrated and isolated by a culture that values money and social status over ideas. Now politics excludes these kids, unless they are content to follow a party line and willing to limit their expression to putting up lawn signs or handing out fliers. Schools are more likely to medicate inquisitive and challenging students under the new diagnosis of "conduct disorder" than to try to channel their energy and creativity toward something rewarding for them, and for the rest of us.

The most popular diagnosis of these kinds of young people, oppositional defiant disorder, was first identified in DSM-V (*Diagnostic and Statistical Manual of Mental Disorders,* fifth edition, published in 2013) as "a pattern of negativistic, hostile and defiant behavior." A child afflicted by this newly discovered "disease" will "often argue with adults," "actively defies or refuses to comply with adult request or rules" and is "touchy and easily annoyed by others."[12] This new malady caught on quickly with educators. It is starting to move alongside attention deficit/hyperactivity disorder, now supposedly suffered by some 15 per cent of American school-aged children. With some 32.4 per cent of children admitted in 2011 to a Fort Bragg, North Carolina, psychiatric hospital diagnosed with ODD, this is an illness with real legs.

It can, according to psychiatrists, be treated with cognitive therapy or powerful antipsychotic drugs like Risperdal (risperidone) or Zyprexa (olanzapine). There is, of course, no mirror malady, one in which children unquestioningly accept authority, follow all orders without talking back, accept without question commercialism and social injustice, and believe everything adults—including the media and politicians—tell them.[13]

Cataloguing non-conformists and treating them as patients makes life easier for teachers and therapists, but it's unlikely to be of much benefit to society or to the people who are labelled. Instead of drugging them, we need to accept that some people simply don't fit into what's become a very stifling society. Some of them are creative, others are simply bored. Schools and parents need to engage with them and help them find some kind of niche.

ANYONE WHO CAN TAP INTO THE MINDS OF YOUNG people and connect with their desires and insecurities can exploit them. The music and film industries are proof of that. ISIS and other terror groups have been quick learners. It's not clear whether their grasp of propaganda in the age of new media is intuitive and home-schooled or if it has arrived with Muslim-born fighters and converts recruited from Europe and North America. Certainly, ISIS is miles ahead of al-Qaeda, which did grasp the idea of propaganda but is unable to shape it to the world of the Internet. Al-Qaeda makes good-quality video, but most of it is extremely boring. Its videos typically consist of preaching mixed with some jihadi home movies. In the early years of this century, ISIS simply gave those videos to the Qatar-government-owned Al Jazeera network, which picked out the more compelling bits and distributed them. Although Western media focused on anything that looked like a threat to the non-Islamic world, the videos were really made for a Muslim audience.

In 2002, Osama bin Laden wrote to Taliban leader Mullah

Mohammed Omar: "It is obvious that the media war in this century is one of the strongest methods; in fact, its ratio may reach 90 per cent of the total preparation for the battles." Another time, he wrote to a friend, "Media occupies the greater portion of the battle today."

Ayman al-Zawahiri, the man who was to take over al-Qaeda when bin Laden was finally found and killed, wrote to his colleague Abu Musab al-Zarqawi, who was running the first big insurgency in Iraq: "We are in a battle, and more than half of that battle is taking place in the battlefield of the media. . . . We are in a media battle for the hearts and minds of our *Ummah* [the Muslim world]."

Meanwhile, in the years after the September 11 attack, the Internet changed from being a virtual world of web pages and blogs to a new medium of communication that allowed users, at very little cost in time and money, to connect with people all over the world and interact with them in real time. Billions of people hooked themselves up to social media. Impressionable Muslims and potential converts made themselves easy to find. And the news media was right there, too. Journalists embraced Twitter because it was interactive. They could quickly track down news sources and interview them. They could mine the tweets of celebrities, politicians and other people, including jihadis, who don't usually talk to reporters. They could also showcase their own work by linking to their employer's website.

Journalists jumped on the Twitter bandwagon before ISIS became a player in the Middle East and North Africa. Individual reporters began spending much of their workday on Twitter, and most major media have at least one staff member paid to stalk Twitter to find trends and news stories and to promote their news outlet's work. Journalists will quote Twitter postings in mainstream news stories, often simply picking up tweets rather than chase down sources for interviews.

So now we have journalists and some academics interacting in real time with ISIS militants on Twitter, the way Stewart Bell of the *National Post* and John Maguire did in the months leading up to Maguire's fall 2015 video. ISIS's Twitter traffic seems grass-roots and authentic, but the messages that go out are very carefully crafted and managed by ISIS's large staff of media managers. Big news comes out of ISIS's headquarters and regional offices. People who are trusted to speak for the "state" craft it and move it to social media and, if there's video, to YouTube and jihad web pages. People who are trusted, especially English-speakers, get to take part in Internet debates with reporters.

ISIS and some of its competitors—there were, at the height of the Syrian civil war, some twelve hundred groups fighting in that small country—are experts with social media, communication apps and file-sharing programs like Twitter and Facebook, as well as Instagram, WhatsApp, Tumblr, Reddit, Paltalk, Viper and Kik. They use encryption software when sharing messages with each other and with potential converts and journalists. Not only does ISIS know how to get the message out, it also knows what "sells" in a world in which the target generation of potential fighters and settlers in the new caliphate were raised on computer-generated video-game, movie and television violence.

The scarred Internet infrastructure of ISIS-controlled territory consists mostly of cellular towers, so ISIS's propagandists prefer Twitter because it's a relatively simple structure that was designed for cell phones. Twitter became established as one of the two dominant social media platforms around 2008. (The other is Facebook, which does not transfer as easily to the small space of cell phone screens.) Twitter forces its users to post messages with 140 characters or less, but it also allows them to link to web pages. ISIS tends to post its video material on YouTube, then get the news out to supporters and journalists by having ISIS propaganda staffers in the Middle East and Europe send out links to these videos to thousands of Twitter followers.

Twitter, which is struggling to prevent its platform from being used by terrorists, does not charge for its services. ISIS, and any other group disseminating propaganda by Twitter, has a ready-made newsletter service to get its news out to the world. Twitter also has a private messaging function that allows people to chat online without being seen by their Twitter followers.

This is something of an evolution from the cell phone texting that was so important to the Arab Spring. The interconnectedness created by cell phones improved the ability of senior and street-level organizers to deploy protesters in Cairo, Damascus and other cities in "smart mobs" with very little likelihood of message interception by the authorities.[14]

Individual ISIS fighters, especially those from the Middle East, tend to stay away from anything political and military and focus their attention on discussions of the meaning of the Qur'an. Most ISIS members on Twitter spend their time discussing religion. The content they put on the Internet hasn't changed much since the 9/11 attacks on the United States in 2001 or the Madrid train bombing in 2004. After the latter attack, investigators found a computer and a thumb drive belonging to the bombers that they hoped would be a mine of information about jihadi terrorism. Instead, it was full of discussions about "good" versus "bad" interpretations, along with some al-Qaeda-approved religious tracts. There were no terrorism playbooks or grand plans. Only a third of the material on the drive had anything to do with terrorism, and it was mostly instructions on how to make the bombs that were used in the attack.[15]

Most material posted by ISIS members is just as mundane. In fact, "ISIS" tweets are a mixture of propaganda and letters home, as well as discussions between ISIS fighters (including the women who support them in ISIS-held territory and back home). These posts may seem tedious, but they connect members to a much larger, very supportive community and help fight the loneliness, isolation and homesickness that many of the foreign fighters must feel. They also act as a sort of permanent pep rally for people who know they stand a very good chance of being killed. Very often, ISIS fighters tweet Osama bin Laden's slogan "We love death more than you love life." But it's the violent material that gets the most notice from the media. It's also the propaganda that many people in the West—potential jihadis and fans of war porn—seek out.

Still pictures of atrocities attached to tweets and video of massacres are part of ISIS's very successful bidding war to become the most notorious and most violent group fighting in Syria, Iraq and, to a lesser extent, Libya and Afghanistan. No other organization in those wars set out to find brutal ways to kill and novel ways to publicize atrocities.

Terrorists tended to be stuck in a body-count bidding war that lacked creativity. Ratcheting up car-bomb body counts may have provided some local publicity, but the world's media tended to ignore these attacks. Al-Qaeda in Iraq and, later, ISIS realized style counts as much as volume. Before it embarked on its execution war-porn program, ISIS leaders realized they needed more horrific ways to kill their opponents to get the attention of the world's media and their audience of potential recruits and donors. Its leaders considered driving "human lawn mowers"—moving blades attached to speeding pickup trucks, which could be driven through crowds—but rejected that idea, perhaps for fairly obvious reasons. Crowds usually contain women and children, and eventually the media tires of people who slice up and disembowel kids. Finding more creative ways to kill is especially important when the victims are poor, racialized people living far from the centres of media power.[16]

Sometimes ISIS has deliberately created video that resembles famous death scenes in movies. A clip showing four men being drowned in a cage resembles the death scene of Vesper Lynd in the James Bond film *Casino Royale*. Both films show the death struggle of people trapped behind bars underwater. And both carry footage shot by divers that show the screaming of the dying. The ISIS film has the extra potency of showing real death. In the 2015 Paris attacks, the assault on the Bataclan concert hall had at least some superficial resemblance to the climactic scene in Quentin Tarantino's *Inglourious Basterds*.

Even with ISIS's well-made war porn, interest in ISIS was fading by the summer of 2015, and attention shifted to the growing refugee and migrant crisis in Europe. That's why ISIS has to bring terrorism to media capitals like Paris. After all, the media will only do so much with crucifixions and beheadings. There always has to be escalation and variation. Abu Daigham al-Britani, a British fighter with ISIS, started out making Instagrams showing himself with severed heads. Then, as Jihad Johnny, he was filmed hacking the head off journalist James Foley and several other Western captives. When that kind of butchery became old, ISIS tried to impress with numbers, slaughtering ten, twenty or more forlorn-looking captives at a time.

ISIS is willing to invest time and creativity. Locking men in a cage that is then suspended over water by a crane, and then drowning them, took a lot of work. The amount of effort required to build the cage and to use three cameras to film the atrocity and to do cutaways of small details like locking the cage is impressive. The work and planning shows in the professional quality of the high-definition video. Editing is important, too, but sometimes ISIS's people became a little too playful. In the second part of the video of the cage-drowning, ISIS men wrap explosive cord around the necks of several victims and blow their heads off. The explosion is shown from several angles and in slow motion, and the editors ran the image backwards to make it look like the flying heads reconnected with the bodies. (A still image from this video was used in a fundraising ad by the Conservative Party of Canada days after it was posted to YouTube.)

Why do they do it? Partly, the videos are entertainment for the troops. They're also a good way to intimidate opponents. Who wants to tangle with ISIS and end up starring in one of these videos? ISIS's reputation for brutality has served it well. Entire towns have surrendered to ISIS with very little fighting because the possibility of being captured has caused their enemies to panic and flee. But ISIS also needs to recruit constantly to fill its ranks if it hopes to expand the territory it holds and expand the "caliphate," something that, by definition, a caliphate needs to do. One of their slogans is: "This Khilafa [caliphate] will have no borders, only fronts."

Although it is cannibalizing al-Nusra (an al-Qaeda-allied group of local fighters, many of whom learned to fight in wars outside Syria) and other jihadi competitors in the region, ISIS can't get many more soldiers from the places that it holds. It needs foreigners to fill its ranks. It's important to remember that ISIS is not really an insurgency, especially in Syria. If anything, it's a colonizing group imposing its ideology and its settlers in occupied areas of that country. ISIS in Iraq does draw on that country's population, but if it is to survive the threats posed by whatever regime evolves in Baghdad, Western air power and the constant war waged on it by Iranian-backed forces and the Kurdish militia, it needs many more men. One fact ISIS propaganda never mentions is that—if the fates of known Western fighters are any indication—ISIS fighters don't usually live very long.

They're not just useful as colonists and cannon fodder. Foreign fighters give ISIS the opportunity to create propaganda in different languages. Foreign fighters, especially those who saw action in Chechnya, Afghanistan and the Balkans, are usually well trained and can be more dependable than local recruits. They have no personal or tribal scores to settle and, in many ways, are so helpless and dependent that they have little choice but to do what they are told.

On the other hand, the presence of foreign fighters in ISIS's ranks provides its enemies with propaganda material. The Russian- and Iranian-backed Assad regime, which, as of fall 2015, holds Damascus and not much else, has used the presence of foreign fighters in ISIS and other opposition forces to tag ISIS as "invaders," which, in many respects, they are.[17]

Because it needs foreign fighters so badly, ISIS is faced with several serious problems. Some of the young people who arrive in their territory, especially from North America and western Europe, are mentally unstable or sociopathic. These people make poor soldiers. The mentally ill recruits are usually undependable and untrainable, and they do not follow orders. ISIS also has to worry about attempts by foreign agents to infiltrate their ranks. There is little time to vet recruits and check their backstories, and no infrastructure to help those who have psychological problems. There are ways to try to expose foreign agents. Ordering recruits to commit atrocities like decapitation might be seen as a way to flush them out. Anyone suspected of not having what it takes to be a good ISIS soldier or who has the whiff of being a spy is assigned to suicide bomber squads. Incompetent soldiers can be put behind the wheel of a vehicle loaded with explosives or fitted up to run into enemy lines wearing a suicide bomb vest.

Those who feel disenchanted with ISIS's tactics or decide that suicide bombing isn't a sound career choice have little opportunity to leave. Some try to return home. A few foreign fighters have joined less extreme opposition groups in Syria. ISIS imposes nighttime curfews and sets up roadblocks behind its lines to try to dampen down desertions. A Lebanese newspaper reported that between September 2014 and February 2015, more than 120 foreign fighters who have tried to leave ISIS were killed by the group. Some, including at least one Canadian, were allowed out to have their wounds treated in hospitals in their own country.[18]

ISIS recruits online, by planting its recruiters at friendly mosques and even, sometimes, by writing to people in prison. Recruits from Muslim countries are usually battle-hardened veterans. Western European recruits—those who go to ISIS's territory and the ones who stay home to kill for ISIS—tend to be socio-economic underperformers. The grim, impoverished high-rise suburban Muslim ghettos of Paris and other French towns were already battlegrounds before ISIS came along. A study of German recruits showed only one-quarter had finished high school and one-third had criminal records. From the United Kingdom, foreign fighters tend to come from more affluent backgrounds. Canadian and American recruits are a mixed bag of college dropouts and a few fairly successful young people.

ISIS attracts them because it has emerged as the most notorious terror group in the world. It indulges in rape, murder and atrocities against civilians and prisoners of war at levels that have rarely been seen since the Second World War. ISIS values the publicity generated by images of those atrocities. Very few terrorist groups get much ink or airtime anymore, especially in the parts of the Middle East and North Africa where ISIS operates. And publicity is oxygen for terrorists. They need it to show they are viable, that they're worth supporting financially, and to prove to recruits that they offer a very good chance of being on a winning team. They also know that Westerners find it troubling when they see people who seem like them wholeheartedly embracing a jihadi terrorist group.

Where does ISIS get its publicity? Not from its military successes, which were largely ignored by Western media even when ISIS took some of Iraq's largest towns. The beheading of journalist James Foley by an English-speaking ISIS terrorist in 2014 generated much more coverage in the West than the capture of Mosul, a city of a million people. Western media deals partly in numbers, partly in images. For instance, a murder charge laid against an attractive young American woman like Amanda Knox (accused of being an accomplice to the murder of her roommate in Italy) will generate far more publicity than a suicide bomb in a busy Middle Eastern market that kills hundreds of people. There's a sort of natural limit on the number of people who can be killed by a car bomb and more traditional forms of terror tactics. The only way to ramp up interest, and coverage, is to become more creative in its violence in the Middle East and to launch attacks on Western targets.[19]

So much of ISIS's war-porn propaganda is directed at the same people targeted by the Canadian army: bored young people who aren't engaged by the consumer ethos of their own society and who feel that adventure is passing them by. They want to step into the video games that have become so important to them and be the heroes that they play on the small screen. As Abu Sumayyah al-Britani, a British fighter with ISIS, posted on Twitter, war is the ultimate in virtual reality.

Call of Duty, one of the most popular video games in the

world, lets anyone who buys the program pretend to shoot people in a very realistic game that simulates modern war, complete with massive, bleeding wounds. ISIS offers what seems to be the chance to play the real game. And, as al-Britani said, recruits get to do it in three dimensions. When they win, there are great prizes: pay, glory, women, loot.

ALTHOUGH THE EXTREMELY VIOLENT PROPAGANDA gets all the media attention, the majority of ISIS messaging is about ISIS governance, justice and public works projects that tries to show ISIS as a benevolent new government. Many of its videos try to give the organization and its fighters a more benevolent face.

Social scientist Jytte Klausen recently wrote that ISIS fighters tweet cute pictures of their cats and their after-battle parties, intermixed with social media posts of almost unimaginable cruelty and brutality. These posts drill home the message that jihad is an obligation for all Muslims, not just people with an obvious cruel streak. ISIS offers the chance to do serious damage to the enemies of Islam, but recruits still get to have somewhat normal lives and plenty of friends. "The content conveys that fighting—and dying—will give your life meaning and is just plain fun and similarly exciting, but 'better' than playing video games like Call of Duty on the couch at home," Klausen wrote. "The secondary messages piggy-backed on Twitter streams range from the dehumanization of other Muslims (Shi'ites in particular) and the bravery of ISIS's righteous fighters." The jihadi community on Twitter acts as bookstores and chat rooms for terrorists. It entertains them, and educates them with sermons on the Qur'an, morality and the justifications to fight. It binds them together and gives them support that firms up their will.

For those who haven't joined ISIS but are steered toward its propaganda network, social media provides a link to recruiters—either in the Middle East or in their home countries—who feed them propaganda and, if the recruit is judged to be serious, gives them the money and contacts to get to Turkey and across the border into Syria or Iraq. The recruiters, mostly Muslim extremists who work for ISIS in its territories or have immigrated to the West, take these conversations private and use encryption software to try to dodge Western intelligence agencies.[20]

Klausen believes ISIS has invented something revolutionary that will remake terrorist strategy, the transformation of social media into a tool of offensive psychological warfare whose mastery is now an important battlefield tactic that can, and has, allowed armies of less than a thousand people to demoralize and defeat tens of thousands of professional soldiers. He's right. Military theorist Sun Tzu recognized centuries ago that battles and wars are won in the mind before the first blow is struck.

Not only has ISIS changed the way war is waged, it's also changed the way wars are covered. Journalists, who have seen their access to battlefields continuously decline since the Boer War,[21] have been driven from it almost entirely and replaced with propagandists.[22] Klausen argues that social media ended ISIS and other groups' dependence on mainstream media to get the message out. Journalists became ideal victims of terrorism, rather than reporters of it.

Beheading footage, far too gory for the mainstream media, is all over the Internet. It's uploaded and downloaded by far-right groups, death-porn addicts, would-be jihadis and anyone else who wants to see it instantly and free of charge. "Slow" media now relies on terrorists for information and images, and what the commercial media gets is a mixture of selected images of violence, ISIS propaganda, half-truths and outright fabrications. ISIS has complete control of the area that it occupies, at least in terms of whether mainstream journalists are allowed in. Except for a team from the online news site *Vice*, very few Western reporters have even tried to get into the region. And ISIS's mastery of the Internet comes at a time when most Western media outlets are in dire financial straits, shedding staff and cutting bureaus, unwilling or unable to pay the high cost of putting and keeping journalists in war zones.

ISIS propaganda about its own invincibility plays well with U.S. media that want to frighten Americans into believing the "caliphate" can only be put down by the use of force by the West. For instance, CNN's website carried no stories of Israel's bombing of Hamas military training targets in Gaza on May 26, 2015, but had at that time an entire page on ISIS's recent successes in Iraq. It included flattering pictures of ISIS fighters shot by ISIS propagandists, taken from the Internet and used for free. On the same day, CNN's website also carried a story about the dismal morale of the Iraqi army after the fall of the Iraqi city of Ramadi. Whatever its successes and failures on the battlefield, ISIS looked like a winner on that website. But ISIS knows that death-porn propaganda kills coverage of its military setbacks. In fact, it released the cage drowning video just after it lost an important town.

ALL THIS PUBLICITY ABOUT ISIS HAS MADE LIFE MUCH tougher for mainstream Muslims in the West. Radicals, many of them converts with simplistic views of Islam and no cultural background in it, have helped create an atmosphere of suspicion that becomes even more heightened every time ISIS makes news. As well, ISIS tries to shame lifelong Muslims into joining its project by throwing propaganda at them, recruiting them around some mosques and writing letters to men in jail.

Tarek Fatah, founder of the Muslim Canadian Congress and

a loud critic of the jihadi crowd, told the House of Commons Standing Senate Committee on National Security and Defence in April 2014 that ISIS and other violent groups have targeted very specific parts of Canada's Muslim community.

The problem of radicalization in the Muslim community depends on which Muslim community you're talking about. If you are speaking about Muslim Kurds or Muslim Baloch or Muslim Darfuris, the problem is non-existent. The same can be said for most Iranian Muslims. However, within the White and Black Muslim converts to Islam, the Somali, Bangladeshi and Attar Muslim communities, and more specifically, the Pakistani-Muslim community, the problem of radicalization is very widespread, deeply entrenched, embedded and framed in an Islam-versus-the-Infidel scenario leading up to an end-of-time Armageddon.

The support structure that exists for Islam-based terrorism or radicalization, all Islamism, which is a starting point to the end part of someone being a jihadi, is multi-faceted. At the base are the Islamist organizations and mosque-based groups that lay the seeds of radicalization not necessarily in the recruitment of terrorists but in the politicization of the sermons that whip up a sense of victimhood of Muslims while cultivating a hatred of non-Muslims and other groups—such as gays and women who demand equality and refuse to wear head wraps or be encased in burkas.[23]

Fatah represents a section of the Muslim community that believes Islamist extremists have nothing to do with their religion and are causing serious harm in countries like Pakistan, where Fatah was born. Fatah wants tougher immigration from jihadi-strong areas, in which all documents, from birth certificates to university diplomas, are carefully checked for authenticity. And he demands that the RCMP be scrupulous about whom it chooses to consult for advice on "Islamic" extremism.

Fatah is not the only Muslim who worries about extremist recruitment. Samy Metwally, an Ottawa-based imam, told a *National Post* reporter that fifteen to twenty people between the ages of twenty and thirty came to him to convert in the three months after Michael Zehaf-Bibeau gunned down Nathan Cirillo at the National War Memorial and shot up the Parliament Building on October 22, 2014. He had never seen more would-be converts, and he worried they, as new Muslims, would be very vulnerable to radical propaganda. "The vast, vast majority of new converts, we have never seen them before, and we never see them again. They disappear and they never come again. That is a big concern. We are concerned about who they are getting information from."[24]

Mohamad Jebara, the chief imam and resident scholar at the Cordova Spiritual Education Center in Ottawa, decided to use the Internet to confront Maguire:

> *John, so you destroyed your Canadian passport. That passport symbolizes a culmination of rights, struggles and values, which Canadians have strived for for generations. In fact, holding a Canadian passport is a privilege and an honour, which many would dream of attaining. I was raised in Ottawa. I skate, rollerblade, cycle, ski, canoe, hike and, yes, I enjoy classical music. I guess that makes me a typical Canadian. But, what is a "typical" Canadian anyways? I memorized the Islamic scriptures when I was 12, and have dedicated the past 22 years of my life to my faith; studying, teaching and defending it. When you say you were one of us, which one of us do you mean? My Canadian identity has not infringed on my Islamic identity—in fact it has made it stronger.*
>
> *John, I'm sorry to have to break it to you, but you've been duped. You've been peddled an empty package. I find it quite ironic that you would cast away the guitar—invented by Islamic Scholar Ziryab in 9th Century Islamic Spain as a soothing tool to help draw people closer to*

God—and replace it with a destructive weapon invented by what you would erroneously refer to as "the kuffar" . . . I will not apologize for being a Canadian Muslim. In fact, my Canadian identity has helped me become a better Muslim. Since you claim to have "maintained a strong GPA," I'm sure you can "put two and two together."[25]

CHAPTER 4

Setting Up the Game

Newspapers are worth an army of three hundred thousand to Napoleon, for the latter would not supervise the interior any better or frighten foreign powers more, than a half dozen pamphleteers in his pay.
—Prince Klemens von Metternich, June 23, 1808[1]

HOW DO YOU GET PEOPLE TO FIGHT? HOW DO YOU GET a kid to give up the life that he—and military recruits are, in most of the world, mainly *he*'s—is familiar and comfortable with and put his life at risk? How do you convince him to fight in any army, let alone one in a foreign country far away? How do you convince a person to kill strangers in cold blood?

ISIS not only succeeds in motivating young people to do these things, it has also become so successful that it's taken the world by surprise. ISIS draws recruits, and it makes them into dedicated fighters who have beaten better-trained and more seasoned soldiers, often when ISIS has been far outnumbered. This is one enemy that is not being underestimated or patronized by Western military analysts. President Barack Obama recently endorsed the judgment of his national intelligence director, who said: "We underestimated the Viet Cong . . . We underestimated ISIL and overestimated the fighting capability of the Iraqi Army . . . It all boils down to predicting the will to fight, which is an imponderable."[2]

ISIS deserves a lot of credit for its recruiting and training successes. Enticing civilians into any army is difficult. Recruitment posters are collectible reminders of the world wars because governments had to put a lot of artistic effort into coercing men to join up. Sometimes, the lure was almost juvenile. During the Second World War, the Canadian army tried to get men to join up with the offer of the chance to tear around in Jeeps. When advertising and public shaming failed, most Western countries used the power of the state to draft men into their armies. Getting them to fight is even harder. So ISIS has come up with ways to turn young men into killers, men fighting a war where prisoners are routinely murdered and civilians are oppressed, raped and enslaved.

First, ISIS's brand of religion, with its simple answers to complex and disturbing modern questions, appeals to people in shattered societies. People in countries that have seen centuries of war and exploitation look out on a world that is rapidly changing and quickly becoming richer, and wonder how they can get a feeling of safety and a sense of being part of a dynamic project. To people who feel they have been left behind, ISIS and other Islamists offer a chance to get to the front of the line, to rule instead of being ruled. The same urge gripped the people of Italy and Germany after the First World War, when they tried to understand the loss of so many men for no obvious reason and struggled with postwar economic misery. Mussolini offered a return to the Roman Empire. Hitler offered German domination of Europe. Abu Bakr al-Baghdadi, ISIS's leader and self-styled caliph, offers the return of the glory days of Islam, when its armies ravaged what was left of the eastern

Roman Empire. In those glory days, Islam seemed on the verge of taking all of Europe. Its armies went deep into France in the eighth century and laid siege to Vienna nine hundred years later.

On the ground, part of ISIS's strategy focuses on the strong bonds that are forged between people in combat. Most foreign recruits come to ISIS in groups. ISIS makes sure these groups stay together and are integrated into an even larger community of fellow soldiers and civilian supporters. Men will fight for each other. As U.S. historian William Manchester put it in *Goodbye Darkness*, a memoir of his U.S. Marine Corps service in the Pacific Theatre in the Second World War: "Those men on the line were my family, my home. They were closer to me than . . . friends had ever been or would be. They never let me down and I couldn't do it to them."[3]

Theorists call this "identity fusion." In a sense, fighters create a sort of new family, often with stronger loyalties than existed in the families they left back home. They are willing to kill and die for each other. Soldiers will roll their eyes when they hear civilian politicians talk about fighting for a cause, yet they will still fight on if the bond between soldiers remains strong and if they have faith in their immediate superior officers. One reason for America's failures in Vietnam is that soldiers and officers were rotated through on fixed terms. Units were constantly adding and losing men. In most other wars, soldiers stayed together for the duration.

Soldiers fight better when they believe in a cause, and will become quite vicious when their home—even if that "home" is a trench holding their war buddies—becomes threatened. The cause has to be more substantial than a vague idea of patriotism or loyalty to a socio-political system. Seeing an enemy fighting ferociously for a cause can instill both fear and respect in soldiers on an opposing side. American soldiers in the Pacific both feared and admired the Japanese soldiers who fought so tenaciously at places like Guadalcanal and Iwo Jima. Defeating these tough soldiers was a source of some pride, and the fact that the Japanese had been so cruel to captured Americans and other Allies made it easier to justify their destruction. So did racial differences, which were played up in American propaganda.

Things were different in Vietnam. Soldiers knew there was little support for the war back home. They were not on a crusade against a cruel enemy determined to exploit a large part of the world. Very few of them believed America's propaganda about neighbouring states falling like dominos to Communism, and if they did believe it, they didn't care. American soldiers told interviewers they believed the cause of democracy was "crap" and "a joke," while praising the bravery of the Viet Cong and the North Vietnamese "because they believed in something and knew what they were fighting for."[4]

That's how insurgents and religiously motivated fighters like ISIS can defeat the forces of the weakened countries of Iraq and Syria and make inroads in Libya and the sub-Sahara. And it's how the mujahedeen defeated the Soviets, and the Taliban wore the Americans down in Afghanistan. Revolutionary and insurgent groups like the Viet Cong and the Afghan mujahedeen have, since the Second World War, beaten armies with ten times more firepower and manpower because they were fighting for a cause, and for comrades, rather than for pay.[5] ISIS builds those bonds among foreign fighters by connecting them through social media. Then they fight in solid, stable units, often alongside friends from back home and with their new wives and children just a few kilometres away. And they do it with ISIS propaganda officers feeding them a steady diet of political and religious propaganda that arrives, most often, on cell phones.

IN A MANY WAYS, ISIS IS A REACTION TO COLONIALISM and imperialism—Western and Turkish, starting at the end of the First World War and culminating in the Iraq War, and now the meddling of Iran, Saudi Arabia, Russia and, once again, the West. Its political roots go deep into the history of the region, drawing partly on a Wahhabist interpretation of Islam, partly on the ethnic politics of the region. ISIS was created by a group of men led by Abu Musab al-Zarqawi. In the mid-1990s, al-Zarqawi and a jihadi ideologue named Abu Muhammad al-Maqdisi plotted attacks against the Jordanian government. They were caught and spent a short time in jail, where al-Zarqawi had his first dreams of creating a caliphate. When he was freed in 1999, al-Zarqawi moved to Afghanistan. At first, he operated as an independent commander and refused to swear allegiance to Osama bin Laden and al-Qaeda. In 2001, al-Zarqawi fled the U.S. attack on Afghanistan and settled in northern Iraq, where he prepared for the foreseeable U.S. invasion. In October 2004, more than eighteen months after the invasion of Iraq, al-Zarqawi finally swore allegiance to bin Laden, though it's clear that he took the oath rather lightly.

Their creation was called al-Qaeda in Iraq (AQI). The group was very good at waging insurgent warfare against the Americans and their allies but not quite as adept at winning local hearts and minds. In January 2006, the group changed its name to the Mujahedeen Shura Council to try to remake its image. Al-Zarqawi didn't live long enough to see if the plan worked. Later that year, he was killed in a U.S. air strike. The Islamic State of Iraq was declared in October 2006, just as the United States began beating back an insurgency that turned into brutal street fighting. The Americans had used their most potent weapon, cash, to buy off Sunni leaders and had given them some political support against the repressive Shia-dominated Baghdad regime, causing a big drop in terrorism in Iraq. After Barack Obama was elected president, the bales of cash that had been distributed by the Americans stopped arriving and a new war between Sunnis and Shiites (and minorities like the Kurds and Yazidis) broke out in northern Iraq.

For four years, ISIS was one of several groups fighting for control of the region between Baghdad and the Turkish border. The deck was shuffled again in 2011 when the Arab Spring misfired and the Syrian regime of Bashar al-Assad was left fighting for survival against several formidable armed opposition groups and more than a thousand small freelance operations. In January 2012, the Islamic State in Iraq created Jabhat al-Nusra, a spinoff organization in Syria. However, ISIS's Iraqi leadership couldn't get along with al-Nusra leader Abu Mohammed al-Julani. The new emir of ISIS, Abu Bakr al-Baghdadi, decided to take over direct leadership of one single organization straddling the Iraqi-Syrian frontier. By then, al-Baghdadi had also weakened his ties with al-Qaeda's leaders in Pakistan. He changed his organization's name to the Islamic State of Iraq and the Levant to reflect its new territorial goals, which included Syria and its historic claim to the Levant coast, which is now partly in Lebanon.

Between 2008 and 2010, ISIS had developed a new generation of senior and mid-level leaders. Most of them, including al-Baghdadi, knew each other from American prisons. They were a mix of Islamic Salafists and members of Saddam Hussein's old fascist Baath Party. Many of the latter had served in the Iraqi army and some of the older ones were veterans of the ugly, now-forgotten war between Iraq and Iran in the 1980s. The Baathists brought discipline, while the Salafists brought ideology. Syrian president Assad's repression of Sunnis gave ISIS the chance to spread across borders, and to draw on foreign jihadis attracted to the *cause célèbre* of the Syrian civil war.[6]

Militarily, the mixture worked. ISIS was able to seize the big city of Mosul in the spring of 2014 with just eight hundred men. It started the campaign with a terrifying propaganda blitz, then sent squads of assassins into the town to kill Mosul's leaders. Once the Iraqi leadership was dead, ISIS drove off more than fifty thousand Iraqi soldiers stationed in the region. ISIS attacked them with "technicals," civilian trucks fitted out with machine guns that could move swiftly on the battleground. Suicide bombers played the role of artillery, a new tactical innovation that proved to be very effective. ISIS captured a big stockpile of real artillery in the city, most of it American-made and donated by the United States to the new Iraq security force. It still, however, uses suicide bombers because of their shock value.

Control of Mosul and the provinces of Nineveh and Salah al-Din in Iraq and a large chunk of Syria has made ISIS the world's richest terrorist group, one with the means to project its power into the Gaza area, where it fights both Hamas and Egyptian forces, and into Libya. In early 2015, its assets were believed to be between $1.3 and $2 billion.[7] Every day, until coalition bombers began attacking its tanker truck convoys and oil prices collapsed, ISIS was taking in $1 million a day in oil revenues. ISIS also makes millions from ransoms for local people and foreigners. It shakes down locals for protection money, loots the belongings of people it sees as enemies and imposes a tax on Christians and Jews who are unfortunate enough to still live in ISIS-held territory. The tax is about seventeen grams of gold per year, the equivalent of the weight of four gold dinars minted twelve hundred years ago.[8] At least 20 per cent of its income comes from collecting antiquities and selling them, or from collecting a percentage from archaeological site looters. This percentage is rising as ISIS work crews strip the ruins of heritage sites like the Syrian city of Palmyra.

The money goes to the salaries of front-line fighters: \$200 to \$600 a month, on top of free food and lodging. ISIS carefully doles out salaries to civil servants and subsidizes farmers. To keep urban residents happy, ISIS cut the price of wheat and bread while at the same time levying a tax on grain. ISIS even operates several mills, which also turn a profit. In some communities, it has also enforced rationing to make sure the people get a fair share of available fuel and food.[9]

Al-Qaeda's leaders aren't happy with the new situation. They backed al-Nusra in Syria and kicked ISIS out of the movement in February 2014, ostensibly for being too vicious. ISIS was to prove just how cruel it could be. That June, the group began a big offensive in Iraq, one that generated a string of propaganda videos of ISIS atrocities against people and ancient ruins and artifacts. The group then declared a caliphate, an entity that exists in ISIS's interpretation of Islam under a very strict set of rules and expectations.

Despite the hype, the world's Muslims have, for the most part, ignored ISIS's claim of a caliphate. If they accepted the claim, they would also have to agree to ISIS's ludicrous assertion that ISIS's warlord al-Baghdadi is the political and spiritual leader of all of Islam. It's also very controversial among jihadis, including al-Qaeda, which rejects the claim completely. The claim does, however, free ISIS fighters from allegiance to any other religious or state power.

AYMENN JAWAD AL-TAMIMI, AN EXPERT ON TRENDS IN the Islamic world, tries to put ISIS into perspective. Westerners wonder whether ISIS simply wants to carve out its own nation from failed states like Iraq and Syria (and possibly Libya), or whether it is seriously trying to start a movement that will engulf the Islamic world, then the rest of humanity. He argues that ISIS's goals are far more ambitious than al-Qaeda's, and talk of world conquest is more than just propaganda. ISIS members believe the end of the world is at hand. Once it dominates and purifies Islam, a culminating battle with infidels of all kinds will be fought in territory that ISIS controls in Syria.

"ISIS's portrayal of its own goals in Syria-Iraq indicate that it seeks to establish an Islamic state that can become the core of a new Caliphate that will eventually strive to dominate the rest of the world," al-Tamimi recently wrote. "Despite their ongoing disagreement with Zawahiri [the leader of al-Qaeda], ISIS abides by bin Laden's dictum that there are only three choices in Islam: conversion, subjugation or death."

ISIS's globalist pretensions are evident in the video testimonies of its members from Syria. In one case, an ISIS fighter named Abu Omar al-Ansari, who participated in the ISIS-led capture of the Mannagh airbase in Aleppo province in August 2013,[10] makes it clear that it is necessary to establish an Islamic state over the entire world, and that the project is not limited to Syria. In another video, American recruit Abu Dajana al-Amriki expressed similar sentiments: "We'll bring the right of Islam to rule all of the entire world." British fighters interviewed by the publication *Vice* have also expressed the same view.[11]

The ideology of ISIS lies partly in its interpretation of Islam. It was formed by Shiites coping with the violence of modern Iraq, and partly in reaction to the wrenching changes in the decades after the moribund Ottoman Empire was put out of its misery at the end of the First World War. Treaty makers set borders that had nothing to do with the heritage or the needs of the local people. The postwar power vacuum was filled briefly by France and Britain, just long enough for European Zionists to get a strong foothold in

Palestine. And, since the end of the First World War, the region controlled by ISIS has rarely been a happy place. The British were the first to use air power against civilians, in raids launched in 1920 against Iraqi "insurgents." The British called this "aerial policing," and kept up the bombing through the 1920s.[12]

But the British and the Zionists weren't the only newcomers at work in the Middle East between the wars. An element of Nazism developed in the region during the Depression, and Adolf Hitler's *Mein Kampf*, translated into Arabic, is still a big seller there. Hitler and his murderous henchman Heinrich Himmler had a strange fascination with Islam. It was, and still is, reciprocated.

It's one of the great uncomfortable facts of history that many of Hitler's soldiers in the last years of the war were foreign fighters. Some, like Soviet POWs left starving in filthy camps, outside the protection of the Geneva Convention and the Red Cross, joined the Wehrmacht to save their own lives. Others believed Nazism could unify Europe into a single, orderly state. The German army also attracted rabid Jew-haters from across the globe who gladly fought a war of genocide. Amin al-Husseini, the Palestinian Arab political and religious leader, was one of the latter.

Al-Husseini visited the concentration camp at Sachsenhausen in 1942 to see how the Germans were using death factories to efficiently kill large numbers of Jews. Sachsenhausen was one of the first camps to have a camouflaged gas chamber, which was far more efficient—and psychologically easier on the murderers—than shooting, hanging or beating the victims to death. Al-Husseini wrote Hitler in January 1941, saying he wanted to build concentration camps near Tunis, Baghdad and Jericho to eliminate the Jews in Arab lands.[13]

Al-Husseini had fled the Middle East when the British put a warrant out for his arrest for stirring up a revolt, and, by 1941, he was living in Germany as an honoured guest of the Nazis. He had met Hitler in 1941, but the Führer had also found time for other guests from the region. Rashid Ali al-Kailani, the former Nazi-allied premier of Iraq and a leader of an Islamist organization, met Hitler on May 15, 1942, after promising the Führer "to fight a common enemy until victory."[14] But it was al-Husseini who was singled out by the Germans to be the leader of the pan-Arab movement, perhaps even leader of a revived caliphate. And he would also, many Nazis hoped, close the door to Jews trying to flee to Palestine, the place named by the League of Nations in 1922 as a refuge for the Jews. Al-Husseini set up housekeeping in Castle Bellevue, the former home of Germany's Crown Prince and now the official residence of the German president.

Germany had been a player in the Middle East well before the First World War. Kaiser Wilhelm II went to Damascus and laid a bronze laurel wreath at the grave of the great Muslim warrior Saladin—it would later be shipped to London as a war trophy by Lawrence of Arabia—and forged an alliance with the Turks that lasted through the war. Arab intellectuals wanted independence from the Turks, but they also looked at newly united Germany, which had forged an empire in 1871 out of a motley collection of states, as an example of a folk-based federation.

In the years between the world wars, Berlin was a haven for Muslim agitators from Pakistan, Iran, Iraq and the Levant, and many of them were involved in the Islamic World Congress, which opened in Berlin in 1931 with al-Husseini as its president. They could worship at the Berlin-Wilmersdorf mosque, which opened in Berlin in 1927. By the time Hitler took power, German diplomats and industrialists had become old Middle East hands and had forged strong links with some of the most vehement Jew-haters in the region.

All of the Arab nationalist groups opposed the Allies during the Second World War, since Britain occupied Egypt, Palestine and Iraq, while France held the mandates to govern Lebanon and Syria. Rebels—in fairness, anti-colonial fighters—in the British territories were secretly supplied with weapons by Berlin and Rome. Germany had a decades-old policy of preventing the Mediterranean from becoming a "British Sea." Max von Oppenheim, the attaché to the German consulate in Cairo, worked for decades to support extremist Muslim leaders and incite jihad against the British.

At the very least, Hitler wanted to tie down a sizable British force that would be needed to beat back any "holy war" launched by the Arab nationalists and their religious allies. But he also had a strong affinity for Muslims, which does seem strange when measured against his disgust for non-Germanic people. Nazi writers came out with a series of books describing al-Husseini as "the little Hitler" of the Middle East and claiming Islamism, like Nazism, was delightfully anti-democratic and anti-Jewish.

During the war, four Muslim-dominated "Eastern Legions" were raised to fight in the German army. Muslims, mainly from the Balkans and Soviet republics—areas that ISIS still draws on for recruits—were welcomed into some SS units, especially the vicious twenty-thousand-strong Handzar SS division recruited in Bosnia. Al-Husseini acted as political officer for these units and recruited firebrand imams, who flooded them with al-Husseini's writings calling for the destruction of Jews in Britain's Palestine mandate and in Europe. The Handzar troops eagerly took up the challenge, committing atrocities against Jews in France and the Balkans.

At the 1944 opening of a German school to train fifty imams to serve as chaplains in Muslim SS units, al-Husseini talked of the common fight of Nazis and Muslims against the Soviets, who had forty million Muslims under Communist control, and the Jews of

Europe and in the Muslim world.[15] Even Middle Eastern leaders in Allied-dominated regions hedged their bets by currying favour with the Germans. King Farouk of Egypt secretly communicated with the Nazis, as did the leaders of Iran. The British sidelined Farouk and, helped by the Soviets, staged a coup in 1941 that installed Shah Reza Pahlavi as Iran's monarch.

But al-Husseini and the rest of the Muslims who backed Hitler had bet on the wrong horse. By the end of 1944, al-Husseini was on the run and most of his personal papers were in American hands. Four days after the fall of Berlin, al-Husseini crossed into Switzerland and was reunited with the cash he had stashed in a Zurich bank. By the summer of 1945, he had been picked up in Paris, but each of the Allies was playing its own game. France wanted to keep its Middle East possessions. The British were trying to create a strong Arab League that would be close allies in the post-colonial world. After U.S. publications like *The Nation* accused him of complicity in the Holocaust and said he was creating a sort of Palestinian Nazi movement, the Americans didn't want al-Husseini either.

He was soon in Cairo, free to wage war on Jews.[16] In 1947, his men retrieved a stash of Nazi-supplied rifles and joined with the Muslim Brotherhood in an attack against Tel Aviv's Jewish quarter. Throughout the 1940s and 1950s, he worked to build up Islamist movements in Pakistan, Iran and the Middle East. He opposed West German reparations to the Jews. At the same time, former Wehrmacht officers were helping to build the armies of the newly independent Arab states. ODESSA, the organization that smuggled Nazi fugitives out of Europe, even set up a Middle East headquarters to help Nazis who had escaped justice by using ODESSA's "ratlines."

Johann von Leers, a former SS officer and Nazi propagandist, found work with the government of Gamal Abdel Nasser in Egypt.

He also developed strong ties with the Palestinian Arab leadership and supplied the newly installed leader, Nasser, with a copy of the Protocols of the Elders of Zion, a supposed Jewish plan for world domination that was, in fact, forged by Russian anti-Semites in 1901. Nasser's brother translated the old hoax into Arabic and it has been a staple of Islamist propaganda in the region ever since. Von Leers also worked with al-Husseini on a book called *The Truth about the Palestinian Question*, which sold quite well.[17]

Nazi expatriates helped build up the secret police in Egypt, supervised its jails and ran the concentration camp where the regime's political enemies were locked up. Similar situations existed in Syria, where Alois Brunner, one of Adolf Eichmann's most murderously efficient staff members, went to work. Israeli agents tried to kill him with a letter bomb in 1977, but failed.[18] A Canadian diplomat found Brunner in Syria in 1987, but no country wanted to try him.[19]

Muslims from the Soviet republics who had joined the Nazi military—like all Soviet citizens who had thrown in their lot with the Germans or had just surrendered to survive—were dead men if they fell into Russian hands, so many of them, too, fled to the Middle East after the war. But as the wartime generation died off, a new group of Soviet leaders came forward who were willing to forget parts of the past. The Soviets had been agitating in the region since the Russian Revolution, promising an end to colonialism. When Russia became a superpower, it began undermining the Western-backed regimes in Israel, Iran, Iraq and Jordan, and tried to make Nasser a puppet. The Soviets, who financed wars of national liberation throughout the developing world, also took Yasser Arafat, a protege of al-Husseini, under their wing. It was a small world after all.

The wartime Muslim leader and the up-and-coming Palestinian

commander met in 1969, when al-Husseini was getting ready to give up leadership of the Palestinian movement. Al-Husseini gave the thirty-nine-year-old Arafat his blessing. One of the first things Arafat did was switch the Palestinian alliance away from conservative Saudi Arabia and toward nationalist Egypt, which, at the time, was a Soviet client. Again, the Palestinian leadership had hitched their cart to the wrong horse. Egypt would make its own peace with Israel. Fundamentalist Shiites were energized by the destruction of the Shah and the creation of an Islamic Republic in Iran in 1979. Some Sunnis like Osama bin Laden would become inspired to fight a holy war against the Soviets in Afghanistan and the Americans stationed in Saudi Arabia to defend and protect Kuwait. A new Islam emerged, defiant of any non-Muslim presence in the Islamic world, and looking for answers to complex questions of modernity in unchanging texts and laws that were written more than twelve centuries ago.

But the Islamic world is a complicated place. National and tribal alliances are complicated. The actions of non-Muslim powers in the region, which need its oil and the capital built up by Saudi Arabia, add to the complexity. ISIS, drawing on the prejudices and fears of some Muslims, offers simplicity, order and fellowship. Its message resonates with Muslims throughout the world. And many people simply like to back a winner.

Since September 11, 2001, radical Islam has looked like a winner. Afghanistan has, yet again, proved to be unconquerable. The World Trade Center attacks were what communications theorist Jacques Ellul calls "the propaganda of the deed."[20] Americans struggled to give meaning to the attack, just as they had struggled to turn Pearl Harbor into the start of a crusade against fascism and militarism. Moderate Republicans and Democrats were pushed to the margins. Even musicians like the Dixie Chicks were boycotted and hounded for speaking out against war. Radicals gained power on both sides.

The Americans put their propaganda machines to work. In 2002, the U.S. State Department launched Radio Sawa, an Arabic soft-rock and pop music station to beam America's messages into the Islamic world.[21] The department also hired a major advertising agency to create extended-length TV commercials in which successful Muslim Americans talked about the good aspects of American society. The commercials were supposed to air during Ramadan, but Al Jazeera would not touch them. They may have been broadcast by a few Indonesian television stations. But the State Department had only $15 million to spend worldwide on the campaign, making it something of a joke in the world of big-money advertising.[22] Much more money and effort was spent by the American right undermining the credibility of United Nations arms inspector Hans Blix, who was actually succeeding at his job of dismantling Saddam Hussein's missiles, poison gas and nuclear facilities.

Pacifists, at first, got little attention. The anti-war crowd reached too deeply into 1960s culture. The hippy era had ended three decades before the World Trade Center attacks and the world had changed. Most of the people pretending to be modern hippies had no real memories of the Vietnam era. And the post–9/11 world was not comparable to that of the 1960s. The Viet Cong had never attacked the United States, let alone killed three thousand Americans on live TV. If any comparison could be made, it would be with the post–Pearl Harbor United States. Most Americans wanted payback and closure.

Once the U.S.-led coalition went into Iraq in 2003, it had to produce the one thing Americans needed: a clear win. That need for victory explains the "Mission Accomplished" aircraft carrier photo-op/press conference held off the California coast just weeks after the invasion. George W. Bush arrived in a fighter plane—a clear middle finger directed at critics who said the president dodged the Vietnam War by joining the Air National Guard. He was kitted out in a flight suit, its strapping forming a bizarre codpiece that suggested the president had oversized genitalia. Real victory, however, could not be sold to the public until Saddam was in the bag. He was, eventually, flushed out of his hole near the end of 2003, given something resembling a trial and hanged at U.S. military base Camp Justice. The judge who passed the sentence would eventually be beheaded by ISIS.

By June 2014, ISIS looked like the real winner. Its capture of the big city of Mosul came at a time when most media and politicians in the West had begun to ignore the Muslim world (outside of Israel and Palestinian territories) again and were focusing on the war that was developing in Ukraine. ISIS would snap world attention back to the Middle East. By then, many Muslim-born foreigners and converts, drawn by the jihadis fight against the brutal, secular Assad regime, had started making the dangerous trip to Syria. ISIS would accept anyone into its new, dynamic project. All they had to do was accept its religious and earthly laws and work to expand the caliphate.

Chapter 5

The Will to Kill

Let the boy win his spurs.
—Edward II at the Battle of Crecy[I]

Millions of words are written about killing, and thousands of movies portray various kinds of slaughter, but very few describe how difficult it is to get people to kill other people. S.L.A. Marshall, one of the United States' official historians of the Second World War, pioneered a very interesting field of study—the mechanics of convincing young men to aim directly at another person and pull the trigger. Marshall interviewed hundreds of American combat veterans and wrote his most controversial book, *Men against Fire*. In it, he argues there is always a small group of men—sociopaths and sadists, for the most part—who are more than eager to kill, and who were drawn to units like the Waffen-SS. The vast majority of men, he says, have a natural repulsion to killing, especially when they can see the enemy. It takes a lot of physical and mental training to kill when self-defence is not involved and, even then, killing leaves most people with psychological damage. Dave Grossman, a psychologist and retired U.S. military officer, has taken Marshall's studies even further, blaming the coercion of men to kill for post-traumatic stress disorder (PTSD) and other psychological problems that dog veterans.

Throughout history, Marshall and Grossman argue, men have been unwilling to kill. Most were never expected to. War was the business of professional foot soldiers, the nobility and, at rare times, feudal levies that weren't worth much in combat. Like their counterparts in the great armies of Rome and its conquerors, members of the warrior class were brought up from birth to be soldiers. (Those of the upper classes who didn't want to fight usually joined the Church.) The few men who showed up on medieval battlefields were there either by choice or because their feudal lord demanded it and could drive them from their farms if they didn't at least pretend to fight. With the invention of guns, soldiers were lined up shoulder to shoulder to create a solid volley, but also to create peer pressure to fire toward the enemy.

Ridgeway was the last battle fought in Ontario. In many ways, it was one of the last gasps of the American Civil War. In late June 1866, several thousand Irish republicans, almost all of them veterans of the Union or Confederate armies, crossed the Niagara River from Buffalo, New York, and took the town of Fort Erie, Ontario. The Irish had been recruited in their home country and from the slums of American eastern seaboard cities by both sides in the Civil War. The North, which came close to war with Britain several times during the crushing of the Confederacy, held out the promise of help for the liberation of Ireland. Turning a blind eye to the Fenians' preparation for the invasion of Canada was a way of partially paying that debt.

At first, the Fenian invasion of Ontario seemed to be successful. After seizing Fort Erie, they moved inland along the railway line and the road that connects the Niagara River with the Welland

Canal at Port Colborne. They planned to take the canal and the railway line connecting Toronto and Detroit, then capture the rest of what's now eastern Canada and trade it back to the British for Irish independence. It wasn't the most brilliant plan ever conceived, but several thousand Irish-Americans and their supporters in Canada were willing to believe in it.

Just south of the small town of Ridgeway, the Fenians fought Canadian militia, mostly students and young working men from Toronto and Hamilton. The Fenians created what could have been a bloody trap for the Canadians. By the end of the morning's fighting, the Canadian line was broken and the Fenians were firing at fairly close range toward the backs of the fleeing militiamen. There should have been dead farm boys and University of Toronto students all over the place. There weren't.

In fact, throughout the battle, the Fenians were almost certainly firing over the heads of the Canadians. After years of reading anti-British propaganda and of being part of the bloodiest war in American history, the Confederate and Union veterans on the Ridgeway battlefield—most still wearing their blue or grey Civil War uniforms—could not shoot into the faces or even the backs of the green Canadian soldiers.

Canadians killed at Ridgeway tended to be men who somehow got into the cloud of overhead bullets. Peter Vronsky, in his book *Ridgeway: The American Fenian Invasion and the 1866 Battle That Made Canada*,[2] describes the Fenians firing volley after volley at the Canadians. The militia had moved toward Fenians hidden in a line inside some woods. Because of a foul-up in communications and dreadful leadership, the Canadian line broke and fell back. Then the Canadian commander heard the Fenians were about to launch a cavalry charge and ordered his men to form a square. That might have been a good tactic in the Napoleonic

Wars fifty years earlier, but in an age of more powerful rifles, it was an invitation to be massacred. Finally, all discipline in the Canadian force broke down and the Fenians chased them from the field, running after and shooting at the militiamen for more than five kilometres, until the Canadians reached the shelter of the town.

It's a dramatic story of hot-blooded, murderous violence. There's only one thing missing: piles of dead bodies. Most of the Canadians killed at Ridgeway appear to have died almost by accident. One Canadian seems to have been shot going over a rail fence, or was hit hiding behind the rails.[3] Another was shot while concealed in gunpowder smoke in an orchard.[4] Yet another was shot in the woods, where he was hidden by trees. One man was killed standing outside the Canadian "square." One unit of Canadians suffered three casualties when they broke away from the main Canadian line and tried to come in behind the Fenians.

The battle ended with a bayonet charge. No one was stabbed to death.

The military and media reports Vronsky draws on talk of volley after volley fired by the main mass of the Fenians and from the advancing, then retreating, Canadians. Yet during the battle and the manoeuvres before and after, only nine Canadians died of wounds inflicted by the Fenians, and one was killed by "friendly fire." One Canadian died of heatstroke while marching in the brutal late-June heat, and twenty-one died of diseases in camp during the campaign.

Getting men to kill is very, very difficult, unless they feel that they, or their loved ones—including friends—face immediate danger.

After the Second World War, Marshall found that about 80 per cent of soldiers would not shoot to kill their opponents and many wouldn't shoot at all. Even most fighter pilots balked at killing: a small proportion of pilots scored the bulk of the kills. Snipers, who hunted other humans, were held in contempt by most foot soldiers. Some Second World War soldiers would shoot to miss, but many found other things to do during battle, like carrying dispatches or loading guns. At Ridgeway, Canadian troops were seen loading guns and passing them to men more willing to fire.[5] People fighting indirectly, for instance by firing artillery or dropping bombs from airplanes, were much more willing to use their weapons. There was far less correlation between their actions and visible damage to human flesh.

ISIS doesn't kill from a distance. In ISIS's war, artillery and air power play minimal roles. Unlike the major wars of the twentieth century, the ISIS war requires killing with small arms, at close range, rather than indirect killing by bombs and artillery shells. That may change as ISIS acquires better weapons, but in its early years it used suicide bombers—often Westerners who had too many psychological problems to make good soldiers—as artillery to "soften up" their opponents and, presumably, horrify them.[6]

The American soldiers of the Second World War were trained the traditional way, shooting for scores on bull's-eye targets. Marshall recommended the American military desensitize trainees by simulating real killing by using realistic, human-shaped targets. The military accepted Marshall's advice and began using human-shaped firing range targets and pop-up figures. So did law enforcement agencies. By the Korean War, most American soldiers were willing to shoot directly at their opponents. While that may not seem like much of an achievement, it was, in fact, a training breakthrough. By the Vietnam War, some 95 per cent of American foot soldiers were shooting at the Viet Cong and North Vietnamese Army.

The age of the video game would arrive a generation later. The jury is still out over whether video games are a cause of violence or simply fill the empty hours of disenchanted young men, but either way, they're ubiquitous. Kids now grow up playing games that simulate warfare better than home-country training ever could. They are desensitized to the sight of killing. Images that used to be considered too shocking and obscene to be viewed by anyone are now part of the daily lives of many young people throughout the world.

In a sense, they are seeing in virtual reality the kind of carnage that used to be common. In Europe, there was a time when gory executions and bloody punishments were normal; brutality on women and children, especially poor ones, was common; and most people didn't live to see adulthood. This was also the norm for African-American slaves until Emancipation, and people in failed states see this public violence today. The combat soldiers who were reluctant to kill during the world wars grew up in a different world. They did see death and violence. Many of them were raised on farms, where killing is a normal part of life. Even in the cities, young people saw much more real violence than they do now. School brawls were common, gangs were part of life and domestic violence was quietly tolerated. But rarely did young people in Western societies see slaughtered human beings until the world wars, and even then it took men months or years to harden. Many never did, and they became psychiatric casualties, diagnosed with "battle fatigue" or "shell shock."

Human death was something like sex, a taboo thing that was filtered through a sort of societal censorship. Dead relatives were laid out in private homes, but only after undertakers had done their best to make them look alive. Newspapers reported on street violence, but their photographers picked out the least gruesome pictures. (They saved the worst to show their friends and colleagues.) Movies were full of violence, but the killing was obviously fake.

Shot people had no holes, no blood, and certainly no sucking chest wounds or gaping exit holes. The people killed in movies were invariably mad, bad guys or racialized people like Plains Indians. They only needed to be shot once to fall down quietly and die without spasms or twitches. There were no compound fractures, no protruding bones, no brains, no gore at all.

George Romero caused quite a stir in 1968, when shooting *Night of the Living Dead*, by going to a local slaughterhouse and buying a few buckets of organs and intestines. Those inexpensive props, never before seen in a mainstream movie, were so novel and boundary-pushing that the movie made Romero a wealthy man. Sam Pekinpah's 1969 film *The Wild Bunch* took this violence even farther. Movies now use computer-generated effects to show dying men blown in half (*Black Hawk Down*, *Stalingrad*), piles of heads (*Kingdom of Heaven*), men and women burning alive (*Elizabeth*) and decapitations with axe and sword (most graphically shown in *Game of Thrones*). Teens are allowed into theatres to see people blown up, stabbed, garrotted, hanged, drowned, burned to death, hit by cars and, of course, shot in vast numbers. We live with a level of simulated violence that was believed to be inappropriate for the generations who lived through the world wars, even though many had seen the real thing close up. It's ironic that the film *The Longest Day*, made for an audience of adults who had fought at D-Day or had seen the news reports, was far less graphic than *Saving Private Ryan*, which was seen by audiences who had virtually no experience with war violence, other than the bloodless gore in the media.

Now video games mirror the desensitization techniques used in military training. The scenes look real. The players must fire reflexively to stay in the game. The targets bleed, they get eviscerated, decapitated and blown apart. At the same time, we've kept kids from playing with each other. They don't fight in schoolyards.

Few live on farms, and those who do rarely see animals butchered, since most places now outlaw on-the-farm slaughtering. Sick dogs and cats in cities are "put to sleep" by veterinarians, not dispatched by a teenager eager to use a .22 rifle. Christmas gifts of BB guns and other weapons used by boys to inflict pain on animals are now fairly rare, and firing one off may well lead to a visit by the police.[7] Meat comes in squared-off chunks or already made into fast food, and, for many people, fur is murder.

So we have moved from a world where real blood and gore were part of life to one in which they are rare. Yet photographs, television, movies, YouTube videos and video games make violence ubiquitous without leaving a mess on the floor. Western culture is now drenched in violence, and everything from decapitation to crucifixion to horrific images of people blown apart by gunfire is available, free of charge, to anyone who wants it.

Today's gang culture is full of violence toward both men and women, and offers the same kind of comradeship and easy power that ISIS peddles. We are fascinated with violence and live in a society drenched with it, but we almost never talk about it. When a white supremacist who worshipped the racist regimes of Rhodesia and apartheid South Africa gunned down nine people in a South Carolina church in the spring of 2015, public discourse almost immediately shifted from the murderer and his victims to a debate over whether the Confederate battle flag should still fly in front of the South Carolina state legislature. When, three years earlier, a demented Norwegian white supremacist named Anders Behring Breivik murdered seventy-seven people, mostly children at a youth camp, the discussion centred on Breivik's wish list of famous victims. Everything else—the pain of the victim, the diseased mind of the killer, the availability of guns, the glorification of natural born killers and vigilantes—was pushed aside.

In his definitive book On Killing, David Grossman cites Alvin Toffler's 1970 book, *Future Shock*: "'This manipulation of reality may provide us with exciting games, entertainment, but it will substitute not a virtual reality, but a pseudo reality, so subtly deceptive as to raise the levels of public suspicion and disbelief beyond what any society can tolerate.' This new 'pseudo reality' will make it possible to replicate all the gore and violence of popular movies, except now you are the one who is the star, the killer, the slayer of thousands."[8]

Police and airline pilots are trained in video simulators that, to the highest degree possible, mimic the sort of emergencies they'll face on the job. That way, they don't have to think of a response. It will be reflexive, originating in parts of the brain that control basic movements. Many video games work the same way. A person who is "trained" only by one of the more violent video games would still likely make a poor soldier, since the games are hardly depictions of real combat. But they do help get rid of the abhorrence of killing and make it much easier for the imaginary warrior to seriously consider dishing out death to real people. Rather than posture and threaten—which is the way most street fights play out and historic battles were fought—the desensitized recruit aims and shoots to kill. Of course, once that video-game warrior is on the battlefield, reality, in the form of a sentient enemy, takes over. One of the striking similarities between Westerners who have gone to fight for ISIS is the shortness of their lifespan in combat. Many of them are killed within a few weeks of arriving in Syria or Iraq. And it seems the younger the recruit, the easier it is to get them to kill, as warlords in central Africa have discovered—and exploited. ISIS trains younger and younger operatives and has formed brigades of child soldiers, some of whom are taught beheading techniques on "blood dolls."

But not all desensitized, violence-addicted young people who don't fit into materialistic Western society join ISIS (or, for that matter, any army). Urban gangs provide the same opportunities for violence and peer support. Military historian and psychologist Dave Grossman, who has written several important books on killing, notes that it's the poor, especially in Black communities, who pay much of the price for the violence that has so enriched game designers, movie studios and even musicians. "Poverty, drugs, gangs, discrimination, and the availability of firearms all predispose more blacks than whites toward violence." Alcohol was used to destroy the culture of American Indians, he says. "The pumping of media violence into ghettos is equally genocidal."[9]

Some abnormal people simply go it alone and shoot up a school or a church, usually in the name of an ideology that is, itself, simple and insane. White supremacy, for instance, is easy to grasp. Its symbols are available everywhere, from stores selling Confederate flags to people making silk-screen swastikas. The neo-Nazis, Ku Klux Klan members and other white supremacists print hate "literature" by the ton, and their web pages are easy to find. And, if things go poorly, there are lots of them in jail to provide companionship and protection. Jails have become recruiting grounds for all kinds of extreme ideology, from jihad to neo-fascism.

Movies glorify the loner-killer righting wrongs, seeking vengeance, doling out justice when the state and the courts have failed. Sports is drenched in violence and violent imagery.

"When our hockey players and other sports figures display a degree of lawlessness, violence and aggression never before seen in such competitions, we should begin to wonder," Grossman wrote in *On Killing*. He thinks we should start asking ourselves why we so often instinctively turn to violence to solve what should be seen as very small problems. Shootings at elementary schools, high schools and colleges are becoming so frequent that a body count of fewer than five or six barely makes them news. To get on the front page of the big newspapers or warrant more than a brief mention on national network newscasts, a school shooter needs killing statistics in the double digits.[10]

Young people, and the people who make violent video directed at them, don't realize how killing shatters the human psyche, how it affronts our brains, which have evolved to protect the species. Soldiers have often spoken or written about the personal damage done to them by killing. Journalist and historian William Manchester, who nearly died on Okinawa in 1945 when an exploding Japanese artillery shell drove a fragment of bone from another American soldier into his back, was tormented with PTSD symptoms the rest of his life. Much of the pain came from reliving the danger, the exhaustion, the loss of good friends, and the horrific injury that had sent him home. But he was also plagued with memories of killing. He finally confronted his demons almost three decades after the war by revisiting the islands where he had fought his war, and wrote about the catharsis in a 1979 book optimistically called *Goodbye, Darkness*.

Guadalcanal had been a tough fight for Manchester, but the fighting was restricted to one end of the island and civilians had found safety away from the battlefront. That fight, though incredibly vicious, was between soldiers, and most of the bigger battles were fought at night. The battles got progressively tougher, more stained with civilian blood and more personal as Manchester and his Marine unit got closer to the Japanese homeland. Manchester, even in the late 1970s, still had very mixed feelings about the "Japs," as he called them throughout the book. They were a brave and ferocious enemy whom he respected as fighters—an opinion that raised the value of the Americans who killed them—but also a cruel enemy who deserved to be punished. They weren't quite people.

In *Goodbye, Darkness*, Manchester uses the language of dehumanization. He claims to have done so to retain the flavour of the war, but more likely it was part of the defence mechanism drilled into him at Parris Island's boot camp. He felt more and more empty as the years went by and the lines between the "good" Americans and the "duplicitous" Japanese became blurred by time and by the new, strong alliance between the United States and Japan. It was difficult to accept that people he was trained to see as monkeys and vicious killers were now among the United States' most valued friends and investors.

What had the suffering been for? What was the purpose of the deaths of so many of Manchester's war buddies? During his trip through the Pacific Islands, Manchester was troubled by the fact that the Japanese had done through corporate investing what they could not do by force: take and hold what they called the Greater East Asia Co-prosperity Sphere. Guadalcanal was, by the late 1970s, a Japanese tourism destination. The Japanese dead on Guadalcanal were honoured with shrines, while there were few monuments for the Marines. On Peleliu, where the Americans had fought a bloody battle for a strategically worthless island, the U.S. monument to the men killed in 1944 had been allowed to crumble. The Japanese monuments, meanwhile, were looked after with great care and adorned with fresh flowers, possibly paid for by the Japanese on the island who were working on a supertanker port project. Manchester took pictures of both countries' monuments and put them in the book to show his readers that the Japanese, who had lost the war, gave care and attention to their monuments, while Americans, who said their soldiers were winners and heroes, had let their monuments fall apart.

He felt let down by his country, so Manchester reached back to the days of the war and wrote about the brotherhood among soldiers: "These men on the line were my family, my home. They were closer to me than I can say, closer than any friends had been or ever would be . . . Men, I now know, do not fight for flag or country, for the Marine Corps or any other abstraction. They fight for one another. Any man in combat who lacks comrades who will die for him, or for whom he is willing to die, is not a man at all. He is truly damned."[11] He had cold contempt for profiteers and fools who did not respect the fighting men on either side. He singled out the quartermaster who left his safe billet on Peleliu to loot the bodies of Japanese soldiers and got himself killed, and the two officers on Okinawa who called their men "bellhops" and were deliberately directed by these same men down a path that led to their deaths. Manchester called this incident "The Execution of the Two Pricks."

Manchester didn't expend much energy thinking about democracy, but he tells how he felt when he learned, during the Battle of Okinawa, that President Franklin Roosevelt had died. "I thought: *my father.*"[12]

And a dark sexuality wafts through Manchester's war stories. He wrote of his sexual arousal when facing extreme danger. At night, on the battlefield, he hallucinated "the Whore of Death," who drifted across the battlefield to seduce young men. She visited him in his dreams as part of the trauma that he fought as a civilian.

Manchester was haunted by one memory in particular: his first kill.

He was the first Japanese soldier Manchester had ever shot at, or had even seen at close quarters. The man did not fit the stereotype of the small, thin, bandy-legged Japanese infantryman. Manchester's target was "a robin-fat, moon-faced, roly-poly little man with his thick, stubby, trunk-like legs sheathed in faded khaki puttees and the rest of him squeezed into a uniform that was much too tight." Manchester came upon this Japanese sniper's hideout, a small hut, from behind and surprised him. When the sniper tried to turn, he was caught up in a harness that he used to steady his Arisaka rifle. The Japanese soldier didn't try to surrender. He tried to free himself and move "crab-like" into a corner.

Manchester's first shot missed and the bullet buried itself in the wall of the hut. The second caught the Japanese sniper in the femoral artery.

Blood poured out of the wound, turned the man's leggings to a bright red, and pooled on the floor. The soldier lived long enough to see the pool and dip his hand in it. He smeared the blood on his cheeks, his shoulders "gave a little spasmodic jerk, as though someone had whacked him on the back; then he emitted a tremendous, raspy fart, slumped down and died. His eyes glazed over. Almost immediately, a fly landed on his left eyeball. It was joined by another. I don't know how long I had stood there staring . . . A feeling of disgust and self-hatred clotted darkly in my throat, gagging me.

"Jerking my head to shake off the stupor, I slipped a new, fully-loaded magazine into the butt of my .45. Then I began to tremble, and next to shake all over. I sobbed, in a voice still grainy with fear: 'I'm sorry.' Then I threw up all over myself."[13]

MANY PEOPLE ARE ATTRACTED TO VIOLENT CAUSES BY the prospect of becoming part of some great mythology. And that's not just an attraction offered by radical Islam. Canadian children are brought up in a society where all people who die wearing the country's uniform are remembered as heroes.

Jonathan Vance, the country's leading expert on war and mythology, often writes about the ways Canada used its myth-making apparatus to make heroes out of young men who had gone overseas for whatever reason—patriotism, adventure or because they had been pressured into joining up—and were killed. In the First World War, most "heroes" were obliterated by shellfire without having much opportunity to look their enemies in the eyes. Others were cut down by machine guns or were gassed. A few had the chance to engage their opponents in single combat, but such fighting, except in the air, was rare. Some wealthy young men who were killed in the war were memorialized in stained-glass windows in churches, invariably as young knights rather than as confused boys blown apart in artillery barrages. Every town and many rural townships had war memorials, almost always showing a young man, rifle in hand, ready for action. Even now, the most remembered poem of the flood of First World War doggerel is a plea for more soldiers to reinforce the vast political and military failure that created and sustained the conflict. "In Flanders Fields" offers no good reasons to "take up our quarrel with the foe," other than to help the dead justify their own deaths, but it at least hints at the possible outcome of that decision. Canadians needed solace for the loss of so many boys, now buried in neat rows in carefully tended cemeteries in France and Belgium. A new generation of heroes went overseas to fight in Europe and in Hong Kong during the Second World War. The names of the dead were added to the monuments commemorating the First World War heroes.

The monuments, strangely, commemorate only those heroes who died. Very few statues and plaques were raised for those who had fought gallantly and survived. Canadians who won medals for courage, including those few who were awarded the Victoria Cross, are rarely commemorated. And when the Ontario government decided, in 2007, during the Afghan war, to rename a stretch of Highway 401 from Trenton to Toronto as the "Highway of Heroes," the definition of "hero" was limited to the dead. There would be no parade down the Highway of Heroes for the living, no matter how gallant they had been. Nor would there be a victory parade (though one was held in Ottawa for Canadians involved in the bombing of Libya).

Medals and decorations were usually awarded in ceremonies out of public view. For kids brought up in Canada after the First World War, the association of heroics and death is quite natural. They were raised in a culture where war and death dominate the media, the history books and even the statuary. At the same time, pacifism is defined as effete. Millions of students would be taught "In Flanders Fields" but few would ever see the postwar poetry written by bitter veterans who were left to struggle with their mental and physical wounds. This one was suggested by veterans in the small Ontario town of Priceville in 1921 as a new verse for "In Flanders Fields":

We thought to catch the torch ye threw,
And to the charge ye left—be true;
But once the strife of arms was past
Then high resolves were overcast
With selfish greed. And lust to gain
Has put to flight the sweet, sad pain
Of sacrifice. And in its train
Went noble deeds. Are ye aghast?
In Flanders' fields.[14]

The message, handed down from the First World War, is fairly clear: to be a hero, don't come back alive. Over time, that glorification of war and martyrdom was resisted by people who believe we should see war as a human failure, not as a glorious contest. Some men, however, would still look to war as a solution to their problems, and the world's.

PEOPLE CAN BE TRAINED TO KILL FOR A CAUSE, FOR A charismatic leader, and for friends and family—pretty much in reverse order. ISIS has set up a system where fighters, so far all of them men, are given all of these reasons to fight. ISIS soldiers fight in small, tight units of friends who volunteer or build strong bonds under fire. It encourages jihadi women to come to the war zone, bear children and stay close to the fighting. And it offers what are claimed to be full, complete, eternal truths, articulated by a leadership that is politically and religiously infallible. That's a pretty potent mix.

Like any cult, ISIS tries to prevent its members from staying in contact with their families back home, especially if the people back home are not radical Islamists. It tries to create ways to make sure its members don't feel comfortable or welcome in the normal world, despite the claims of people like John Maguire that they were normal people fighting for a just cause after they had made a logical decision.

Yet normal people don't destroy UNESCO World Heritage Sites and make propaganda movies of their work. The Prophet Mohammed and the early leaders of Islam did not set out to erase traces of the past, but ISIS does. It bulldozed at least part of the ancient cities of Nimrud and Hatra. It has destroyed mosques and shrines built more than a thousand years ago because it believes any physical monument to the dead is idol worship. When it took Palmyra, one of Syria's most important archaeological sites, it murdered the retired curator of the ruins and filmed executions in the old Roman theatre. Then it got to work blowing up two of the ancient temples on the site. Presumably, it has also looted the ruins, since, after oil prices collapsed in 2015, the illegal trade in ancient antiquities has become one of ISIS's most important income streams.[15] The United Nations says the people behind the destruction are war criminals, but no one has seriously tried to drag them into a court of law. So far, the International Court of Justice has not indicted ISIS and its leaders for its crimes against culture, which include the destruction of some of the archaeological sites of several of the first cities ever built and the systematic destruction of the religious and cultural heritage of the people it conquered.

Terrorists, like gangsters, build tighter bonds between foot soldiers by making them partners in crime, and ISIS has pushed this practice to a higher level. Crucifixions, drowning people in cages, throwing them from the tops of buildings, beheading by knife or with explosives, burning people alive, rape, kidnapping and slave-trading are acts of such cruelty that most societies would not accept—or take back—anyone involved in them. So those involved in ISIS's worst crimes know that they are burning the bridges between them and the rest of the world. That transition from college boy or farmer into moral outlaw helps bind them together. Some commentators say ISIS's use of early Islamic punishments is an expression of its faith and the group's determination to roll the clock back to the days of the Prophet. This argument is unconvincing. Mohammed and his followers did not behead men with Bowie knives or fire rocket-propelled grenades at captives locked in cars. These killings are done to shock and intimidate, and to create a wide moral and legal gulf between ISIS killers and the rest of the world.

The bonds of atrocity are strong enough to last a lifetime and to survive after the cause is long lost. Nazi SS units developed tough bonds that survived the war. Nazi government and military leaders with money and political connections in Spain and the Vatican established "rat lines" to get their men out of Europe and into safe countries. Despite being wanted men, the Nazis kept up a support system until they died. Those engaged in atrocities were bound by the danger, stigma and guilt that come with them. They also know that their crimes can only be understood by those who have committed similar acts and justified them in the same way. It's difficult enough for soldiers to deal with the trauma of fighting and killing, but atrocities push things up to a new level.

There was a reason the Nazis switched from killing Jews and other victims in mass shootings by German soldiers to an industrial system manned, at the front lines, by prisoners and foreigners. Only the most frighteningly psychopathic Germans were able to cope with committing atrocity upon atrocity. Even a society that regarded Jews as subhumans and educated children to believe they lived in a death struggle with Soviet Communism could not find enough young men who could endure the stress of committing the mass murder of civilians and prisoners of war. German soldiers committed many atrocities in the Soviet Union, but it was brigades of SS soldiers, many of them Ukrainians, Poles and men from the Baltic republics, who provided most of the manpower for genocide.

A soldier who commits atrocities "*must* believe that not only is his atrocity right, but it is proof that he is morally, socially, and culturally superior to those whom he has killed," Dave Grossman says. The military theorist says atrocities are the defining act of denial of their perpetrators' humanity and the ultimate act of affirmation of their superiority. To have any hope of surviving as a rational being, someone engaged in killing must violently suppress any thought that he has done anything wrong. "Further, he *must* violently attack anyone or anything that would threaten his beliefs. His mental health is totally invested in believing that what he has done is good and right."[16]

It helps that many young people, whether raised in the Middle East, Iraq or elsewhere, have seen so many atrocities long before they decide to commit them in a three-dimensional world.

Canadian communications scholar Michael Strangelove says carnage videos, whether they're made by ISIS or posted online by others, take what used to be called the CNN Effect and extrapolate it. Life, including war, exists to be recorded.

Canadian propaganda expert Paul Rutherford has described how the U.S. propaganda videos of targeted attacks during the Iraq War made the American public see the war as a Disney-movie-type experience in which the killing, as in James Bond movies, is off-screen or bloodless.[17] Like a Bond movie, the Iraq War had a megalomaniac villain threatening to destroy the world with super-weapons. This was somewhat deliberate. The British, for example, launched "Operation James" against the port city of Basra, with targets "Pussy" and "Galore."[18]

Sex and death often fight it out for Internet market share. "Aggression and sex not only involve intense emotions, they draw upon the same unbridled drive for pleasure, especially in the case of the masculine libido," Rutherford wrote in a recent book that examines porno-violence. "War can replace sex. One of the trivial results of the Iraq War was how it changed, briefly, the pattern of searches on the Internet: reports came out that the hunt for sex sites, consistently the favorite on the web, had been upstaged by the hunger for war news."[19]

Even during the 2003 invasion of Iraq, Al Jazeera was still a major journalistic force and an important conduit of al-Qaeda propaganda. Now Arabic speakers could tune in to the news and see something other than the Arabic services of networks based in countries that were fighting Iraqis, or view the broadcasts of American cable news networks. Technology had made coverage much easier. Just over a decade before, transmission of images in the first Gulf War required large, expensive satellite uplink systems.

By 2003, one reporter could carry the gear needed to file from rural Iraq. Ten years after *that* war ended, a person could record a battle, atrocity or speech on a phone worth a couple of hundred dollars and immediately upload it to the Internet. The 9/11 attacks and the invasion of Afghanistan and Iraq War were the glory days of American cable news and of TV news services worldwide. They were the go-to place for porno-violence. Since then, they have been in financial decline, and war is unlikely to revive them, since CNN, Fox and MSNBC will always have to trim ISIS videos to make them fit for broadcast. Those who really like that stuff will turn to the Internet to see the real thing. And the networks will always have to rely on ISIS for handouts, since they can't get their own reporters into ISIS-held territory.

The Americans used video to undermine the Iraqis during their two invasions of that country, while al-Qaeda weaned itself off preachy videos given to Al Jazeera, the Qatar-government-owned news agency whose Arab-language service has been attacked by the government of Egypt and by Western critics as a mouthpiece for Islamic extremists, and learned how to make movies.

The Martyrs of Bosnia, a propaganda video created by jihadis fighting in the Balkans during the civil war in the former Yugoslavia and released in the late 1990s, was a breakthrough film. It came out in both English and Arabic. In 2001, *The State of the Ummah*, a professionally produced al-Qaeda movie, was posted on the Internet just in time for the 9/11 attacks. It showed flattering pictures of Osama bin Laden and his fighters. The film was mined by Western media for imagery of the terrorist group. Still, the combat was obviously staged.

By the time the United States returned to Iraq in 2003, inexpensive digital recorders had flooded the market and cell phones were starting to be equipped with video recorders that made films that were good enough for websites like YouTube.

Unfortunately, many American soldiers chose to record their own atrocities. In 2007, the Defense Department banned soldiers from uploading to YouTube, but it lifted the ban two years later. It also tried to control content—and, likely, inspire soldiers to shoot more palatable video—by creating its own video site, TroopTube, in 2008.[20] The Taliban in Afghanistan already had its own YouTube channel: Istiqlal Media.

When various factions in Iraq launched their "insurgency" against the U.S. military forces in their country, many of the attacks were captured on video. High-definition short films of army trucks being blown up with improvised explosive devices (IEDs) and American soldiers being gunned down and blasted with rocket-propelled grenades were uploaded to eager consumers throughout the world. Some of that footage has made it into mainstream newscasts and documentaries. American soldiers learned to watch for kids with cameras and cell phones as an early warning sign of trouble.

Now, jihad videos are everywhere. Some are full-length movie features with the same kind of design and camera work as movies shot in Europe or North America. Some are how-to videos for training, instruction and recruitment. Others are documentary-style videos recording battles, executions, confessions and media releases. Many are tribute videos that commemorate the death of significant group members. The vast majority, however, are long, preachy sermons that stress orthodoxy and conformity to the extreme jihadi version of Islam. The University of Arizona's AI Lab Dark Web research project has located and archived more than fifteen thousand videos from terrorist websites, about half of which are related to IEDs.[21] The video *Thunderstruck*, a mashup of videos showing U.S. military vehicles attacking civilian targets, was posted in 2006 by al-Qaeda in Iraq and had nearly 650,000 views by 2010. The video was headlined: "What We Should Start Doing to the Whole Middle East." It has been followed by a series of other professionally shot, well-edited, full-length war-porn videos directed at young men.[22]

By 2008, there were already complaints that YouTube had become the broadcaster of choice for violent jihadis. "Although YouTube has made efforts to control video content, the site is still heavily used by extremists for video sharing," Frank Cillufo, homeland security director at George Washington University, said. "The reality is by shutting YouTube Jihadi videos down, it is more or less a game of whack-a-mole: they pop up somewhere else."[23]

Jihadi video makers came into their own during the war between Gaza-based Hamas and Israel in 2008. Hamas uploaded high-quality close-up colour video of dead and injured civilians and property damage. Israeli imagery was shot from planes, helicopters and drones and tended to be in black and white. Israeli video was posted on a well-designed web page, but it lacked the immediacy and availability of the Hamas footage. Israel did try to catch up through the war, filming Hamas fighters firing rockets and mortars at Israeli civilian targets from schools, hospitals and UN compounds.[24] By 2015, Israel was sending out links to videos on social media. The Israeli Defense Forces (IDF) tried to build a reputation as a humane organization, one that sent military field hospitals to Nepal after the 2015 earthquake and treated civilian casualties from the fighting in Syria. While framing itself as benevolent, the IDF also made it clear it was ready to take on any threat from ISIS.[25]

Westerners, who had invented modern propaganda, have been slow to rise to ISIS's challenge. When they've done so, their propaganda has often misfired. On June 7, 2006, the Americans dropped two five-hundred-pound bombs on Abu Musab al-

Zarqawi's hideout. The bombs killed al-Zarqawi's spiritual adviser and his sixteen-year-old wife. The ISIS founder briefly survived, and the Task Force 145 team leader who called in the attack got to the wreckage and tried to resuscitate him. He failed, but the Americans took the body for an autopsy, then released pictures of al-Zarqawi that revolted his followers and many others in the Muslim world.[26] The Americans learned from their mistake. When Osama bin Laden was tracked down and killed, there would be no pictures and no public funeral.

EVEN AL-QAEDA WAS SHOCKED BY THE LEVEL OF VIOLENCE in the ISIS propaganda. "Among the things which the feelings of the Muslim populace who love and support you will never find palatable . . . are the scenes of slaughtering the hostages," al-Zawahiri, the leader of al-Qaeda, said in a letter to al-Zarqawi, the leader of ISIS. "You shouldn't be deceived by the praise of some of the zealous young men and their description of you as the shaykh of the slaughterers . . . We are in a battle, and more than half of this battle is taking place in the battlefield of the media."

As ISIS grew, it released *Salil al-Sawarim* (The Clanging/Clash of the Swords), Part 1, in 2012. It was a boring mishmash, but Part 2, made by a different filmmaker, moved ISIS much farther ahead. The film documented an assault on Haditha, Iraq, from the planning, through the training of the attackers, to the fight itself. The raw film was edited to show the story of two of the young fighters who died in the assault. Sometimes the filmmakers actually had the sense to use humour. One short film showed ISIS fighters rescuing a camel that fell into a pit. This was described in a caption as an action to "liberate a prisoner in the desert."

Most of the propaganda was directed against the governments and soldiers that ISIS was fighting in Iraq and Syria, but ISIS propagandists soon realized they could generate much more support outside the region by going after the United States. Each Clash of the Swords was better produced and more violent, showing battles, the massacre of prisoners and much shorter lectures. Some included music sung by people who could carry a tune.[27]

Then, in August 2014, ISIS ramped up the violence in its propaganda to a level that has never been seen from any country or group. After a series of short videos were released, no one could seriously argue that ISIS was not a terrorist group, at least in the sense that it used violence to instill panic in its enemies. And, of course, it used violence to attract a certain kind of violent young man, Muslim-born or convert. *A Message to America* is probably, in mainstream Western culture, the best-known ISIS video. It shows journalist James Foley, who had been kidnapped while covering the rebellion against the Assad regime, held by gunmen for two years and traded among militants fighting in Syria, being forced to read a screed attacking American plans to carry out air strikes against ISIS. The setting and imagery were carefully chosen. Foley was shown on his knees in the desert gravel, wearing an orange jumpsuit similar to those issued to Muslim prisoners held by the Americans at Guantanamo, Cuba. A small microphone was clipped to his collar.

"I call on my friends, family and loved ones to rise up against the real killers, the U.S. government," Foley said in the last moments of his life. "For what will happen to me is only the result of their complacency and criminality." He criticized his own brothers in the U.S. military and ended with, "I guess, in all, I wish I wasn't an American." Even those who had seen the gruesome al-Qaeda video of the murder of journalist Nick Berg a decade before were likely not prepared for what came next. The executioner, his face covered, began speaking with a London accent. After killing Foley—the graphic details were edited out, but the reporter's severed head was shown tossed onto his body—the killer reappeared, dragging terrified American journalist Steven Sotloff. "The life of this American citizen, Obama, depends on your next decision," the executioner said. (A video of Sotloff's murder was released a few weeks later, but he may well have died moments after Foley. If not, he must have lived the last few days of his life in utter terror.)

A string of these videos was issued in the next few months, most of them ending with the same cruel cliff-hanger. The video showing the slaughter of Abdul-Rahman Kassig, an American convert to Islam who had been kidnapped while giving medical aid to Syrian refugees, was tarted up with graphic, stomach-churning footage of the beheading of captured Syrian soldiers. This time, viewers could see the faces of the killers: they appeared to be Europeans and, perhaps, North Americans.

The stream of ISIS propaganda videos turned into a flood, with five or six loaded onto the Internet every day. They had worked. Media throughout the world talked about the thousands of young people, many of them Muslim first-generation citizens, and many of them young people from families with no Muslim heritage and, like John Maguire, raised in middle-class homes in secular Western countries, dropping everything in their lives and trying to sneak into the most dangerous place on the planet.

Richard Barrett, senior vice-president of the Soufan Group, a security consulting company, said in 2014 that he estimates there are 12,000 to 15,000 foreign fighters in Syria and Iraq. Radio Free Europe/Radio Liberty put the figure at between 17,000 and 19,000 foreign fighters in 2013, about 32 per cent coming from Europe and Turkey. The United Nations estimates there are 20,000 foreign fighters. About 2,000 are from Chechnya and Dagestan; around

4,000 are from the West. The rest are from the Middle East and northern Africa.

Almost all of the foreign fighters who joined the U.S.-backed mujahedeen war against the Soviets in Afghanistan during the 1980s came from the Middle East. Barrett has counted eighty-three countries that foreign fighters have left to join ISIS or one of the other groups fighting in the two countries. Yet many of them knew each other before arriving in ISIS territory and befriended ISIS militants on platforms like Twitter and Facebook: "Their literacy with social media is so much greater than even before. That is why the whole understanding and awareness of what's going on in Syria-Iraq has been able to spread so widely."

Barrett says extreme Islam really is "a gloss over a much deeper desire for a sense of identity and purpose and belonging, and they want to participate in something, too." He believes people attracted to jihad want to be part of something dynamic, but they also want to be led and they want to be told what to think. Fulfillment comes from breaking the bonds to a world that has become boring and offers no interesting goals. They may be all right economically, but that's not enough to make them happy.

"I think converts from the West are going particularly because a convert by definition is seeking for some sort of broader truth, and they're being offered it in spades by the narrative coming out of Syria-Iraq." ISIS tells volunteers that it doesn't care about their background. It doesn't care if they've had trouble with the law or at school. It simply offers them a new life in a better world, on the winning side of a struggle for a new civilization, Barrett says.

Twitter and other social media are vital links for these people, not just to feel bonded to a community but also for instruction. They can get step-by-step advice on how to radicalize, and help with the problems that arise as their lives change. At the most extreme, they can get assistance to travel to the Iraq-Syria war zone. Once in what Barrett calls the "Twitter bubble," they find it very hard to leave.[28]

Brian Michael Jenkins, an expert on ISIS, told a U.S. congressional committee that ISIS propaganda is very successful.

"European authorities are already being overwhelmed by the volume of persons travelling to and from Syria," he said at a meeting of the House Homeland Security Committee in March 2015.

Thus far, the number of Americans involved appears to be manageable with current resources and laws, although that number is growing. According to official estimates, between 130 and 150 Americans have gone to or attempted to go to Syria in the past three years—already more than the total number who have gone to or tried to go to all the other jihadis fronts since 9/11, a few more than 100.

Western governments must also deal with the threat of action by frustrated homegrown jihadis who are inspired by al-Qaeda's or ISIS's exhortations to act but are unable to travel to Syria. ISIS's claimed recreation of the caliphate has galvanized extremists worldwide. ISIS's use of deliberately barbaric forms of violence resonates with a unique, self-selecting audience of people who are not repelled by such atrocities and may even seek to participate in them. Intensive media coverage of terrorist attacks like those in Brussels, Ottawa, Sydney, Paris and Copenhagen or of stabbings or driving automobiles into crowds provides further incitement to jihadist fanatics and jihadist loons.[29]

ISIS IS ACTIVELY ENGAGED IN SEXUAL SLAVERY AND mass rape. ISIS not only considers rape to be legal, it encourages its men to buy women from sex slave markets. Many of these slaves are young women from the Yazidi minority. ISIS attacked the Yazidi in 2014, after the city of Mosul fell. Some five thousand Yazidi women were captured when ISIS attacked their villages in northern Iraq. Most of the men, along with any boys old enough to have armpit hair, were massacred, while the women, babies and young girls were packed off to warehouses, where potential customers inspected them like livestock. Some of these crowded barns hold as many as two hundred women and girls. Children as young as eleven were sold with the approval of ISIS's Islamic courts, which notarized bills of sale. The courts also uphold the "right" of ISIS soldiers to claim captured women as their personal property. They, or their heirs, may sell them or give them away.[30]

When the Yazidis were attacked, military analysts in the West believed ISIS was simply expanding and engaging in its usual genocide. In fact, the Yazidi campaign, which ended with the intervention of Western air power, may have been a huge slave raid from the beginning. In an online posting called "The Revival of Slavery before the Hour," the author of the English-language article wrote:

> *Prior to the taking of Sinjar [the Yazidi homeland], Sharia students in the Islamic State were tasked to research Yazidis to determine if they should be treated as an originally* mushrik *[indigenous religious] group or one that originated as Muslims and then apostatized . . . The apparent origin of the religion is found in the Magianism of ancient Persia but reinterpreted with elements of Sabianism, Judaism, and Christianity, and ultimately expressed in the heretical vocabulary of extreme Sufism.*

By not being part of Islam or one of its direct ancestor religious groups, Yazidis are, in the mind of ISIS, fit only for slavery or death.

That was enough justification for ISIS to decide that, unlike

Christians and Jews, the Yazidis could be not be spared in return for a *jizyah* payment:

> *Also, their women could be enslaved, unlike the majority of the apostates who the majority of the* fuqaha *[scholars] say cannot be enslaved and can only be given an ultimatum to repent or face the sword. After capture, the Yazidi women and children were then divided according to the Sharia amongst the fighters of the Islamic State who had participated in the Sinjar operation, after one-fifth of the slaves were transferred to the Islamic State's authority to divide as* khum *[spoils of war].*

The author of the ISIS text on Yazidi slavery insists that children are not separated from their mothers, although eyewitness accounts gathered by the *New York Times* from escaped slaves put the lie to that claim. Some women were bought by wholesalers, photographed and sold by catalogue for a few hundred American dollars.

The re-establishment of slavery in the Middle East helps ISIS's end-of-time prophecies come true. ISIS's scholars cite Islamic writings that say that, before the last great battle, "the slave girl gives birth to her master." The cryptic line is interpreted to refer to ISIS's belief that a child of a slave fathered by the slave's master is a free person, with the social rank of the father. Slavery is also supposed to be a way to combat adultery and fornication, since the rape of slaves is not seen as real sex.[31]

ISIS has enslaved Iraqi and Syrian women, and many other women unlucky enough to fall into their hands. The women who are captured know they are in for a terrible ordeal. A few manage to escape, and report that ISIS fighters and leaders indulge in sexual sadism and torture. Women in the region know the awful details and some have had others strangle them rather than live through that.[32] At least one escapee has managed to get revenge by killing her master,[33] but such justice is rare. More common are stories like that of American aid worker Kayla Mueller, kidnapped by ISIS while she was leaving a Doctors Without Borders hospital. She was tortured and repeatedly raped by ISIS leader Abu Bakr al-Baghdadi as a spoil of war before she was killed in the spring of 2015, either by al-Baghdadi or an American air strike.[34]

In July 2015, ISIS's Research and Fatwa Department issued a how-to manual for the slave trade. It expanded legal slavery to include the holding and raping of Jewish and Christian women. Pretty much any woman, outside of ISIS, who is not pregnant can be enslaved and raped. Rapists claim it is *ibadah* (worship) to force their captives to have sex, and insist they are required to rape and degrade all women considered by ISIS to be infidels.

ISIS's organized rape has caused some foreign fighters to have second thoughts about the caliphate, although most defend rape and slavery when confronted online by critics and journalists. The issue has caused some cleavage within ISIS, which answered the grumbling in May 2015 with an editorial in its official publication, *Dabiq*.

"What really alarmed me was that some of the Islamic State's supporters started denying the matter as if the soldiers of the Khilafa had committed a mistake or evil," the editor wrote. "I write this while the letters drip of pride. We have, indeed, raided and captured the *kafirah* women and drove them like sheep at the edge of the sword."

AND, OF COURSE, THERE'S DEATH. IN SYRIA ALONE, about seventy-five thousand anti-government fighters have been killed since the civil war broke out in that country. ISIS has a certain appeal for the suicidal, whether they want to go out as suicide bombers or as cannon fodder. Either way, they become martyrs. And lots of Canadians have joined their ranks.

John Maguire became a martyr soon after making his briefly famous video. He was not the first. Six months earlier, the Al Hayat Media Center released an eleven-minute video starring Timmins resident Andre Poulin. He had converted to Islam in northern Ontario, then had moved to Toronto and talked several other Canadians, Muslim-born men, into going to Syria.

The video, called *The Chosen Few of Different Lands,* was a slick job advertisement for martyrs. Opening shots of the eleven-minute high-definition digital clip showed shots of mountains and wilderness meant to portray Canada. These led into a film similar to the cult movies that Nazi propaganda minister Joseph Goebbels used to make about street-fighter Horst Wessel, whose tawdry death at the hands of Communist gangsters turned out to be a lemons-into-lemonade moment for Hitler.[35]

Poulin, in his new identity of Abu Muslim, started his video with a spiel that would be copied, tone for tone, by Maguire months later. It was a proclamation of his normalcy, his sanity, his lack of criminality:

"I had money, I had family, I had good friends . . . It wasn't like I was some social outcast. It wasn't like I was some kind of anarchist, or someone who just wants to destroy the world and kill everyone. No, I was a very good person, and, you know, mujahedeen are regular people too . . . We have lives, just like any other soldier in any other army. We have lives outside our job." Poulin said he did not want to live in Canada and pay taxes "used to wage war on Islam."

"We need engineers, we need doctors, we need professionals. We need volunteers. We need fundraisers. There is a role for everyone."

The action shifts to the Syrian government military base in Minning. Poulin charges at the enemy at the side of his comrades, but the digital editors have made him easier to spot by highlighting him so he sort of glows. It's fitting imagery for what happens next. Poulin gets in front of his colleagues and runs at what's supposed to be a Syrian army position. Then he's hit by a big explosion. Sorrowful comrades prepare his body for burial as the film's narrator drives the message home.

"He answered the call of his Lord and surrendered his soul without hesitation, leaving the world behind him," says a voiceover with a mid-Atlantic English accent. "Not out of despair or hopelessness, but rather with a certainty of Allah's promise." The video ends with a gauzy, heavenly image of Poulin saying, "Put Allah before everything."[36]

And that's apparently a pretty good ending for a troubled kid from a hole-in-the-wall Canadian mining town. Poulin had dabbled in Communism and anarchism. He acquired a taste for blowing things up. Before Poulin left Canada, he had been arrested twice for threatening the husband of a woman he was sleeping with.[37] But he died a hero, and his comrades say he's enjoying a sweet life in heaven. The film was there for everyone to see. According to ISIS, and probably in his own mind, Andre Poulin went out a winner.

CHAPTER 6

Twitterversal Soldiers

ABU TURAAB, A CANADIAN FROM THE TORONTO SUBurb of Mississauga, helped ISIS make its name as a purveyor of porno-violence. He was an early ISIS recruit, joining it in 2010. He came back to Canada for medical treatment when he was wounded in 2012, but by April 2013, he was again in ISIS territory, posting gory pictures of severed heads and taunting the West with words. According to *National Post* reporter Stewart Bell, who wrote a remarkable series of stories based on online interviews with jihadis, Turaab became a darling of Western media for spouting quotes from martyred ISIS propagandist Anwar al-Awlaki. The latter, before he was killed in a drone strike in 2011, wrote a blistering call to arms that almost certainly inspired two Islamists to attack soldiers in Canada in the fall of 2014. Turaab helped push al-Awlaki's message, using many of his words and calling American troops "criminals and high school dropouts." He tweeted in August 2014 that he couldn't wait "for the day IS beheads the first American soldier. Soccer anyone?" He used the same poor joke after ISIS beheaded American journalist James Foley: "I guess it's time to play soccer boys").

"I wonder how my homie @StewartBellNP feels after watching the latest IS video? ;)" he wrote on the day of Foley's execution. "Seeing these so called Muslims' [*sic*] send condolences to James Foley's family is disgusting. No dignity whatsoever."

He was also something of a poet, one who was able to shrink his art into 140 characters: "Roses are red, violets are blue, IS is coming, to a town near you." Turaab, who managed to combine soldiering with full-time propagandizing, quickly lit up the screens of Western intelligence agencies, Twitter managers and groups that try to counter ISIS propaganda. His page was taken down, but his writing and pictures still find their way to Twitter and other social media. "You'll never kill the desire, nor the love the believers have for jihad and fighting to raise the word of Allah the highest," he wrote. "And that is why you will fail time and time again." Bell tracked Turaab through social media. "I traded the snow for the desert sand," he wrote to Bell a few weeks before he posted his soccer fantasies. Turaab said life with ISIS was better than "paying taxes to Harper in Canada."

Turaab was actually a suburban kid who had left Canada when he was in his late teens or early twenties, telling his parents he was going to travel to Turkey. He was disgusted with what he saw as the lack of opportunity in Canada. Like many ISIS recruits, he said he was unwilling to take on the crippling debt that most students are burdened with. "You're [*sic*] education system is a failure," he told Bell. "$50,000 for a four year course? And then you'll be stuck paying it off and that's if you find a job." Bell asked Turaab on Twitter if he was Canadian. The answer: "Not anymore."[1]

Turaab is one of ISIS's busiest recruiters. He is part of the team that works the Internet, Muslim groups in the West and even prisons to recruit Westerners to join the cause. His recruitment operation is typical of ISIS's operatives. Mohamed El Shaer, a young man from Windsor, Ontario, was befriended and recruited online by Turaab, who fed El Shaer a steady diet of propaganda through social media, then forwarded money and help to make it to ISIS territory, even though the Canadian government had revoked El Shaer's passport. (ISIS has the graphics and printing capacity to make its own currency, but it's not clear whether it has the expertise to forge passports.) Turaab posted a picture of the two men together and captioned it: "Canadian Muslims guess which 'High Risk Traveller' made it into the Sham [one of ISIS's names for its territory]?"

The brotherhood was not to last. Less than three weeks later, ISIS posted a picture of some of its dead fighters, lined up in a grassy field, their AK-47s lying over their chests on the LiveLeak website. Amarnath Amarasingam, one of Canada's leading researchers on foreign ISIS recruits, spotted Turaab's body among the dead.[2]

Turaab was not an innovative man, at least when it came to pushing ISIS on Twitter. ISIS has a whole division to work social media, which it calls *I'lamiy nasheet* (the energetic journalists). Most of the Twitter posters operate under *noms de guerre* or ridiculously fake names. One American who recruited for ISIS called himself Douglas McAuthur McCain. He was killed fighting for ISIS in 2014.[3]

In the years just after the 9/11 attacks, jihadis preferred to talk among themselves on online forums whose participants were vetted by administrators. This solved some of al-Qaeda's security problems, but it also limited the group's audience. Social media changed everything. Jihadis didn't need Al Jazeera or any other mainstream "slow" media. Mainstream journalists were no longer needed to get words and images out. In fact, they had greater value as stars of atrocity videos, and ISIS-held territory became utterly unsafe for any journalist.

ISIS's reputation as a skilled recruiter has become mythic. In January 2015, several news outlets fell for a story from the prank website *Daily Currant* that said ISIS would pay off the U.S. student loans of new recruits. Supposedly, ISIS also offered snazzy new cases for iPhones. It said:

> *ISIS spokesman Haji Mutazz told Al Jazeera, "You become debt free and fight in the name of Allah at the same time. Great deal for everyone. You fight, we pay for your philosophy major." The U.S. Army has a similar program, but recruits must serve before they can attend college. "Our program is for those who already went to college and have no way of paying off their debt. We will pay off their debt," Mutazz said. "It's a much better deal."*

The beauty of a well-played prank lies in its timeliness and believability. When it comes to recruitment and propaganda, ISIS seemed so far ahead of the curve that it appeared believable to thousands of people that ISIS had dreamed up a scheme to save American college grads from student loan collectors.

ISIS took shape when blogs and private forums fell out of style, and jihadis had already started to migrate to Twitter, Facebook, YouTube and other social media. They have created Twitter pages for each town under ISIS control. Most jihadi press releases appear on archive.org first. The Taliban, too, uses Twitter. Starting in 2011, Abdulqahar Balkhi was the Taliban's man on Twitter. He often got into personal flame wars with the person who handled the account of NATO's International Security Assistance Force. By 2012, the Somali terror group al-Shabab joined Twitter. Its flame wars would spill over into the real world, and people would die for what they wrote about al-Shabab.

Much of the material posted by ISIS is porno-violence spam

targeting the Arabic-speaking world. During the 2014 World Cup, when billions of people were engaged with media in what has become the biggest sporting event in the world, Arabic-speaking users of Twitter were spammed with images of ISIS massacres that were worked into tweets discussing the games. The pictures showed the execution of hundreds of Iraqi soldiers and civilians after ISIS captured Mosul, the second-largest city in Iraq. The threat—later carried out—of a U.S.-led air campaign set off a Twitter fight on the hashtag #AMessagefromIStoUS. There are some celebrity ISIS tweeters, including Abu Talha al-Almani, a rapper who used to be known as Deso Dog and is now fighting with ISIS in Syria. Still, none of the jihadis have a particularly large following. In 2014, four out of five tweets were used to disseminate jihadi dogma. Threats against the West were quite rare. In fact, pictures of pets outnumbered them.

"The inanity of the pictures from the Syrian war zone is often jarring," Jytte Klausen, a communications expert who follows jihadi media manipulation, wrote recently. He found a picture of a French boy standing in a store with a gun in one hand and a jar of Nutella in the other. One clearly staged picture shows an ISIS fighter studying the Qur'an with a dead body laid out behind him. The ISIS foreign fighters have clearly burned their bridges. After the spring of 2014, most ISIS fighters felt free to ditch their balaclavas and show their faces in the pictures they post on Twitter and other social media.

"The most graphic pictures send a message of unconstrained power: the power of fighters is supreme and the enemy is worthless," Klausen writes. "Particularly Osama bin Laden's old jingle about 'we love death more than you love life' is reformulated for Twitter." ISIS spends the time to make dead jihadis look good, touching up pictures of them and photographing them with half smiles on their makeup-covered faces before burying them. The bodies of beheaded and crucified people are photographed left in heaps on the street or still hanging from crosses.

"Executions communicated via Twitter are a new medium of psychological warfare," Klausen said. "Pictures of crucified men started to circulate on extremist social media sites in mid-June [2014]. One was hung out on a clothes line. Another man was put up on metal bars. And then, at the end of the month, there followed a picture of eight men hung on crosses in a dusty town square. Few news outlets reproduced the pictures but type 'crucifixion' and 'Syria' into Google and they are easily found."

These images tell potential recruits that fighting for ISIS can give your life meaning and adventure. Enemies are dehumanized and destroyed, ISIS fighters are glorified and a complex world starts to look very simple.

Such imagery makes up about 10 per cent of the content that jihadis feed into the Internet. Twitter is the medium of choice, serving the same essential purpose for terrorist organizations that bookstores and Internet forums played in the past: proselytizing and recruitment of followers, firming up the resolve of believers by engaging them in the distribution of propaganda and educating them in dogma. But social media have added new capabilities that dramatically expand the organization's reach and efficiency.

"The transformation of social media into an offensive strategy of psychological warfare is ISIL's particular innovation of terrorist strategy," Klausen says. "Across the Middle East, phones have become the most commonly-used instrument for obtaining reliable news. In this context, ISIL's broadcast of Twitter feeds of executions and crucifixions carried out in Aleppo and Deir Hafer turned social media into a tool of offensive psychological warfare and battlefield tactics."[4]

Twitter is the favourite way for ISIS and other jihadis to disseminate the online preaching of Anjem Choudary, the London-based Islamist firebrand who recognizes al-Baghdadi as caliph. Choudary has praised the 9/11 hijackers and advocated the imposition of Sharia law in Britain. Choudary was one of the founders of Islam4UK, and has promised his followers that the Sharia flag will fly over the prime minister's residence at 10 Downing Street by 2020. In August 2015, he was charged with supporting a banned organization, ISIS, and was freed on bail. Jihadis also push the writings and speeches of Ahmad Musa Jibril from Dearborn, Michigan, and Musa Cerantonio, of Melbourne, Australia.

ISIS has even created its own computer apps. A young Palestinian who claimed to be a graduate of a Los Angeles art school developed programs for Twitter and Android smart phones. The Android app delivered verses from the Qur'an. The Dawn of Glad Tidings Twitter app was much more sophisticated. Until Twitter was able to expunge it, the app allowed ISIS to co-opt the Twitter accounts of all supporters who signed up for the app. When ISIS sent out a piece of propaganda, the tweet was retweeted by every account that had the app. To those unfamiliar with Twitter, this program created a sort of automatic chain letter that greatly amplified ISIS's audience on a powerful social media platform. It also acted as spyware, gathering personal information from its users. It mimicked the Thunderclap app used by the Barack Obama campaign in 2012, which is still popular with American political candidates.

When ISIS launches an offensive, it lets the world know through Twitter. During the successful attack on Mosul, ISIS and its followers sent out as many as 44,000 tweets a day. These tweets put ISIS propaganda at the top of the list of Twitter search results, both in Arabic and in English. One ISIS hashtag, the Arabic equivalent of #the-FridayofSupportingISIS, drew more than twenty thousand mentions in one day. ISIS does work hard to keep its fighters from going off-message, which is one of the potential downsides of using social media that allows anyone with a cell phone to publish worldwide. For instance, ISIS recalled a video (and, presumably, punished its creator) that showed the author chopping off a man's hand. ISIS leaders apparently feared a backlash from that video, which was graphic even by ISIS's standards.[5]

ISIS supporters who choose to be off the grid can, instead, read the slick, well-designed printed publication *Dabiq*, a magazine stuffed with denunciations of *shirk* (polytheism) in the Islamic world and official justifications of ISIS atrocities. It portrays Muslim people, wherever they are, as victims of Zionists and crusaders and promises them a better life if they adopt ISIS theology and swear allegiance. The publication is named after the town of Dabiq, near Aleppo, Syria, where ISIS theologians claim an apocalyptic battle will happen soon. It will be a fight between true Muslims and the people who would oppress them, who are described by ISIS as "Rome."[6]

Islamists throughout the world have learned from ISIS. The al-Shabab group in Somalia draws heavily for financial support and recruits on Somalis living in North America and Europe (especially from the large Somali community in Minnesota). Omar Hammami, a Syrian-Irish-American from Alabama, became the English-language voice of the organization, starring in al-Shabab's English-language propaganda video "Ambush at Bardale," in which American recruits rap about jihad. When Hammami showed signs of heresy—arguing for a caliphate, complaining about the way foreign fighters were treated by al-Shabab and asking annoying questions about the group's spending practices—he became a marked man. Hammami knew it and turned to al-Qaeda's message boards for help. He was shut down by the heavy hand of al-Qaeda's moderators. So he went on YouTube to beg for support from al-Qaeda members and other jihadis. Then he went on Twitter as @abumamerican to try to drum up some American media attention, which he hoped might save him. Instead, he drew down onto himself waves of threats from pro-Shabab militants. This started yet another flame war as Hammami's American colleagues in Somalia and abroad joined Twitter and took his side. Hammami was so frightened that he took to the Somali wilderness, coming out once in a while to plug in his phone, charge it up and launch another Twitter attack. It didn't take long for al-Shabab to hunt him down and kill him.[7]

AMARNATH AMARASINGAM IS AN ISIS RECRUITMENT expert doing post-doctoral research at Halifax's Dalhousie University and working with Lorne Dawson to head an ISIS research project at the University of Waterloo. He says ISIS members deeply believe in their cause. When they execute someone in the name of Allah, they aren't hamming for the cameras. Religion is an obsession that ISIS members talk about constantly, and they believe the End Time is something that will happen soon enough for them to be a part of it.

Much of ISIS's theory is drawn from Salafism, a conservative form of Islam that seeks to purify Muslims from what its followers see as doctrinal and ritual corruption. Salafists believe Islam was at its purist in the days of the Prophet Mohammed and in the years when Islam was fighting for survival in the deserts of Arabia. ISIS is grounded in the thought of early-twentieth-century writers like Abul Ala Mawdudi, an Indian Islamic scholar and founder of Jamaat-e-Islami, and Egyptian radical thinker Sayyid Qutb. These men saw the creation of an Islamic state as "a necessary prerequisite for the fulfillment of a Muslim's faith" and as an opportunity to free themselves from a corrupt society where they are forced to pay taxes that are used to pay for wars against Muslims. He says that less than 1 per cent of Muslims are Salafists, and many of the Salafists stay silent about ISIS. The rest, he says, "are very vocal, very loud on line, but I don't think there are that many."

Amarasingam says mainstream Muslims are more tolerant of differences between people, see the Salafists as xenophobic, and believe the creation of an Islamic state is politically untenable and theologically misguided. For true believers, however, ISIS offers the fulfillment of a spiritual need.

But, he says, Muslims cannot pretend that ISIS preaches some kind of heresy that places its members outside Islam: "There has been a pendulum swing between the right, which often claims that ISIS is the very embodiment of Islam, and the left, which suggests that ISIS has nothing to do with Islam. The truth is somewhere in the middle: ISIS is an extreme offshoot, a breakaway sect, which deviates in significant ways from mainstream Islam, but remains based on claims to Islamic authenticity . . . qualified Islamic."

Amarasingam and Dawson monitor about a thousand Twitter accounts. They've archived over a million tweets. They've also gone to the homes of the parents, siblings and friends of foreign fighters to try to learn why they joined ISIS. The two researchers look at ISIS's broader support networks and the way it gets its messages out. They've been able to communicate with about fifty fighters in Iraq.

"In general, [for foreign fighters,] it's a quest for meaning, a quest for significance," Amarasingam says. "There's an explanatory gap over why they go. There are hundreds of thousands of young people with divorces in the family and other problems. Why do these few people go down that path? We have seen foreign fighters who have family issues, drug issues, personal issues. We also see people who are normal and see fighting for ISIS as a religious obligation."

Amarasingam and Dawson monitor several jihadi groups on the Internet. About half are in English, and the rest are mostly in Arabic. Amarasingam says ISIS members discuss religion among themselves but will also debate with people in organizations like al-Nusra, which ISIS is trying to incorporate in a hostile takeover. "There's a lot going on in that community. All of the fighters say they feel at home on Twitter, in a brotherhood, in a community of believers. They feel they can't say what they want in Canada or the U.K. but they are free to express themselves on Twitter. These are mostly young people, from thirteen to late twenties."

At the same time, they must dodge Twitter's online police. The company now has people fluent in Arabic chasing down any ISIS accounts that drift into glorifications or plans of violence.

"Many people were attracted by what they saw as a legitimate war against the corrupt and brutal Assad regime," says Amarasingam. "From their point of view, the solution is to install an Islamic state. In many ways, the people attracted to ISIS from the West are reacting to the situation in Syria in a very Western way. They were told, as they were brought up and went to school, to stand up for what's right and against injustice. But they don't make the connection between ISIS and human rights violations."

The fighters get defensive when Amarasingam confronts them about ISIS seizing captives as slaves and war booty. But when cornered, the ISIS fighters toe the line. "They think they can do whatever they like. I've talked to a lot of fighters who defend slavery. Even the most normal ISIS guy—if there is such—will defend slavery," Amarasingam says.

While ISIS can't be shamed out of existence, it does have one serious weak point. Caliphates are expected to expand, and ISIS seems to have reached a plateau, at least in Syria and Iraq. That may explain why it is trying to get jihadis in Afghanistan, Libya and Somalia to swear allegiance. "ISIS has to maintain the territory it captures. It has to have land," Amarasingam says. "That's why I think bombing is useless. You can't take back land by bombing. Losing the land would be a huge blow, especially if al-Baghdadi is killed and they can't find someone credible to replace him. Their broad argument is that they are a state that needs to be protected. That's how they get recruits. But a caliphate can't exist without land."

THERE IS A RELIGIOUS ELEMENT TO ISIS'S BRUTALITY. There's even a text that justifies it, and, of course, it's available online. *The Management of Savagery*, by al-Qaeda ideologue Abu Bakr Naji, was posted in 2004. It is the go-to source for jihadis who want to justify their excesses. Naji, who was killed in an American air strike four years after finishing his most famous work, wrote a detailed description of the military and political efforts that would be needed to create an Islamic state. The "savagery" of the title is his description of the world outside the grip of al-Qaeda and, presumably, ISIS. It needs, he says, to be managed properly once it is incorporated into the caliphate.

He anchors his arguments for primitive warfare, brutal punishment and a revived caliphate on the writings of Taqi al-Din ibn Taymiyya (1263–1328). The latter's work laid the foundations of Saudi Arabia's Wahhabi movement. It's ironic that the Saudis are, after Syria and Iraq, the most likely targets of ISIS's forces. Naji believed Islam had to reach back to the generation after Mohammed's death. The first caliph, Abu Bakr, had to crush the "apostate" tribes—the people who had embraced Islam, then changed their minds when the Prophet died. Today, according to the writings of Naji, and in the minds of ISIS's leaders, almost all Muslims have compromised their faith. All Shiites, Sufis and Ismailis are outright heretics. So are secular Sunnis and most other members of that branch of Islam, because of their bad habits or any sign of what ISIS calls "idolatry" that crept into the faith. That can be as simple a transgression as planting a gravestone.

To fulfill its religious obligations, the cause must always advance, Naji wrote. He continued:

> *The rate of operations escalates in order to send a living, practical message to the people, the masses, and the enemy's low-ranking troops that the power of the mujahids is on the rise. All of those people do not know these principles and the escalation of the operations leaves an imprint in their minds—whether with respect to the number (of the operations) or their specific character or their spread or all of that—and establishes that the mujahids are continually advancing and the enemy is in retreat and that the fate of the enemy is defeat.*
>
> *This encourages the masses and revives hope within them and facilitates permanent support for the movement and the automatic escalation of the movement. Therefore, when we plan our operations, we should begin with small operations and then (undertake) larger ones, and so forth, even if we are capable of undertaking the largest (operations) from the very beginning, just as the al-Qaeda organization arranged operations to ignite confrontation. This is to say nothing of many other benefits that come from the escalation of actions, including the advancement of the youth and accustoming them to confrontation and other things.*

SOCIAL SCIENTISTS HAVE IDENTIFIED FOUR WAVES OF modern terrorism, each one lasting about a generation. The four terror waves—anarchist, colonial, left-revolutionary and Islamist—had very different political agendas but, by and large, their tactics have been quite similar. The swift changes in the way people communicate and travel have accelerated the global reach of terror groups, spreading their ideals among radicalized diaspora communities. In the most recent wave, the diaspora that is most receptive to jihadi messaging is Muslims living in the West in countries where they have not integrated well (France and Germany are high on that list). Through these waves, ideas have been communicated at steadily increasing speed, while available weaponry has become more lethal.[8] ISIS is one of the first terror groups to try to establish its own territory and to try to assume the mantle of a caliphate, which is, essentially, a claim of leadership of Islam that snubs the religious and political leaders of the rest of the Muslim world.

Since the death of Mohammed, several Muslim regimes have tried to establish lasting caliphates to unify and expand their civilization. There are good reasons to do this, including ending the divisions between the various branches of Islam, but these efforts have led to war, assassinations and the shattering of community unity. ISIS is the first group, since the Ottoman Turkish caliphate was dissolved almost a century ago, to seriously try to hold itself out as a caliphate. In its propaganda, ISIS argues that anyone who accepts its leadership must move to ISIS territory and fight to expand its reach. ISIS's insistence on acceptance of its political and religious leadership has resulted in the brutalization and ethnic cleansing of Christians, Jews, Yazidis, Zoroastrians and Druze from their long-time homes by a group that welcomes foreigners to settle in the conquered lands.

Al-Qaeda early on understood the potential of the Internet for building a global movement. In a 2002 letter to Taliban leader Mullah Mohammed Omar, Osama bin Laden wrote: "It is obvious that the media war in this century is one of the strongest methods; in fact, its ratio may reach 90 per cent of the total preparation for the battles." In documents found at Abbottabad, the al-Qaeda leader's long-term hideout in Pakistan's version of West Point or Sandhurst, a letter was found in which bin Laden had told a friend, "Media occupies the greater portion of the battle today."

During the first jihadi insurgency in Iraq, Ayman al-Zawahiri, bin Laden's second-in-command and, later, successor, reiterated the lesson and wrote to Abu Musab al-Zarqawi: "We are in a battle, and more than half of that battle is taking place in the battlefield of the media. And that we are in a battle in a race for the hearts and minds of our *Ummah*." Naji, in *The Management of Savagery*, also dwells on the importance of using the media as a weapon.

For years, the media has carried a steady stream of atrocities. Reporters and editors often feel they see nothing new. Terrorist attacks that, thirty or forty years ago, might have got blanket coverage now don't even get a mention in newspapers, TV newscasts and news web pages. ISIS was among the first terror groups to realize that killing needed to be taken to a new level if the group was to have any impact.

Klausen says Abu Daigham al-Britani, a British national, was one of the first ISIS fighters to use Twitter to circulate an Instagram of himself holding a severed head. He posted the picture in April 2014. By that summer, during and just after the World Cup, ISIS started cleverly hijacking hashtags to flood Twitter with images of beheadings, severed heads on fence posts and rows of crucified men hung on crosses, their deaths watched by ISIS fighters and local townspeople. The *I'lamiy nasheet* posted a picture of a seven-year-old Australian boy holding a severed head given to him by his father, an ISIS executioner. No one had seen anything like this on mainstream social media, and it had profound effects in the Middle East.

Most mainstream Westerners took little notice of this first round of ISIS porno-violence propaganda, probably because it featured poor brown people, but it was working well with the target group, people like John Maguire. ISIS coverage went mainstream with the execution of journalist James Foley. Several Westerners had suffered the same cruelty since Nick Berg was beheaded by al-Zarqawi in 2004. Then, people—especially those who saw the unedited version of the videos posted online—were horrified that Berg had been murdered with a knife, rather than a sword or axe. (Any beheading image is distressing. The image of a captured American pilot being executed with a sword by a Japanese officer had certainly galvanized people in Allied countries during the Second World War.) ISIS raised the stakes in the Foley murder. They forced him to wear what looks like Guantanamo prison garb. Foley read a soul-crushing anti-American statement before he was murdered. And his killer, whose face was concealed, spoke with a London accent.[9]

The people who run Twitter came to believe that being a soapbox for jihadis was not part of its business plan. Twitter, helped by intelligence agencies and by ISIS opponents, fights cyber war with ISIS and other jihadis. After the Paris attack of November 13, 2015, they were joined by the hacktivist group Anonymous, which claimed to have found and killed fifty-five thousand ISIS accounts in three days.[10] ISIS responded by calling Anonymous's hackers "idiots" and offered its supporters advice on how to avoid detection.[11] In July 2014, Twitter killed the Dawn of Glad Tidings app. This infuriated ISIS, which relied on the app to get its message out. Shayba al-Hamd, one of ISIS's front-line twitterati, protested: "As the accounts of the caliphate's supporters become scattered, their effectiveness rises and falls, and the control the supporters have decreases." He called Twitter's actions "devastating" and, without any obvious sense of irony, a "dirty war." The ubiquitous social medium, so popular with ISIS just months ago, had shown its true colours, but ISIS would triumph over the American nerds: "The Crusaders tremble at the media power of [the Islamic State], which has taken up permanent residence in the depths of Twitter." To press the point, ISIS began publishing the names and photos of Twitter executives and warned of their imminent beheading.[12]

During 2014, the ten most popular ISIS-controlled accounts, including those of @Shamiwitness, who retweeted links to beheadings and to ISIS propaganda showing alleged U.S. atrocities, were either shut down by Twitter or became dormant. @Shamiwitness had twelve thousand followers, a respectable number for a Twitter account, and a blog on the Microsoft-owned Blogspot site.

Facebook also decided to purge its servers of ISIS propaganda, and were so effective that many of its jihadi clients moved over to Twitter. And U.S. senator Joe Lieberman pressured YouTube into creating an easy way for people to flag violence porn.

Social media offers ready-built networks that can connect jihadis to each other, and to potential recruits, free of charge. As well, social media either attracts or creates the kind of people who can be enticed by organizations that offer the chance to remake their lives. A recent study of Ottawa, Ontario, teenagers found almost a quarter of them are online "almost constantly." Those who are heavy social media users are more likely to have poor mental health, anxiety and depression, suicidal thoughts and unmet mental health needs. These findings matched earlier studies.[13] Correlation does not prove causation, and it doesn't matter much, when discussing jihadi recruitment, whether social media simply attracts troubled teens or creates them.

And at what point can a government stick its nose into private online conversations? Just before he retired as Canada's foreign minister, John Baird talked about that problem: "This is a huge challenge because you have people sitting in Kemptville, in their parents' basement, almost self-radicalizing. And obviously, our capacity to deal with a lone wolf, it's very difficult. I am a huge advocate, a huge advocate for Internet freedom. So I think we're struggling with how do we tackle that, because our values on freedom of the Internet are very strong . . . And it's not just [ISIS]. Look at the radical elements in the Syrian opposition. It's pretty ugly."[14]

Some of ISIS's opponents are learning the same propaganda skills. The Kurdish Peshmerga has its own Facebook page, the Lions of Rojava, where former Canadian Forces infantryman Dillon Hillier connected with a recruiter who helped him get to the fighting front. The Lions page has a showcase of heroes, people who have died fighting for the Kurdish cause. Foreign fighters—men and women—are given prominence. But some critics say the Peshmerga has sometimes been just as reckless as ISIS with people's lives. In 2015, they were criticized in Britain's House of Commons for recruiting an autistic man from a small town in England's East Midlands. The Conservative MP for the region, Robert Jenrick, called the Peshmerga's fighters "brave" but he called on Foreign Secretary Philip Hammond to speak with the Kurdish regional government about the Peshmerga's recruitment practices.[15]

ISIS'S ONLINE RECRUITERS TARGET WOMEN AS WELL AS men. ISIS wants women as settlers, and knows the nearby presence of women and children strongly motivates soldiers. ISIS demands *hijrah*, immigration to the caliphate. Al-Baghdadi, in his first speech as caliph, said: "O Muslims everywhere, whoever is capable of performing *hijrah* to the Islamic State, then let him do so, because *hijrah* to the land of Islam is obligatory. We make a special call to scholars . . . especially the judges, as well as people with military, administrative and service expertise, and medical doctors and engineers of all different specialties and fields."

ISIS recruiters approach women online, tell them they're attractive and entice them to become "bedroom radicals." One jihadi tried to seduce a British woman with a message telling her she was beautiful, and went on to say, "Now's the time to cover that beauty because you're so precious." The woman, called Ayesha by London's *Independent*, told the newspaper's reporter she found the message doubly exciting. She felt flattered, and the message also appealed to her identity as a Muslim. It was the "best way [she] could have been targeted."

She thought the jihadis were cute, too:

"As a teenager I wanted to get my piece of eye candy and I'd take a good look, and all the YouTube videos, for some reason, they [the militants] were all really, really attractive. It was glamorous in the sense it was like 'oh wow, I can get someone who practices the same religion as me, who's not necessarily from my ethnicity and that's exciting.' It was like, get with him before he dies. And then when he dies as a martyr you'll join him in heaven."

At the same time, she was swayed by her online seducer to see Western women as "disgusting" and "like men." Ayesha learned to see her home country as a "kuffar [non-Muslim] nation" that had killed many Muslims. It was "our enemy." She said, "You don't trust the state, you don't trust the police, you don't send your children to state schools." Propaganda published across social media accounts through ISIS's media arms included guides for women on how to be good jihadi brides.[16]

Ayesha was just one of many women approached in the West. To see if ISIS frequently targets women in North America, a Canadian TV news producer, Vassy Kapelos, played the part of an underaged girl interested in joining ISIS. It took just minutes for her to be approached on Skype by a man claiming to be an ISIS fighter looking for a wife. "Abu Antar" seemed to know a lot about Canadian air travel. He told Kapelos to lie to her parents about going to a sleepover with friends, and fly to Calgary, then on to Frankfurt and then Istanbul. There, she would be contacted by a middleman who would smuggle her into Syria.[17]

These pickups work, especially in families with plenty of stress. A startling number of anecdotal cases of young people leaving the West to join ISIS involve the divorce and remarriage of a parent. This was the case with John Maguire, and also with Sharmeena Begum, then fifteen, who left Britain at the end of 2014 just weeks after her father remarried. Friends of the teenager said she was enticed by ISIS propaganda after eighteen months of severe personal troubles. Her mother died of cancer, and her father found a new wife. Begum was one of four students of the Bethnal Green Academy in East London who slipped out of the United Kingdom, travelled to Turkey and made the overland trek to ISIS territory. Kadiza Sultana, sixteen, and fifteen-year-olds Shamima Begum (no relation) and Amira Abase left London in February 2015. They were guided to ISIS territory by a Turkish national working for the Canadian Security Intelligence Service (CSIS) but supposedly acting on his own. Before he was arrested by the Turkish government, the man was making $800 to $1,500 for each person smuggled across the border.[18]

And in October 2014, three ethnic Somali teen girls from Brampton, Ontario, tried to make it to Syria to join ISIS. The women, aged fifteen, sixteen and eighteen, got as far as Istanbul. "The parents realized they were missing, contacted CSIS and the RCMP," Hussein Hamdani, a lawyer who was called in by the RCMP as a liaison between the families and law enforcement, said at the time. He said the RCMP alerted the Turkish authorities about the missing teens. "They were able to track them on the plane to Istanbul," Hamdani said. "When they got to the Istanbul airport, that's where the Turkish authorities captured, arrested, returned, deported them back to Canada and they've been here ever since."

GOOD SPIN IS A TICKET TO HEAVEN. AT LEAST, THAT'S what Abu Qatada, a Jordanian-based Islamic scholar, tells his supporters. Qatada has a big following among the jihadi fighters in Syria. In the summer of 2015, Qatada's followers, especially those who work in propaganda and spin, wanted to know whether media work was as valuable as front-line fighting. They seemed to be afraid that they would not get the afterlife rewards that are supposed to come to fighters who kill with bullets and knives instead of words. They wrote to the spiritual leader, then posted his answers online. Qatada, who was deported from the United Kingdom for his fire-breathing sermons, assured them that Allah puts the highest value on their work, and reminded them of stories of the Prophet Mohammed searching rather fruitlessly for a satirist to attack one of his enemies and more successfully for good storytellers to spread the news of his victories. In fact, people who are good at media work should be pried out of jihadi forces and put to work doing spin. "Indeed from amongst the greatest obligations on the leader is to set aside even if by force, men who will support the truth through speeches just as the fighter establishes the truth by his rifle," Qatada wrote to his followers. "And if Jihad was void of this great action, we would not have been able to clarify ourselves nor to reply to our enemies, nor would we have been able to recruit the youth and men who would fill the battlefields and the front lines."[19]

So, even in Qatada's world, a story barely exists if it is not told.

Chapter 7

Dreams of Green Birds and War

In the dream, I saw myself in a huge, flat area. I saw an army mounted on white horses moving towards me. All of them were wearing black turbans. One of the horsemen, who had shiny eyes, came up to me and asked me, "Are you Osama bin Muhammed bin Laden?" I replied, "Yes." He then asked me again, "Are you Osama bin Muhammed bin Laden?" I again replied, "Yes, that is me." He again asked, "Are you Osama bin Muhammed bin Laden?" Then I said, "By Allah, I am Osama bin Laden." He moved a flag towards me and said, "Hand this flag over to Imam Mahdi Muhammas bin Abdullah at the gates of al-Quds [Jerusalem]." I took the flag from him, and I saw that the army started marching behind me.

—Osama bin Laden recounts a dream he had at the age of nine[1]

GENERATIONS OF ADVERTISING WRITERS HAVE TOLD people to follow their dreams. ISIS and its supporters take this directive very seriously. Dreams have played an important role in the development of ISIS and the jihadi groups that came before it, and they're used by ISIS leaders as guides to some of their most important strategic decisions.

ISIS fighters and the leaders of the organization use *Ishtakara* (dream prophecies) to help them make life-and-death decisions. A person who wants dream advice from Allah says an *Ishtakara* prayer dating back to the time of Mohammed, then looks for guidance in his or her dreams. It's a prayer that is used by people seeking meaning and guidance. In a variation, some people pray for guidance, then open the Qur'an to a random page to see if there are any signs that can help them. Dreams and visions are described by the same word in Arabic, but the dream advice is expected from night dreams, not some kind of visionary revelation or miracle. Those seeking that advice need clarity of mind. They don't use drugs to stimulate their dreams, since they're hoping to hear from Allah directly.

Dreams have played an important part in the strategic planning of campaigns in the Islamic world and attacks against the West. Abu Bakr al-Baghdadi, the founder of ISIS, is supposed to have planned to withdraw his forces in Mosul in late 2014 at least partly because he was told to in a dream. Anti-ISIS media, including the website of the Kurdish Democratic Party, reported in March 2015 that the Prophet Mohammed appeared to al-Baghdadi in his sleep and warned him the Iraqi army would drive him out. In fact, the Iraqi offensive faltered and fell apart well before government forces got to Mosul, and ISIS was able to take back the towns it lost.

The Iraqi army had already retaken Tikrit (hometown of Saddam Hussein) and seemed to be on the verge of attacking Mosul, part of an important oil-producing region. Iain Edgar, a social worker turned anthropologist who recently retired from Durham University in England, notes that while the dream story was not corroborated by ISIS, it is a grave sin in Islam to lie about a dream. Many Muslims believe there is a special region in hell for people who commit this sin. So either al-Baghdadi did, at least for a time, plan to flee Mosul because of a dream, or Kurdish propagandists risked hellfire for a temporary media win.

Edgar started studying the role of dreams in Muslim culture more than a decade ago. He has interviewed people throughout the Islamic world. "Ask a Muslim about dreams, and usually you will be told of a significant dream that has influenced their life through focusing their attention on a possibility not previously recognized by their conscious mind."

He identifies four kinds of jihadi dreams:

Divine guidance, news of future events, and insights into the world hereafter.

Dreams that give legitimacy to the actions of the dreamers, their followers, and for all Muslim people.

Dreams that connect the jihadi with the Prophet Mohammed and the quasi-mythical Golden Age of Islam in the centuries after the founding of the religion.

Dreams consisting of symbolism that must be deciphered, containing imagery of the Prophet and his companions Hassan and Hussein, along with much more obscure material.[2]

"Sacred figures are important," Edgar said in an interview. "So are works in command dreams [dreams that send the dreamer on a mission or seem to make a decision]. So are colours. You have to go by the feelings as well. They're used for marriage a lot. They let their subconscious decide."

Dreams are often used to make business decisions and sort out many of life's mundane, day-to-day problems.[3]

Elton Simpson's attack on the American Freedom Defense Initiative's Muhammad Art Exhibit and Cartoon Contest in Garland, Texas, in May 2015, was partly inspired by a dream. The cartoon show, organized by anti-Muslim activist Pamela Geller, was, probably quite accurately, seen as a deliberate provocation by jihadis and many people in the mainstream Muslim community. Simpson and another gunman, Nadir Soofi, were shot dead after the would-be assailants were outgunned by the Texan art patrons.[4]

Simpson was a convert to Islam. He appeared on the FBI's radar in 2006, during its investigation of Hassan Abu-Jihaad, a former U.S. navy sailor who was eventually convicted of terrorism-related charges. Simpson was caught in an FBI sting in 2011 and convicted of lying to federal agents about his plan to travel to Somalia to join the Islamist group al-Shabab. Simpson was fined $600 and placed on probation for three years.

Simpson was already a busy member of the jihadi social media network, talking with fellow extremists in the United States, in Europe and in ISIS territory. He was obsessed with *hur*, the reward supposedly given to martyrs in paradise. As the date of the attack grew closer, he became more concerned with the number of women that he would supposedly receive.

But the real motivator, according to Amarnath Amarasingam, the Canadian researcher on Islamic recruiting, was a dream that Simpson described to members of his online spiritual community. Simpson had the dream months before the art show was announced. In it, he saw a woman in a hijab looking down at him from the sky. This is a fairly common dream among jihadis, who take it as a clear sign that they will be "martyred" soon.

On May 3, Simpson posted his final message on Twitter pledging his loyalty to ISIS. Abu Hussain al-Britani, one of ISIS's Twitter stars, immediately posted the tweet, which quickly spread through the ISIS social media network with the hashtag #texasattack. As soon as the shooting started, al-Britani was tweeting a blow-by-blow, then celebrating the martyrdom of Simpson and his accomplice.[5] ISIS also, for the first time for a killing on American soil, claimed responsibility for the attack. "Two of the soldiers of the caliphate executed an attack on an art exhibit in Garland, Texas, and this exhibit was portraying negative pictures of the Prophet Muhammed," an ISIS spokesman said on the group's radio station.[6]

Simpson's dreams were no surprise to the Western intelligence agents who track jihadis. Osama bin Laden mentioned dreams in the first video released after 9/11. In the video, publicized by Al Jazeera, bin Laden said: "Abu'l-Hassan al-Masri told me a year ago: 'I saw in a dream, we were playing a soccer game against the Americans. When our team showed up in the field, they were all pilots.' He [al-Masri] didn't know anything about the operation until he heard it on the radio. He said the game went on and we defeated them. That was a good omen for us."

Other 9/11 planners like Ramzi bin al-Shibh and Khalid Sheikh Mohammed, as well as "twentieth hijacker" Zacarias Moussaoui, were also inspired by dreams. Moussaoui's dream of flying a plane into a building—which he supposedly had before he was brought into the 9/11 plot and told by bin Laden to follow his dreams—was an important part of the evidence in his trial.

Al Jazeera journalist Yosri Fouda interviewed al-Shibh and Sheikh Muhammed, who told him the Prophet often appeared in the dreams of al-Qaeda leaders. This was, they said, proof they had Allah's blessing. Bin Laden and his lieutenants talked of dreams about Mohammed Atta and the rest of the 9/11 hijackers, with moments in the dream of pity for Atta's relatives in Egypt.

The al-Qaeda leader mentioned his dreams in the three interviews that he gave Robert Fisk of *The Independent*. Bin Laden told Fisk: "Mr. Robert, one of our brothers had a dream. He dreamt that you came to us one day on a horse, that you had a beard and that you were a spiritual person. You wore a robe like us. This means you are a true Muslim." The story of the dream terrified Fisk, who worried about being labelled an apostate if he did not accept the dream as divine prophecy (and, presumably, immediately convert). "Oh Lordy," he wrote years later, "I don't know if Bin Laden was seeking a convert, but I quickly dissociated myself from this self-apparition, explaining to him that, far from being an aspiring cleric, I was a mere *Independent* reporter trying to tell the truth."[7] Fisk said to bin Laden, "I am not a Muslim, I am a journalist." Bin Laden replied, "If you tell the truth, you are a good Muslim."

Bin Laden's boyhood flag dream, his account of which starts this chapter, instructed him to lead an army in preparation for the arrival of the Mahdi, the redeemer of Islam, who will rule in the final days of man. In many ways, bin Laden saw himself as the servant of a greater leader who would arrive later, a role very similar to that of John the Baptist in Christian teaching. That dream, reported on many Islamist websites, provides hope to those who followed bin Laden that his death, like that of John, would not hinder the arrival of the important messenger.

Bin Laden had that dream when he was nine years old and told his father about it. Mohammed bin Laden, a wealthy and well-connected owner of a multinational construction company, immediately took the boy to some of the top clerics in Saudi Arabia. In a scene similar to the New Testament story of the adolescent Christ in the temple, little Osama showed his brilliance to the theologians. "O Mohammed bin Laden," one of the clerics supposedly said after kissing away the boy's tears, "this son of yours will prepare an army for Imam Mahdi and for the sake of protecting his religion, he will migrate to the region of Khurasan [in western Afghanistan].

"O Osama! Blessed is he who will do Jihad by your side and undone and disappointed be he who leaves you alone and fights against you."[8] From that time, the younger bin Laden was marked as a special man.

RICHARD REID, THE BOMBER WHO TRIED TO BLOW UP an airliner with explosives hidden in his shoe, also acted on his dreams. His jihad dream involved waiting on the side of the road for a ride, but when a pickup truck came, it was full and Reid could not go on that trip. He was upset and had to go later in a smaller car. Reid believed the first pickup truck was a symbol for the 9/11 attacks. He was, he said, "upset about not being sent" and looked for a new mission.

A Western intelligence agent told Iain Edgar: "Everyone we are watching in our area is into dreaming as crucial to their jihadi membership, progress, and their final decision, via *Ishtakara*—Islamic dream incubation—as to whether to go on militant jihad." Another agent came up to Edgar at a convention and said everyone being watched by his intelligence organization was obsessed with finding revelations and advice in dreams.

ISIS founder Abu Musab al-Zarqawi was, according to one of his cellmates in a Jordanian jail, inspired to convert to radical Islam when his sister dreamed of a sword with the word "jihad" on one side and the Qur'anic verse "God will never abandon you and never forget you" on the other. Many of his subordinates in al-Qaeda in Iraq reported similar dreams. The most potent of these dreams—after those featuring the Prophet Mohammed—involve the sighting of green birds, which symbolize martyrdom and the promise of paradise. The bird itself is believed to represent an angel of death. Its colour, one of the heraldic colours of Islam, symbolizes the favour of Allah.[9]

Rahimullah Yusufzai, a high-profile former BBC and magazine journalist who now edits a newspaper in Pakistan, has reported on jihadis' use of dreams. He was one of the very few reporters allowed to interview Mullah Mohammed Omar, the spiritual and military leader of the Taliban. Omar was an almost mythical man, so reclusive that his death (in April 2013) went unreported for two years. It was Omar who created the group, led it to power and kept it going after 9/11. Yusufzai met the mullah about a dozen times as the Taliban was taking shape. Omar was blind and very shy, but he gained a reputation as a man whose dreams were accurate. Everyone knew Omar founded the Taliban after being told to do so in a dream.[10]

Yusufzai learned that no big Taliban military operation took place unless Mullah Omar got instructions for them in dreams. Yusufzai was in on the ground floor of modern jihad, learning of the Taliban long before they took power in Afghanistan. His credentials and his fame in the region as a BBC journalist and a writer for *Time* and *Newsweek* gave him ready access to the Taliban leadership during a time when the movement was still taking shape and fighting for control of Afghanistan. Yusufzai wrote:

> *The story I was being told everywhere was that because of his courage, because of his very timely decision to fight the Mujahideen that had made him very popular and the Taliban flocked to his banner as they thought he had this vision, this dream, he was challenging the Mujahideen and because he had been instructed to fight the Mujahideen, they thought he was going to succeed... The whole project was maybe built on this dream, he had this task or duty to perform and he must lead his Taliban, his fighters, and he must restore order and peace and enforce Sharia, Islamic law . . . I was told by so many Taliban leaders, commanders, fighters, "Look, you know, Mullah Omar is a holy man and he gets instructions on his dream and he follows them up."*

The genesis of the Taliban Islamic movement was this vision, this night dream that Mullah Omar had.[11]

ISIS fighters often use Twitter to launch discussions of their dreams. One Twitter poster, End of Times Dreams, @endtmdrms, acted as a broker between dreamers and people who were recognized as authorities on the meaning of dreams. Simpson, one of the assailants in Garland, Texas, discussed his martyrdom dream with people linked to the End of Times Dreams account. The owner of the account arranged to have the dream analyzed just a few days before the attack on the cartoon show. The results of that analysis aren't available because Twitter removed all of Simpson's posts and discussions after the attack.

After Twitter shut down the End of Times Dreams account, it was replaced by @Entdrm13, which survived until late July 2015. Jihadis took its advice very seriously.

"Show me the dreams and ill be glad to die i believe dawlah are khawarij and i will fight based on my belief," one ISIS supporter wrote to the second End of Times Dreams account. Another described how "a sister wrote Anwar Awlaki came to her in a dream and said mahdi [the returning Prophet] is in your time, or something like that." The followers of the site and other Twitter dream analysis accounts often talk about End Times, wondering whether they will come as a battle between Muslims and non-Muslims, or in some other form, such as a nuclear war. Most of the people in these Twitter conversations appear to be ISIS or al-Nusra fighters or supporters. Invariably, the dreams are interpreted as signs of battlefield success or some other kind of triumph over various enemies, whose faults and evil plots are described in some detail. There are also warnings of potential setbacks, which are expected to be used as advice to escape from danger. There are solo political dreams, centring on issues such as whether the Somali terrorist group al-Shabab and other, smaller Islamist groups in East Africa will swear allegiance to ISIS's caliphate.

In July 2015, the dream of a Russian-speaking ISIS fighter was posted on the Internet. The timing was fortuitous. ISIS was taking a pounding by Kurdish forces backed by U.S. coalition–led air power. There was speculation in Western media that ISIS was on the verge of military collapse. The dream was supposed to calm the fears of ISIS fighters. ISIS's team of propagandists quickly got to work sharing it on many more websites and posting messages on Twitter and Facebook linking to those sites. This was the dream:

> *THE DREAM OF A CERTAIN BROTHER!*
> *Assalam aleikum Muslim brothers and sisters and mujahideen! Recently, one of the brothers of the Islamic State dreamed a dream. In the dream, he saw the Communist Kurds took Tel Abyad and got as far as Ayn al-Isa. And he saw the Prophet of Peace [in Russian, the word "mir" can mean both "peace" and "world"] above them, who thrust his sword into the ground. And the brothers said to him, fight with us against them. He replied that he would not fight. When they ask him about the reason for his refusal, he replied that you are being profligate with food [i.e., wasting food], throwing food away and not giving it to the poor, you are not getting up for the night time namaz [prayers]. May Allah reward you with a blessing!*

The dream offered a simple solution to ISIS's military problems: stop wasting food and remember your nighttime prayers. If the fighters were more careful, the Prophet would fight alongside them.

Edgar, the British anthropologist who pioneered the study of ISIS dream culture, found another ISIS dream on the Internet. This one was not nearly as literal as the July 2015 dream that assured ISIS of divine support if its fighters were more careful with resources. It was a dream that an ISIS fighter had about Umar (or Omar) al-Shishani, a Russian who rose to be ISIS's military commander in Syria. Al-Shishani is beloved and respected by foreign fighters, especially those thousands of ISIS soldiers who have come from countries in the former Soviet Union. This dream, reported by a Chechen fighter, was also published by ISIS as part of its dream-based propaganda:

> *One brother-mujahid (Abu Yusuf) had a dream: "I was standing on the front line, as if guarding the brothers. It seemed as if brother Adam was among them, and definitely Umar Shishani. Suddenly, I heard the noises of dogs, suddenly it became dark, and Umar and the other brothers were asleep. I was alert, and started to look attentively in all directions, and I saw a large animal like a lion, dull gray in color. Alongside it was a masked man, looking like the brothers, who petted the lion.*
>
> *I went up to Umar and said,*
>
> *'Umar, there is a lion and a suspicious man in a mask.'*
>
> *He went with me, 'show me,' he says, and I showed him.*
>
> *I asked him, 'Can you shoot them?' At that, Umar said, 'Wait a minute and look at them.'*
>
> *But suddenly they saw us, the man in the mask saw us first. And he swiftly ran at me, saying, now I will kill you.*
>
> *I asked Umar for permission to shoot.*
>
> *But Umar instead of speaking fell silent. The man in the mask ran very close. I wanted to shoot but it seemed I had not taken the safety off my gun. But Umar, defending me, started to shoot at him. I also opened fire and we started to shoot together and killed the one in the mask. But the lion was not dead. Then Umar said, 'there's a tree, jump up on it.' All the brothers jumped. Me and Umar remained on the ground.*
>
> *Umar said that these lions can climb trees. So be careful. We also climbed the tree. And the lion jumps after us and says to me in human speech, 'if I catch you, I'll kill you.' He jumps from side to side. I jump up after him. I jump, catch the lion's head and turn it this side and that. And*

> *I say to myself, 'I'm only afraid of Allah, not you.' And I actually killed the lion."*
>
> *Ma sha'llah. And at that time I dreamed the same dream. We explained the dream according to the Quran and the Sunnah [the transmitted oral teachings of the prophet Mohammed]: the lion is the taghut [rebellion], the man in the mask is a munafiq [hypocrite], the tree is IS.*

Jihadis often report numerous people having the same dream. Simultaneous dreaming is seen to be a sign that this is, in fact, a true dream created by Allah, not the work of the Devil or of a troubled mind. So many Taliban and al-Qaeda fighters and leaders supposedly dreamed of aircraft and pilots before 9/11 that bin Laden worried that the plan might be compromised. He mentioned these dreams in the first video released after 9/11. Some of the "lion" dreams seem literal, but several obscure Qur'anic references are buried within them.

Bin Laden seems to have had an obsession with recording his life on audiotape. After he fled from Afghanistan in 2001, hundreds of these tapes were pilfered from the bin Laden compound in Kandahar, Afghanistan, to be used for pirated pop music. More than fifteen hundred of the tapes were tracked down before they could be destroyed, and they're now kept at Yale University. Flagg Miller, a University of California (Davis) Professor of Religious Studies, has translated and transcribed them. Miller, fluent in Arabic and an expert on Islamic beliefs, wrote a widely praised book *The Audacious Ascetic: What the bin Laden Tapes Reveal about Al-Qa'ida.* Miller says references to dreams can be found throughout the tapes. Bin Laden and other members of the al-Qaeda leadership talked about the importance of dreams and the ways dreams could be used to develop a more pure form of Islam.[12]

Most Muslim dream conversations are about more practical

things. Some dreams resolve or explain day-to-day problems. A few even offer marriage advice. Many more are seen to be insights into theology, a topic that obsesses many of the ISIS fighters. Some dreams are believed to offer a peek at the delights that await martyrs when they reach paradise. And since martyrdom is both a motivator for ISIS recruitment and a real, immediate possibility for ISIS fighters and the women who follow them on *hijrah* to ISIS territory, these dreams are very important. They're carefully analyzed on social media and discussion groups and, quite often, acted upon.

It's possible that some ISIS fighters take dreams so seriously that they're willing to play out ones that would seem anathema to their very existence. One story floating around the Middle East—an account that may be a sort of urban myth—is about an ISIS fighter who took great delight in killing Christians until he had a dream about a man in white who, the fighter said, was Jesus. The fighter supposedly quit ISIS and became a Christian. The dream bears a rather uncanny and suspicious resemblance to the story of St. Paul's conversion on the road to Damascus, and to the tales of the conversion of Roman officials during the years when the Christian church was persecuted.[13]

Muslims aren't required by their faith to believe in the prophetic power of dreams, and many of them don't. Discussions of dreams on Internet sites can range from careful analysis of symbols, colours and apparent messages to harsh debates over Sigmund Freud's theories. One Muslim discussion board, Ummah, has frequent conversations about dream interpretation.[14] In one, a man dreamed about meeting a Black teenage stranger. He and the young man went into a women's clothing store. A blue-clad Caucasian woman working in the store told the two men they should use a side entrance. Instead, they went through a doorway into a large room where they were supposed to meet an important person. It turned out to be Osama bin Laden, who was greeted warmly by the dreamer. "I was delighted when that happened, by the way the room smelled of a very light but very pleasant fragrance." The dreamer told his young companion, "No one will ever believe this." Then he woke up.

One observer asked if the dreamer was experiencing *fitna*, a word that broadly translates into "troubles," with women. The dreamer admitted he had, but said he thought the dream's importance lay in the latter part. Another commenter warned the dreamer that a young man usually symbolizes an enemy of some sort. The clothing store probably represented problems with women. And blue isn't a good colour. Seeing a "martyr" means a Muslim is trying to follow good traditions and is striving for Allah's pleasure. Another poster said dreams, according to Freud, are representations of unconscious desires and thoughts. Almost immediately, a commenter shot back: "Freud was on drugs when he came up with this stuff."

Dreams also seem to have had a role in the politics of Egypt's Arab Spring. After he led a coup overthrowing the Muslim Brotherhood government of democratically elected president Mohamed Morsi in 2013, then-general Abdel Fattah el-Sisi had several dreams that he found noteworthy. An audiotape of el-Sisi, a formerly unknown general whom Morsi had, unwisely, named minister of defence in 2012, was leaked to the media. In the tape, the general talked of the dreams he believed showed that his rise to power was endorsed by Allah.

The general was the star of one dream in which—like al-Zarqawi, the founder of ISIS—he wields a sword engraved in red with the central tenet of Islam: "There is no god but God." Another dream had him wearing a large Omega watch set with a green star. In yet another dream, Anwar Sadat, who was murdered by Islamist radicals in the Egyptian army in 1981, told el-Sisi, "I always knew I would be president of the republic." In the dream, el-Sisi told Sadat, "I also know I will be president of the republic."

Soon afterwards he confirmed his destiny by holding a referendum that was almost certainly rigged by beings of the temporal, rather than the heavenly, sphere.[15]

PROF. EDGAR HAS TRAVELLED THROUGH THE ISLAMIC world studying the importance of dreams, and became certain they played an important role in many people's lives. Some dream accounts, like the Kurdish media story about ISIS losing heart in Mosul because of al-Baghdadi's dream, may be manipulative, but most are careful, honest interpretations of dreams. And people from all walks of life, in conservative Islamic countries and secular nations, seemed eager to share them.

"I was surprised," Edgar said in an interview. "In all the Islamic dream interpretation books, they tell you that you should only tell your dream to someone you trust or who has knowledge, because a mistake in interpretation can be very dangerous. For instance, you could be sent on jihad.

"In Pakistan, because I was interested in dreams, doors opened. People told me their dreams very easily. There was one person, the national poet of Pakistan, [who] said he didn't believe [in them], but everyone else did. In Turkey, even if they were fairly secular, if they had a dream of a family member being ill, they would ring them. It was part of the culture."

Before discounting all of Islamic dream culture, ask yourself what you might do if you had a vivid dream of a set of winning lottery numbers, or a dream that an out-of-town relative was sick and needed your help right away. Many Westerners do take dreams literally, and stories of dream warnings before disasters are quite common.[16] Christianity, when it dominated Western culture, suppressed dream interpretation, fearing that the Church could not control mystics who claimed to get revelations from dreams. The Church made this decision despite the New Testament's claims of prophetic dreams, like the one in which Joseph, the father of Jesus, is warned to flee to Egypt with his wife and infant son before Herod can kill the baby Jesus. However, it did accept, with strong suspicions, daytime visions like Joan of Arc's supposed instructions from various saints, who told her to fight at the side of Charles VIII. It more eagerly embraced more symbolic visions like the one reported by seventeenth-century Jesuit missionary Jean de Brébeuf, who saw a gigantic cross over the homeland of the people he called the Huron, "big enough to crucify us all." The Huron-Wendat were destroyed by their enemies, the Haudenosaunee, soon afterward. Brébeuf was tortured to death and the Pope elevated him to sainthood.

In the secular world today, dreams are seen as an expression of repressed emotions like fear and desire. Dreams that seem to come true are remembered and talked about, dreams that don't come true are forgotten, and strange recurring dreams are parsed and analyzed by those who have them and, sometimes, by their psychologists. And books on dream interpretation are hugely popular, with some claiming sales of over a million copies.[17] Many Muslims put about as much stock in dream prophecy as do people in the West, believing there may be *something* to it. ISIS fighters and other extreme jihadis believe dreams, even the most obscure and scrambled, need to be parsed to determine they are messages from God.

"In a sense you dream about what you love and who you love," Edgar said. "If you watch soap operas all day, you'll dream about characters in them. There's a book about dreams of Britain's queen. There's a book about people's dreams of Princess Diana. It's how popular culture circulates internally, through the personal and the collective unconscious, and into reality."

One of Edgar's students told him she had enrolled in a master's program after doing *Ishtakara* with her mother, grandmother and two best friends. Other Muslims living in the United Kingdom told him they had refused to move to another city to take a better job, and several said they had chosen their husbands based on advice they got from dreams. Dreams are also a way to keep in touch with the dead. This is not unique to Islam. The idea that the dead are still close at hand is a powerful remedy for those who are grieving.

Al-ru'ya, the "true dream," is important in Islam, as true dreams were to the authors of the New Testament. Three dreams are described in the Qur'an, two by Mohammed and one by Joseph. One of Mohammed's dreams gave him advice before the Battle of Badr near Mecca in 624 CE. Joseph's dream of seven fat and seven lean cows, which is also described in the Old Testament, is important to the story of the eventual enslavement of the Israelites in Egypt. In the Hadiths, the recorded sayings of Mohammed, a chapter is devoted to the teachings of Mohammed about true dreams, those that come from Allah. The presence of the Prophet in a dream is a clear sign that it is a "true dream."

Edgar says authentic true dreams in the Islamic tradition cannot advocate action that is against Islamic teachings in the Qur'an and the Hadiths. Islam teaches that the Devil can easily delude humans through dreams. Shias similarly regard dream sightings of Ali, Hussein, Hassan and the rest of the twelve imams as true dreams, if the dreams themselves do not advocate anything that is forbidden by Islamic teachings. Sufis often regard their major sheikh in a similar light if seen in a dream.

Dream interpretation should only be done by those with spiritual knowledge and who love the dreamer, but the large number of books, websites and discussion groups that offer dream advice show that people are not always careful about dream interpretation.[18]

Mohammed warned Muslims to beware of false dreams, which may come from the Devil, and of dreams that are simply a person's expressions of their own desires. The challenge is to be able to tell these three types of dreams apart, ignore the Devil's false dreams and the mundane dreams that are generated by desire, and to understand the true dreams.

In Islam, dreams can be a way of communicating with the dead. They can offer advice, add insight, warn, inspire, reveal theological truths and foretell the future. They are especially potent for their supposed ability to show what will come in the afterlife, giving fighters a taste of the paradise that awaits those who die in a righteous cause, and the horrendous eternal punishments that are in store for their enemies. David Cook, who has collected more than five thousand dream stories that were written down through Islamic history, wrote: "All of these dreams—only a small section of those available—are common through the Muslim martyrdom tradition. The general themes of martyrdom literature serve to confirm the status of the martyrs after their death, to demonstrate their satisfaction with their fate and to influence others to follow them."[19]

True dreams are important because, while most sects of Islam preach that prophecy ended with the death of Mohammed, Allah gives people snippets of knowledge about the future and insights about the present through dreams. Iain Edgar found Arabic television has many dream-interpretation programs. Websites offer people the chance to have their dreams analyzed by strangers. Books, some of them more than a thousand years old, offer people advice on understanding the symbolism in their dreams.

"During my fieldwork research, especially in Pakistan, Turkey, Bosnia and the U.K., I rarely met a Muslim who didn't relate his night dreams as a potential porter to the divine," Edgar wrote in 2015. "Moreover, I found this dream tradition to be similar across all the main branches of Islam: Sunni, Shia, Salafi and Sufi, as well as amongst the minority Alevi and Ahmadiyya sects."

Muhammad Amanullah studied staff in the religious studies department of a Malaysian university: the majority reported true dreams, and 50 percent believed that they had seen the Prophet in a dream. A recent anthropological study of female adult conversion in the U.S. confirms the crucial significance of night dreams in the conversion process.[20]

Canadian author and journalist Stewart Bell got to know some friends of Abdul Rahman Jabarah, an Iraqi-Canadian who joined al-Qaeda. Jabarah was killed by Saudi Arabian soldiers in 2003 shortly after Jabarah and several of his colleagues blew up Western housing complexes in Riyadh. One of the jihadi friends who wrote a glowing, over-the-top eulogy told Bell of a dream he had about Jabarah:

"We were sitting and Abdul Rahman was in front of us. I asked him 'Weren't you killed?' and Rahman Jabarah answered: 'No, I wasn't killed. Rejoice, for God, may he be glorified and exalted. Do not consider those who died for God's sake dead—but alive.'" Jabarah revealed he was "among those whom God used in the Jihad." He was raised on the Jihad and became a martyr on its course.

"We will never forget you, O guiding martyr. Nor will the families [to] whom you gave their grants. The brothers who lived with you and whom you taught will never forget you. May you receive award and compensation, with God's help.

"Farewell, martyr."[21]

Chapter 8

The Ones Who Stay Behind

To those who are involved and listen to this movie, this is in retaliation for Afghanistan and because Harper wants to send his troops to Iraq. So we are retaliating, the Mujahedin of this world. Canada's officially become one of our enemies by fighting and bombing us and creating a lot of terror in our countries and killing us and killing our innocents. So, just aiming to hit some soldiers just to show that you're not even safe in your own land, and you gotta be careful.

So, may Allah accept from us. It's a disgrace you guys have forgotten God and have you let every indecency and things running your land. We don't, we don't go for this. We are good people, righteous people, believers of God and believing his law and his Prophets, peace be upon them all. That's my message to all of you in this, Inshallah, we'll not cease until you guys decide to be a peaceful country and stay to your own and I—, and stop going to other countries and stop occupying and killing the righteous of us who are trying to bring back religious law in our countries.

Thank you.[1]

—Michael Zehaf-Bibeau in his video message to Canadians, filmed a few minutes before he shot up Parliament Hill

IT'S SUCH A CANADIAN THING, TO SAY "THANK YOU" TO the people you tried to murder.

Kristel Peters was pushing her nine-month-old baby past Canada's National War Memorial on her way to visit her husband at a downtown Ottawa construction project when the world went crazy. "I saw a man who seemed to be dressed in black," she told a reporter many months later. "He had a big rifle. I thought that it was a show until I realized that a person fell at the time."

Michael Zehaf-Bibeau was standing over Canadian army reservist Cpl. Nathan Cirillo, firing bullet after bullet into his back. Cirillo, wearing the kilt of Cameron Highlanders, was a ceremonial guard at the memorial and the Tomb of the Unknown Soldier at its base. The Canadian military had opposed the idea of posting unarmed guards at the monuments, saying they would attract this kind of attack, but Stephen Harper's government had insisted on it after a drunk had urinated on the War Memorial during a Canada Day street party. Cirillo could not defend himself, and his partner, also carrying an empty rifle, could not save him. The wounded man tried to crawl away and find shelter at the Tomb of the Unknown Soldier, but Zehaf-Bibeau kept following and firing into the corporal's back. When it was clear Cirillo was dying, Zehaf-Bibeau turned toward the Langevin Block, the building that's home to the Prime Minister's Office, and shouted the word "Iraq." Peters, the thirty-five-year-old mother, finally realized what was happening, turned in terror and ran toward a place she thought would be safe: Parliament Hill.

Zehaf-Bibeau was right behind her. Peters saw him and pushed her baby's carriage to a police car parked on the far end of the Parliament Building lawn. "I told the officer there was a shooter out there," Peters later said. While the police officer was on her radio reporting the War Memorial attack, Zehaf-Bibeau raced by in a commandeered limousine, headed for the Centre Block, where the House of Commons and the Senate meet. The RCMP officer gave chase, leaving Peters, alone and very afraid, near the Centennial Flame.

Canada was lucky that the man who attacked the nation's Parliament was as inept as Zehaf-Bibeau. He had scouted the Parliament Building before his attack, but he didn't really know his way around. When he did storm the building, he ran in the one direction where there are rarely politicians: toward the library. If he had come an hour earlier, he would have stumbled across almost every member of Parliament and senator as they walked into two giant meeting rooms for their weekly caucus meetings. He would also have come across a mass of reporters trying to scrum the politicians. By the time he was in the Hall of Honour, the long hallway that separates the House of Commons and Senate sides of the building, the caucus meetings were underway behind closed doors and the reporters were gone.

And he was packing the most useless gun imaginable for a terrorist attack. His Winchester 1894 .30-30 carbine was named after the year it came on the market. It was a fine gun for shooting at gophers on the prairies but was no good for hunting people. It's slow to load, holds a small number of bullets and is nowhere in the league of the AK-47s used by the men who attacked the Charlie Hebdo office in Paris in January 2015. And even that rifle's design is seventy years old.

Zehaf-Bibeau was hit in the hand by a police bullet as he ran through the hall. Four Mounties—Const. Curtis Barrett, Sgt. Richard Rozon, Const. Martin Fraser and Cpl. Danny Daigle—moved in on Zehaf-Bibeau in a diamond formation. Two more lurked nearby, and Kevin Vickers, the Sergeant-at-Arms of the House of Commons, rushed into his office to get his Browning pistol. Vickers was the man in charge of security in most of the building, and he was clearly enraged by Zehaf-Bibeau's attack. Zehaf-Bibeau had reached the end of the hall and lodged himself in a small alcove at the entrance of the Library of Parliament, with a stone pillar for protection. Vickers, now armed with a semi-automatic handgun, lurked on the other side of the pillar, close enough to hear the terrorist breathing. Vickers signalled to Barrett that Zehaf-Bibeau was hiding on the other side of the post.

When Zehaf-Bibeau got up to take a shot at the RCMP officers moving toward him, Vickers fired the shot that knocked Zehaf-Bibeau down. In the melee, Zehaf-Bibeau fired one last shot before being hit by thirty-one of the fifty-six rounds fired by Vickers and the RCMP. Zehaf-Bibeau's shot had gone wide, hitting the base of a wall carving that commemorates nurses who served in the First World War. He lay dead on the floor, the fatal head shot fired by Barrett. Zehaf-Bibeau had survived less than two minutes inside the Parliament Building, and just ten minutes had passed since he had killed Corp. Cirillo. Two of his unfired bullets lay near his body, and police found a damaged round in his pocket.

Except for the RCMP officers who gunned him down, no one at that time suspected Zehaf-Bibeau had been such a failure as a terrorist or that he had acted alone. Most people in downtown Ottawa believed Parliament Hill was targeted by a sophisticated group of terrorists, and that some of them had fanned out to attack high-profile places in the parliamentary precinct. A few feet from where the librarians normally worked, police were handcuffing the bloody, bullet-perforated corpse of Michael Zehaf-Bibeau.

RCMP security agents throughout the city rushed VIPs and their children from offices and schools to safe places like the bunker at the Department of National Defence. The cell phone system around Parliament Hill either collapsed or was put out of service as police from across the city rushed into the downtown core to look for Zehaf-Bibeau's accomplices. Fortunately, there weren't any.

A great secret, well known to anyone who worked on Parliament Hill, had finally been exposed to the world. Security was a joke. Anyone with any kind of weapon could storm in, as long as they did not care whether they were killed. Canadians had come to expect their Parliament Building to be accessible. At the beginning of the Chrétien era, anyone could drive onto the Hill, park without too much hassle, wander around looking for famous politicians, have a picnic and enjoy the view. There was some security inside the building. People hadn't had free run of the Centre Block since Paul Joseph Chartier accidentally blew himself up in a third-floor washroom with ten sticks of dynamite on May 18, 1966. (Chartier had planned to toss the dynamite into the House of Commons from the visitors' gallery.) At least one other similar plan was thwarted by police during the Trudeau years.

Jeffrey Arenburg, the Nova Scotian who gunned down Ottawa sportscaster Brian Smith in a 1995 random killing, lurked around the Hill before he went off to the local CTV studio to shoot the first on-air journalist who walked out the door.

In 1997, a distraught man drove a Jeep up the Hill and plowed into the same doors that Zehaf-Bibeau had pushed his way through. Soon afterward, someone left a car full of propane canisters on the Hill. Ten years earlier, a guy hijacked a Greyhound bus and drove it onto the lawn. In 1984, Denis Lortie, who shot up the Quebec National Assembly with guns he stole from the Diefenbunker nuclear shelter in suburban Ottawa, stopped by Parliament Hill but decided there were better pickings elsewhere.

There had been no increase in the level of security after the murder, just two days before, of Warrant Officer Patrice Vincent by Muslim convert and self-styled jihadi Martin Couture-Rouleau.

He and another soldier were run over near the military base at Saint-Jean-sur-Richelieu, just south of Montreal. Both of these attacks were inspired by the call sent out through ISIS's propaganda machine to attack the West. "All these attacks were the direct result of [Islamic propagandist Abu Muhammad al-Adnani's] call to action, and they highlight what a deadly tinderbox is fizzling just beneath the surface of every western country, waiting to explode into violent action at any moment given the right conditions."[2]

The Ontario Provincial Police report into Zehaf-Bibeau's death concludes that "anything similar at Parliament Hill with the present security in place would have devastating results. There have been terrorist-related incidents worldwide and in Canada since Oct. 22 that are indicators that similar attacks are possible and probable."

Police searched Zehaf-Bibeau's car, which was parked near the War Memorial. He had been careful to make sure the licence plate sticker on the old car was up to date. Inside, police found the video made by Zehaf-Bibeau just minutes before he gunned down Cirillo.[3]

Two days after the attack, Zehaf-Bibeau's mother, Susan Bibeau, a senior federal public servant, wrote to the *Ottawa Citizen* to explain the horror and confusion she felt: "I feel mad at my son for what he did, I feel shame for what my son did, yes as someone wrote to me I must have been a bad mother, you can never express it as deeply as I feel it at this time. There will always be guilt. Emotions are complicated, never in a single dimension."[4]

Her son was mentally ill, able to function on the streets of Canada but too confused and disorganized to get to Libya, where he wanted to join a jihadi group. She and Michael had been estranged for more than five years, and when they did talk, it was mostly her listening to one of Michael's lectures about her materialism. In one of his last emails, Michael told his mother he was "only writing because his religion dictated to him to be good to his parents, it was his duty." Susan Bibeau continued:

> *As mentioned my son wanted to have little to do with me, he was troubled and spoke of religion, and religion is not a subject I can easily relate with. So our conversations were one sided where he would talk about religion and I would listen.*
>
> *What did he talk about at our final lunch, he talked about religion, how it was good. How I was wrong to pursue the materiality of this world. He had come to Ottawa to try and get his passport. He ultimately wanted to go to Saudi Arabia and study Islam, study the Koran. He thought he would be happier in an Islamic country where they would share his beliefs.*

The son told his mother he had applied for a passport but was being stonewalled. This, he believed, was a test by the Devil.

It's hard not to feel sympathy for a mother who had struggled to help her son, only to be met with a storm of abuse, criticism and religious preaching.

> *He refused any of my help, he preferred staying in the homeless shelter rather than coming to my house. I will always be left with the question if I could have said something else, insisted more to help . . . The emptiness and pain are overwhelming.*

There was probably nothing she could have done to save her son. He was born in 1982 to a French-Canadian mother and a Libyan father. Drugs and a warped interpretation of Islam had taken over his life by the time he was old enough to vote. The young man's mental problems appear to have begun as a child growing up in a fractured family in Montreal, where his father came in and out of the picture. By the time he got to high school, Zehaf-Bibeau seemed to have a bright future, but four years later, it was obvious Zehaf-Bibeau was on the skids. He embraced hard drugs like PCP, and people who knew him said he was becoming paranoid. He was arrested and accumulated a damning criminal record, for beating people up and carrying a weapon.

"My son used to spend hours playing those war video games, in looking at the event it reminded me of that except that now it was real life, people were real and got hurt," Susan Bibeau wrote soon after the attack on Ottawa.

The family was not particularly religious. "Bello" Zehaf, Michael's mostly absent father, owned nightclubs in a trendy part of downtown Montreal and, at most, fasted during Ramadan. The boy went to high schools filled with children from other privileged families and didn't talk about religion. But as the years went by, Zehaf-Bibeau faded into street culture and somewhere along the line embraced Islam.

Three years before the attack, Zehaf-Bibeau was living in Vancouver and its suburbs, hooked on crack and looking for meaning at one of the more progressive mosques in the Lower Mainland. The Masjid Al-Salaam mosque, in Burnaby, prides itself on its outreach programs for Muslims and non-Muslims, and on an education program aimed at countering anti-Islamic prejudice. Zehaf-Bibeau made it clear to the mosque's managers that he did not think non-believers should be allowed in. "He had a problem with this," Aasim Rashid of the B.C. Muslim Association, which oversees the mosque, told *Maclean's* magazine's Michael Friscolanti. "He told the administration: 'This is a mosque. This is supposed to be for Muslims. What are you doing?' One of the officials sat him down and told him, quite forcefully: 'This is how we operate.

If that is bothersome for you, maybe this is not the right mosque for you.'"

The views of a drugged-up, sullen and obviously troubled convert were unlikely to gain much traction within the mosque. Frustrated, and desperate to get some treatment for his crack addiction, Zehaf-Bibeau walked into a Vancouver McDonald's and pretended to rob it. Very quickly, he was arrested and brought in front of Judge Donna Sinnew.

He begged her for help. "I'm a crack addict and at the same time I'm a religious person," he told Judge Sinnew, according to a transcript released by the court. "I want to sacrifice freedom and good things for a year maybe, so when I come out I'll appreciate things in life more and be clean." The Crown prosecutor recommended the judge save taxpayers' money by releasing Zehaf-Bibeau, but the judge ordered him to be sent to jail. In the end, though, Zehaf-Bibeau got no help for his drug addiction and mental problems.

After two months of going through cold turkey withdrawal, Zehaf-Bibeau copped a plea to a minor charge and was released. He went back to the Burnaby mosque. He wasn't welcome, especially when he was found hiding in the mosque after hours. When it turned out he'd stolen a key, Zehaf-Bibeau was turned out of the mosque for good. He did try to get some psychiatric help, but cash-strapped mental health agencies proved to be useless. He ended up in a homeless shelter in downtown Vancouver, staying there until the summer of 2014.[5] Then he went to Ottawa to live in a shelter within sight of Parliament Hill and close to the passport office that, he believed, was working on the documents he needed to travel to Libya to join in the fighting that had broken out since Muammar el-Quaddafi was overthrown. While in Ottawa, he struggled with his addiction and his religion.

"Religion and Islam was his way of trying to make sense of the world, I don't think he succeeded. It did not bring him peace," Zehaf-Bibeau's mother later wrote. "If I try to understand the motivations of my son, I believe his passport was refused and that pushed him into action. He felt cornered, unable to stay in the life he was in, unable to move on to the next one he wanted to go to. He was mad and felt trapped so the only way out was death.

"I believe he wanted death but wanted it not at his own hand because that would be wrong according to Islam. Maybe he also wanted to strike back at the government who had refused him, the fact that he killed a soldier and went to Parliament would indicate that, they are symbols of government. Regardless of the motivation, that was wrong and despicable."

While security agencies like CSIS had ramped up surveillance in Ottawa and had hauled several members of the city's Muslim community into court on terrorism charges, Zehaf-Bibeau was not on their radar. He probably was unknown to ISIS, too. In his video, Maguire mentions Zehaf-Bibeau's rampage, saying, "The storming of Parliament Hill in Ottawa [was] carried out as a direct response to your participation in the coalition of nations waging war against the Muslim people." But, while he gave a shout-out to Martin Couture-Rouleau, the man who had run down the soldiers in Saint-Jean-sur-Richelieu, he seemed to have forgotten Zehaf-Bibeau's name.

Couture-Rouleau was hooked on ISIS propaganda. A muscular man from a small town near Montreal, he had failed in business. A power-washing company he owned collapsed, but Couture-Rouleau found solace among his new, virtual friends in the Middle East. He changed his name on his Facebook and Twitter accounts to "Ahmad Rouleau" and "Abu Ibrahim al-Canadi." He wasn't alone. At least a half-dozen of his friends had converted to Islam. He had offered to pay their airfare to ISIS territory or Afghanistan, but it's likely none of them tried to travel. Couture-Rouleau did. Security officials stopped him from boarding a plane to Pakistan in 2013, but he still hoped to get to Iraq somehow. In June 2014, the RCMP came for Couture-Rouleau's passport, so whatever jihad he planned to do would have to happen in Canada. Prosecutors had looked at the police files and decided there was nothing they could charge him with. Instead, police tried to deradicalize him. RCMP Supt. Martine Fontaine and a local imam visited Couture-Rouleau less than two weeks before the attack. "He said he wanted to perhaps take steps to change things in his life," Fontaine later said.

It's likely Zehaf-Bibeau and Couture-Rouleau were inspired by a call to arms made by Abu Muhammad al-Adnani, ISIS's chief spokesman, in late September 2014. Certainly, ISIS's propaganda machine wanted people to think so.[6] Al-Adnani was reacting in a rage to allied bombing of ISIS military and economic targets. He wanted jihadis who hadn't yet made the trek to ISIS territory to lash out against Western targets.

In a forty-two-minute audio speech posted on the Internet and linked to by ISIS's Twitter and Facebook network, al-Adnani urged ISIS supporters to kill Canadians, Americans, Australians, the French and other Europeans. It didn't matter if they were civilians or soldiers.

> *Rely upon Allah, and kill him in any manner or way however it may be. Do not ask for anyone's advice and do not seek anyone's verdict. Kill the disbeliever whether he is civilian or military, for they have the same ruling. Both of them are disbelievers. Both of them are considered to be waging war. Both of their blood and wealth is legal for you to destroy, for*

blood does not become illegal or legal to spill by the clothes being worn.

Do not let this battle pass you by wherever you may be. You must strike the soldiers, patrons, and troops of the [unbelievers]. Strike their police, security and intelligence members, as well as their treacherous agents. Destroy their beds. Embitter their lives for them and busy them with themselves. If you can kill a disbelieving American or European—especially the spiteful and filthy French—or an Australian, or a Canadian, or any other disbelievers from the disbelievers waging war, including the citizens of the countries that entered into a coalition against the Islamic State, then reply upon Allah, and kill him in any manner or way however it may be. Do not ask for anyone's advice and do not seek anyone's verdict. Kill the disbelievers whether he is civilian or military, for they have the same ruling. Both of them are disbelievers . . .

If you are unable to find an IED or a bullet, then single out the disbelieving American, Frenchman or any of their allies. Smash his head with a rock, or slaughter him with a knife, or run him over with your car, or throw him down from a high place, or choke him, or poison him . . . If you are unable to do so, then burn his home, car or business. Or destroy his crops. If you are unable to do so, then spit in his face.

The Canadian Prime Minister's Office said it would not be "cowed by threats while innocent children, women, men and religious minorities live in fear of these terrorists." There were, however, no obvious changes to Canada's security strategy.[7]

Within days, an Australian teen stabbed and wounded two police officers when he went to a police station to ask why he had been denied a passport. Zale Thompson, who had also loaded himself up on ISIS propaganda, took a hatchet from a backpack and attacked four police officers in the New York City borough of Queens, wounding two of them before he was shot to death.

But al-Adnani's pitch wasn't the only motivator, and the two men who supposedly acted on it weren't the first Canadians to try to wage freelance jihad. Muslim converts John Nuttall and his girlfriend Amanda Korody, two other street people struggling with drug addiction, came up with a plan to use pressure-cooker bombs in an attack on the British Columbia legislature during Canada Day celebrations in 2013. It's hard to know how much of the plot was their scrambled thinking and how much of it was devised by the very large contingent of RCMP deployed against the couple. The two were convicted of conspiracy to commit murder and possession of explosives for terrorism. The bomb, if it had been put together, would have been lethal. Two similar bombs had devastated the Boston Marathon.

Their lawyer, Marilyn Sandford, claimed: "This was a crime completely manufactured by the RCMP. We also have arguments that the police themselves committed crimes. They were involved in exactly the same activities as our clients were to a large extent, at least some of them." But in Canada, entrapment is not, in itself, a defence that can be made in front of a jury. After Nuttall, forty, and Korody, thirty-three, were found guilty by the jury, their lawyers had to try to convince the judge in a second phase of the trial that there had been entrapment during the five-month police operation involving 240 officers. The two were identified by CSIS as a couple who were inspired by al-Qaeda to launch terrorist attacks. When the police found them, they were living in a basement apartment, using methadone to cope with their heroin addictions and spending most of their time playing video games. Their lives revolved around a bizarre fantasy world that they shared, one populated by aliens and angels and supernatural "Muslim" figures and fuelled by witchcraft and conspiracy theories.[8]

Their case raised the spectre of police shooting fish in a barrel, creating elaborate, media-ready "plots" to ensnare the damaged and drug-addled. Would Korody and Nuttall have harmed anyone if the police hadn't made advances to them? The question seems unanswerable, but the odds are likely on no.[9]

THE DOMESTIC ATTACKS, ALONG WITH FEAR AND disgust at ISIS's Middle Eastern atrocities, were put to good use by the Canadian government. The Conservative Party used a screen grab of al-Shabab fighters in Somalia to create a Facebook post asking for support for new anti-terrorism laws that give police and spy agencies much more power, along with criminalizing jihadi propaganda. Video of ISIS atrocities shot by the Islamists was used by the Conservatives in a pre-election television ad that supposedly showed Liberal leader Justin Trudeau to be naive about terrorism. Trudeau opposed Canadian involvement in the air war against ISIS.

But are jihadis and wannabe Islamic martyrs the biggest domestic threat to Canadians? CSIS, the Canadian intelligence agency, believes white supremacists and anti-Muslim thugs pose a greater danger to public safety inside the country. They're more likely to cause "lone wolf" attacks. In fact, neo-Nazis and other white racists cause about 17 per cent of such attacks worldwide, while Islamic extremists commit about 15 per cent. Of those that are ideologically motivated, Black power groups accounted for 13 per cent, anti-abortion activists committed 8 per cent and about 7 per cent were committed by people motivated by nationalism or separatism. In 40 per cent of attacks, there was no clear ideological motivation. "Lone actors tend to create their own ideologies that combine personal frustrations and grievances, with wider political, social, or religious issues," note the 2014 documents prepared for Michael Peirce, assistant director of CSIS. "This study confirms that lone actor terrorism runs the gamut of ideological persuasions."

In fact, the CSIS analysts said, the idea that the Western world is at war with Islam plays into terrorist recruitment strategies. "International terrorist groups place a high priority on radicalizing Westerners who can be used to carry out terrorist attacks in their home countries. The narrative that the West is at war with Islam continues to exert a very powerful influence in radicalizing individuals and spreads quickly through social media and online fora."[10] Other CSIS documents, obtained by the Canadian Press, warned the Canadian government in September 2014 that there is an emerging anti-Islam movement in Canada, similar to movements in Europe, that may well be at least as dangerous as jihadis inside Canada. The crisis of refugees and migrants flooding into Europe from the Muslim world threw more fuel on the flames of racism and white supremacy, and, by the summer of 2015, the right-wing government of Hungary and neo-fascists in the rest of Europe began collecting on the fear they had sown over the years. After the Paris attacks in November 2015, U.S. states and European countries began closing their doors to the refugees, even though the attack on the French capital had been carried out by men born in Europe. Perhaps that's what ISIS wanted, and it explains the fake Syrian passport found on the bodies of one of the terrorists.

Chapter 9

Saving the Children

O ye who believe! Let not a folk deride a folk who are better than they . . . nor let women . . . [deride] women who may be better than they are; neither defame one another, nor insult one another by nicknames. Bad is the name of lewdness after faith. And those who turneth not in repentance, such are evildoers.

—Qur'an, Sura "The Private Apartments," Verse 2

On January 16, 2013, more than thirty militants belonging to a terror group with strong links to al-Qaeda stormed a natural gas processing plant near In Amenas, Algeria, and charged at the living quarters of the 130 foreigners who worked there. In the final moments of the attack, one of the militants tried to blow himself up with a homemade bomb. He was Xristos Katsiroubas, from London, Ontario, fighting under the name "al-Taher" (The Pure One). Rather than become a human artillery shell, Katsiroubas lived long enough to act as a negotiator and translator for the Signatories in Blood brigade as they tried to cut a deal with British Petroleum, which co-owned the plant. He was also filmed building bombs and setting up a heavy machine gun, and at least one hostage says Katsiroubas fired it at an Algerian military helicopter. And he helped string Western hostages together with explosive cord, setting the scene for the gory climax of the attack.

His high school buddy Ali Medlej, a Lebanese-born Canadian, was later identified by one of the few surviving hostages as one of the leaders of the assault. The Canadians, in their early twenties, were not a couple of young dupes. The bloodshed in that obscure corner of the Algerian desert, which claimed forty hostages and twenty-nine terrorists, was, in a very large way, their fault.

Katsiroubas was one of the militants who helped guard the hostages. After two days of fruitless negotiations with petroleum company executives and Algerian officials, Katsiroubas became frustrated and testy. Algerian soldiers had managed to place themselves between two clusters of terrorists, and the Signatories in Blood couldn't talk the Algerians into pulling back. Katsiroubas's group of terrorists, at the foreign workers' building, decided to make a run for their colleagues in the gas plants. They forced thirty-four foreign workers into SUVs and charged toward Algerian army lines, straight at bullets fired from a military helicopter and the Algerian soldiers. When the SUV carrying Katsiroubas and several hostages flipped over, the Canadian tried to set off a homemade bomb made of a land mine and plastic explosives. It didn't work. Somehow, though, the militants did manage to crowd together with the hostages and set off their explosives. After the shooting and blasts were over, just five hostages were still alive. Katsiroubas was among the militants who blew themselves up when the Algerian army stormed the gas plant.[1]

When he was a student at London South Collegiate Institute, Katsiroubas had made friends with Medlej. Other students later said Katsiroubas was a small kid with a sense of humour who had joined the school's Peacemaker team. The two high school kids were soon on the RCMP radar. For four years, they were watched by Canadian intelligence agents, but they still managed to make it to North Africa in 2011 and join the Signatories in Blood brigade. A third Canadian man, Aaron Yoon, went with them but was in a Mauritanian jail serving a two-year sentence for terrorism when the gas plant was attacked.

Does Canada do enough to defuse radicalism and prevent its nationals from travelling to failing states to join extremists? The answer is obvious.

In February 2015, Lorne Dawson, co-director of the Canadian Network for Research on Terrorism, Security and Society (TSAS), told a senate committee examining security threats to this country that Canadian police and policy makers simply don't understand jihadi recruitment well enough to create effective countermeasures. At about the same time, Conservative senator Daniel Lang told delegates to a public policy conference, "We need to recognize that radicalized thoughts lead to radicalized actions." Dawson told the senators that extremists can be found fairly easily, but it's far more difficult to predict which ones will actually break the law. Research on radicalization, Dawson said, shows very few radicalized people will ever have anything to do with violence.[2] Most draw spiritual sustenance from their religion without feeling a need to kill for it.

But attacks by extremists seem to generate interest in Islam as a go-to religion/political cause for people who are dissatisfied and who don't feel attracted to the anarchism of groups like Black Bloc. The imam of Ottawa's largest mosque reports fifteen to twenty young people approached him for conversion to Islam in the first few weeks after the October 2015 attack on Parliament Hill.

Researcher Amarnath Amarasingam says ISIS's claim to be the new caliphate offers Muslims and non-Muslims an intriguing and exiting new project. It "was seen as the fulfillment of a prophecy." It became incumbent on Muslims around the world to fight for this and build the new fledgling state. "Those who join are looking for 'significance, meaning and belonging.'"

Amarasingam believes ISIS can't be rolled back unless options for better government exist in Iraq and Syria, along with other Islamic nations that are unable to maintain political and social stability.

In testimony at the U.S. House of Representatives Armed Services Committee in July 2014, counter-terrorism expert Brian Fishman was prophetic. He warned ISIS's violence could spill out of the Middle East. "The Islamic State aims to upend and then replace all existing order in the Middle East—and has a disconcerting amount of power to invest in that grandiose mission," he told the members of Congress. "The Islamic State has essentially upended sovereignty and the post-Ottoman national borders in the Middle East . . . in conventional terms, the Islamic State is the most powerful jihadi entity in the world—and it has no real competition, including al-Qaeda. But unlike al-Qaeda, the Islamic State is focused *primarily* on regional power projection rather than global terrorism. Nonetheless, the Islamic State is so large and multifaceted (including several thousand foreign fighters) that it would be surprising if subgroups did not intend such strikes—and U.S. policy toward the Islamic State should account for that risk."[3]

Remaking Middle Eastern states into safe, decent places to live—in effect, keeping the faith of the misfired Arab Spring—would blunt the political attraction of ISIS to people in failed states, stem the flow of refugees and migrants, and possibly reduce the threat of terrorism in the West. However, whether defeated by democracy or by force, the jihadi movement would almost certainly manifest itself in some other failed state in the Muslim world, and people like John Maguire and Michael Zehaf-Bibeau would either travel overseas to join them or use their propaganda as an excuse to lash out at home. The West used force in Afghanistan, Iraq and Libya. American drones have killed people in Yemen, Pakistan and other Muslim states. Most of the time, the use of force has set the stage for more failure. But Islamism—the use of selected parts of Islamic dogma to justify totalitarianism, repression and, in some places, genocide—is the flavour-of-the-month for the disgruntled, just as fascism and communism were through the twentieth century. Fascism had to be crushed. Communism died of Western containment and its own internal failings. Especially after the November 2015 attacks in Beirut, the Sinai and Paris, the debate in the West became focused on whether to use force to crush ISIS or simply contain it while local forces did the actual fighting. After the 2015 election, Canada chose to pull out of the air war and has left it to armies and militias in the region, along with the Americans, French and Russians, to contain ISIS.

CANADA'S MUSLIM RELIGIOUS LEADERS KNEW THAT Maguire's video would make it even more difficult for Canadian Muslims to live peacefully. They have to deal with the storms generated in Canadian mass and social media, and on Internet sites, each time terrorists claim to act in the name of Islam. The extremists force Muslim leaders to, yet again, assure the public that the crimes are committed by a very small group of people on the fringe. In fact, imams in Ottawa, Toronto and Calgary are some of the most outspoken critics of people who use a skewed version of Islam to justify violence.

After Maguire's video hit the news, imams in Ottawa-Gatineau released a statement objecting to Maguire's statements:

> *We categorically and unequivocally condemn all kinds of attacks against innocent people in Canada or any other place in the world. The teachings of our faith leave no room for such actions. As such, we call upon our fellow brothers and sisters in faith to outright reject the call to violence by ISIS. We vehemently stress that Muslims have absolutely no duty to migrate to ISIS-controlled areas or to assist in any way, shape or form in promoting their cause. We believe that Muslims can legitimately continue to live in Canada while obeying all laws of this great nation and sincerely practicing and exemplifying the teachings of our faith within the Canadian context.*[4]

Ottawa imam Imtiaz Ahmed said Muslims need to watch for trouble in their own congregations:

> *If we hear someone expressing sympathy for ISIS, we should tell the authorities. We don't want these young men to hurt themselves or their fellow Canadians. We have seen new converts going abroad. Maguire looks intelligent, and he got good grades in university. What makes him think what he is doing is right? Who would have thought that the proverbial boy next door could become a radical militant? Obviously he is getting ideas from somewhere—at university or on the Internet. We have to find out where. But these people have an agenda of harming Canadians and harming our country, so we should be the first to report them.*

Another Ottawa imam, Mohamad Jebara, wants police and Islamic leaders to work together to help young Muslims understand that ISIS propaganda does not represent Islam. It's the only way, he said, to prevent all of Canadian Muslims from being marked by the sins of a few angry people: "A nation can take reactionary measures to address such pressing issues by bombarding those who instigate bigotry and hatred. Prevention is far superior. Inclusive compassionate education is much cheaper and far more effective than missiles. It's far more successful than hatred and far more productive than sitting back, allowing extremists to spread their hateful dogma and then reacting to their atrocities."[5]

SECULAR MUSLIMS ARE ALSO COMBATTING EXTREMISM. Syed Sohail Raza is director of Muslims Facing Tomorrow, which he describes as a grassroots organization with a focus on separating mosque and state, and assisting Muslim youth in engaging and embracing Canadian values. The challenge, he says, is to convince Muslims to turf the radicals from their midst and to not be seduced by the easy answers offered by extreme fundamentalists.

At the same time, the ideas of militant Islam need to be rooted out of their home soil. Muslims Facing Tomorrow also operates in foreign places where radicalism appears to be taking hold. His group helped make a documentary called *Honor Diaries*, which discusses challenges faced by women in Muslim majority areas. They have taken on the dangerous job of pushing extremists out of communities in very dangerous places. Muslims Facing Tomorrow has even convinced villagers in Muslim countries to change the school curriculum away from totally religious to include academic and skills subjects, along with religion.

"We have successfully carried out a pilot project in Bangladesh in declaring a village radical-free in 2013. In a period of one year, we now have 12 villages that call themselves 'radical-free,' and there are signs outside the village saying the same," he told Canadian legislators in early 2015. "Now, I must let you know that this was done without the involvement of law enforcement agencies. It was done by empowering the moderates, by giving them enough literature, audio and visual, so they could explain to the masses why it is necessary to lead a peaceful coexistence."

So Raza can speak with some authority about defusing radicalism in Canada. "We must follow the three E's: expose, educate and eradicate. Expose the elements, individuals and organizations involved in radicalizing our youth; educate with or without the help of law enforcement agencies but in partnership with the government. It is imperative to educate our youth without falling into the victimhood narrative. Eradicate. This can only happen when the Muslim community gets out of the denial mode and law enforcement agencies are serious about eradicating this menace." He takes a tough line on some Canadian Muslim groups, which, he says, are fronts for radicals, and he takes a tough line on returning jihadis.

Raza says anyone who returns from fighting with ISIS should be charged. Canada should be more vigilant fighting financing of terrorism, and authorities should shut down any religious place of worship that perpetuates hate. To understand what's happening in the Muslim diaspora, law enforcement agencies should consult with secular and moderate Muslims. Political Islam or Islamism should be explained to Canadians and studied in detail by politicians, law enforcement agencies and educational institutions, with an emphasis of avoiding the "victimhood narrative" and emphasizing "reasonable accommodation."

Raza says the RCMP has never returned his phone calls.

"As a Muslim, I'm more concerned about resolving this than anyone else in this room," he said, "but we have to partner with somebody. We're trying on our own. It doesn't seem to be working."[6]

PEOPLE IN THE COUNTER-JIHAD BUSINESS HAVE SPENT A lot of time and money looking at ways to identify radicalized young people and deprogram them. They see radical Islam as a cult that cleverly recruits troubled and bored people, isolates them and exploits them. Jocelyn Bélanger, a psychology professor at Université du Québec à Montréal (UQAM), studies deradicalization. He advised the Senate National Security Committee to advise the government to come up with policies that don't treat radicalized young people as potential criminals or psychiatric patients, but as people with social needs that have not been met.

"I think the evidence is very clear about mental health and terrorism: there's actually no link." He said foreign fighters with mental health issues who join terror groups are normally "weeded out of these organizations. We know that people that have mental illness are stigmatized in our society. And now too, on top of that, we say that they may be radicals or future terrorists, imagine the labels we are putting on those people."[7]

Canada does have some historical experience dealing with young people who grew up steeped in a radical, violent philosophy. The country was dotted with POW camps during the Second World War. Canadian soldiers and propaganda experts waged a tough war with hard-core Nazis to win over German soldiers. It wasn't easy. At first, the Canadians tried segregating the prisoners, weeding out the most diehard Nazis. That did not work. Canadians also, with the help of anti-Nazi POWs, wrote propaganda and distributed it in camps. POWs were shown films and made to sit through speeches. None of those tactics worked, either. The only prisoners who seemed to change were the men who were taken out of the camps to work on farms and logging camps across the country. Not only did they realize they'd been lied to by the German propaganda machine, many of them liked Canada so much that they immigrated to this country in the late 1940s and early 1950s. Some even chose to live in remote northern Ontario towns close to their now-closed POW camps.[8]

Maybe the wartime deprogrammers had found part of the

solution. People like John Maguire and Xristos Katsiroubas grew up in cities and towns. They never had the chance to put their energy into anything that was productive or adventurous. Instead, they lived in a world where kids spend their time at home or in low-wage, low-skill part-time work.

Stephane Pressault, psychology professor at the University of Ottawa, said that many of the radicalized youth need better links to society. "I think the common sign is really social isolation. How can we engage these individuals who are isolated, who are not in the mainstream and following the majority of Muslims in Canada? It's something that the whole [psychologist] community is thinking about. How do we engage these young people who may be prone to that?"

Jocelyn Bélanger, the UQAM professor and radicalization expert, agrees. "The loss of significance deeply hurts. The highway to significance, if you wish, is fighting for radical ideology—which provides significance through a demonstration of power, harming victims and inducing fear in others." That's why, he says, ISIS propaganda is so effective. "Their ideology dictates the actions required to become a hero, a martyr, a rock star."

We don't do a good job of encouraging young people. Most people think of themselves as good parents, and the teaching profession is much more sophisticated than it was a generation ago, but this is very much a society where kids are expected to be unheard and often unseen. Joel Westheimer, an American expert on youth alienation, says the school system simply has no ability, or desire, to deal with children who are "different":

> *The goals of K-12 education have been shifting steadily away from preparing active and engaged public citizens and toward more narrow goals of career preparation and individual economic gain. Pressures from policy*

> *makers, business groups, philanthropic foundations, and parents, and a broad cultural shift in educational priorities have resulted in schools being primarily seen as conduits for individual success and, increasingly, lessons aimed at exploring democratic responsibility have been crowded out. Much of the current education reform is limiting the kinds of teaching and learning that can develop the attitudes, skills, knowledge, and habits necessary for a democratic society to flourish.*[9]

In his book *Pledging Allegiance: The Politics of Patriotism in America's Schools*, Joel Westheimer argues that, after the 9/11 attacks, the American government began implementing policies that actually restrict critical analysis of historical and contemporary events. "In 2003, Tennessee senator Lamar Alexander introduced his bill, The American History and Civics Education Act, by warning that educators should not expose students to competing ideas in historical texts. Civics, he argued, should be put back in its 'rightful place in our schools, so our children can grow up learning what it means to be American . . . In April, 2008, the Arizona House of Representatives passed SB 1108 specifying that schools whose teachings 'denigrate or encourage dissent' from 'American values' would lose state funding."[10]

In Florida, the Education Omnibus Bill specified "the history of the United States will be taught as genuine history . . . American history will be viewed as knowable, teachable, and testable." Only "facts" could be taught about the period of discovery and colonization. Representative Shelley Vana, a former executive of a local teachers' union, wondered, "Whose facts would be taught, Christopher Columbus's or the Indians'?"[11]

Purging the schools of "political correctness" is part of a movement to get kids—and their teachers, along with anyone else who makes trouble for power people—back into line, Westheimer says.

"There is a certain irony to the argument that schools in a democratic nation can better prepare students to be democratic citizens by encouraging deference to authority and discouraging lessons about social movements and social change." He says plans by Jefferson County, Colorado, to suppress teaching of anything but "positive" American history and downplay the country's legacy of civil disobedience and protest "isn't about making better citizens. It's about removing the very idea behind good citizenship—the very American premise that we choose our leaders, hold them accountable, and demonstrate peacefully to make our views known and to question authority."[12]

At least, Westheimer says, Canadian educators are rejecting much of the American curriculum, which is geared toward improving Scholastic Aptitude Test (SAT) scores.

"The Canadian Principals Association went to the unusual step of issuing a 'statement of concern' regarding student testing and its impact on thinking and learning. School-based administrators throughout Canada, they wrote, 'are increasingly concerned that current policies and practices on student testing are leading to . . . a secretive or unintended shift of priorities to focus on a narrow range of student knowledge and literacy/numeracy skills.'"[13]

We also do a somewhat better job of caring for our children, though certainly not enough to deserve to be smug. The very programs Westheimer praises are under attack by people who that believe kids aren't learning enough in the classroom and that programs trying to give poorer kids a hand up are subsidies for scam artists and lazy parents.

"In Ottawa, the Q & A section of the Ottawa School Breakfast program lists as their number question 'Why is the school breakfast program important?' Children who arrive at school hungry do not perform well in the classroom. Numerous studies have shown that students who are fed are more alert, develop greater self-esteem, have better attendance, and fewer discipline problems. Children who receive a healthy, nutritious head start to the day show a marked improvement in academic achievement."[14]

MANY PARENTS OF WESTERNERS WHO HAVE JOINED jihadi groups would like to see some sort of support for deprogramming people who show signs of being radicalized. So do the critics of ISIS within the Muslim community. So far, the deprogramming—treating people on the road to extremism as though they have been seduced by a cult, and trying to help them understand and resist what's happening to them—has taken place very sporadically. Not only do most activists and agencies lack the money for long and expensive interventions, they have to accept that someone who reads jihadi literature and agrees with it has committed no crime. People have a right to their religious beliefs, and many of the rights we have were won by people who refused to conform to the beliefs of the prevailing sources of power and moral authority.

Canada's controversial Bill C-51 gives security agencies the authority to "disrupt" situations that appear to involve recruitment. The law, passed in early 2015, is vague about what that word means, but it does appear, at the very least, to allow CSIS agents to approach the families and friends of suspected recruitment targets to try to get help to dissuade those targets from getting more deeply involved in foreign or domestic terrorism.[15] That may seem like a common-sense thing to do, but federal agencies normally aren't supposed to breach the privacy rights of Canadians by spreading warnings about them.

Craig Forcese, a law professor at the University of Ottawa and an expert on counter-terrorism, says the government should be "throwing money hand over fist at the RCMP's fledgling program to confront violent extremism. The problem can't be solved through prosecutions and penitentiaries," he recently told a parliamentary committee.[16]

Like many European police forces and governments, the RCMP started a Countering Violent Extremism (CVE) program that provides education and engages in collaboration at the community level. The program, initiated in 2014, is limited to people who have not committed violent acts. It has about thirty trainers across the country now.

Shirley Cuillierrier, director general, Partnerships and External Relations, RCMP, says the police need to balance the rights of people to freedom of conscience and expression with the needs of society, which expects to be protected from violence:

"When I reference radicalization to violence, I am not speaking of individuals who have radical beliefs or who have passionate views. Every citizen has the right to his or her own beliefs. What I am specifically referring to is the process by which individuals come to believe that inflicting violence upon others will advance their cause. It is when it is heading toward, or reaches that point, that it becomes a particular concern for law enforcement and society at large."

And, as usual, the challenge is to identify which people share ISIS's beliefs but want to live peacefully, and which have decided to follow ISIS's call for violence.

"Indicators vary, from withdrawal from positive social interactions and activities to isolation and segregation. They could manifest as expressing increased hatred or espousing the virtues of violence and expressing an 'us versus them' mentality," says Cuillierrier.

"I think the tides are turning in terms of community engagement and community leaders coming forward . . . We've had mothers come forward and say, 'I didn't know that was going on, and now I recognize what I should have seen, perhaps I would have acted differently.' That's a switch in thinking."[17]

The RCMP has to balance factions within Canada's Islamic community. It also has to build trust with people who feel pressured by mainstream media, right-wing antagonists, and even some Muslim converts. Calgary imam Syed Soharwardy says police haven't made a dent in ISIS recruitment, which he calls brainwashing. "Why has intelligence failed to stop them? Who funded them? This is a very important question. A national enquiry would be able to find that out." Soharwardy's hard line attracted the attention of John Maguire, who sent him threatening Facebook messages in August 2014, calling him a deviant Muslim supporting an infidel government. "He said, 'Syed Soharwardy, shame on you; you are a deviant imam; you are supporting an infidel government and shame on you. We are fighting for Islam and we are trying to establish the Islamic government, and you are misguiding people.'"[18]

Deputy Commissioner Scott Tod of the Ontario Provincial Police says his force learned a lot from its 1995 standoff with First Nations people at a former provincial campground at Ipperwash in southwestern Ontario. The police shot Dudley George, one of the protesters, and the inquiry that was held after George died showed that police needed far better skills to deal with people who have grievances. Tod said his force, which was still setting up a program when Maguire made his threatening video and Zehaf-Bibeau attacked Parliament Hill, learned very quickly that it had to resist the urge to turn community involvement into intelligence gathering.

Part of the RCMP's Countering Violent Extremism program centres on finding ways to defuse ISIS's sophisticated online propaganda systems. The RCMP is trying to develop the same social media counter-terrorism systems that have worked well for the U.S. government. Not only do intelligence agents at the State Department's Center for Strategic Counterterrorism Communications help social media companies identify ISIS propagandists, they also take them on. Sometimes, they debate them, but it turns out that mockery is an even more effective way to isolate them.

The RCMP has been careful with its words. It is encouraging people who work on deradicalization programs to discuss extremism without making connections to the Muslim religion. Alienating Muslims as some sort of "other" will probably generate more radicals. Still, some Muslim leaders believe that there's so much suspicion, Muslim young people are afraid to talk about the pressures placed on them for fear of being labelled.

The federal public safety ministry has also created a website called Extreme Dialogue, which is supposed to discourage young people from radicalism. It also developed the Cross-Cultural Roundtable on Security, which brings together community leaders with extensive experience in social and cultural matters. The roundtable was created in 2005, as part of the federal government's response to the 9/11 attacks, to engage the government and communities in long-term discussions. It meets three times a year. The same government department started the Kanishka Project, which funds more than thirty academic studies that are trying to improve the understanding of terrorism in the Canadian context. The researchers are tracking how terrorism changes over time and looking for new counter-terrorism strategies, trying to find ways to adapt counter-terrorism tactics. The Kanishka Project has given money to the Canadian Resource Centre for Victims of Crime, which has been exploring ways to help victims of terrorism. The centre created the website www.TerrorVictimResponse.ca.[19]

Daniel Gallant, a former Nazi skinhead who started turning his life around in 2002 after spending time in jail for attacking a First Nations man with a hatchet, says many of the government's laws and programs are designed to pressure young extremists into turning themselves in. Gallant, who now runs a deprogramming counselling program in British Columbia, believes the government shouldn't gear its programs just to people flirting with radical Islam. "What we're doing is creating a pressure-cooking atmosphere. It's as if our government is saying, 'let's bring it to a boil, get 'em out and then nab them.' If we come at them hard and punch them, we are going to entrench them further into extremism."[20]

Other critics of the system say that it's designed to criminalize ISIS recruits, not help them. But the situation in Canada is in a state of flux as much of the law and order agenda of the Harper government is swept away. Justin Trudeau's Liberals were silent about Islamic radicalization and ISIS recruitment in Canada during the 2015 campaign. They have the opportunity to look at what's worked and what's failed in Europe, and develop programs that keep Canadians safe while undoing some of the damage caused by radical Islamic propaganda.

Chapter 10

Isn't There a Law against That?

A steady stream of anti-terrorism bills has flowed through Parliament since the September 11, 2001, attacks in the United States. Since June 2015, Canadian authorities have had the power to seize the passports of suspected jihadi extremists and to strip the Canadian citizenship of dual citizens convicted of terrorism, treason, spying or taking up arms against Canadian soldiers. (Those laws may now be repealed or toned down after the change of government in November 2015.) Canada followed the lead of Australia, where the government passed tough legislation after journalists trolling the Internet found pictures of an Australian citizen holding the severed heads of Syrian soldiers.

New Zealand, however, has no such law to strip people of its citizenship. Prime Minister John Key told the *New Zealand Herald*: "Obviously that's [tough laws] not our preference, but we can't stop what Australia chooses to do. We can only reflect on whether we believe it's appropriate to leave a New Zealand citizen in a stateless position, and I think the view we've taken is we don't support that."[1]

During the 2015 Canadian federal election campaign, then-prime minister Stephen Harper promised even tougher laws against what he called "jihad tourism," saying his government, if re-elected, would make it illegal for most Canadians to travel to places where groups like ISIS are fighting. Even more money would be pumped into the country's intelligence agencies, and border security agents would start collecting the biometric information—fingerprints, eye retina scans and voice prints—of all travellers coming into the country, on top of the screening that's done of anyone arriving in Canada on a visa. "We'll make sure people are who they say they are," Harper said. "You can fake your name, you can fake your documents, but you cannot fake your fingerprints." The announcement was greeted with some skepticism. Christianne Boudreau, whose son Damian Clairmont was killed while fighting in Syria, said the government wasn't able to stop her son from leaving Canada to join a Syrian insurgency affiliated with al-Qaeda.

"Anybody can pick up and travel and book a flight to anywhere, and if you really want to go badly enough, you can book your flight to Europe and then from there book yourself into somewhere else," she said. "It's window dressing. It's not realistic."[2]

The government had already created a High Risk Travel Case Management Group. Members of police forces across the country track people who seem close to joining terrorist groups. Michael Zehaf-Bibeau, who attacked Parliament Hill, and Martin Couture-Rouleau, the man who deliberately ran over two Canadian soldiers in Saint-Jean-sur-Richelieu, Quebec, were spotted by the task force and thwarted from leaving Canada. They struck here instead. Hopefully, that systemic failure has been fixed. The group also does "targeted early intervention" with people who have not yet crossed the threshold to violent extremism.

Canada has an Integrated Terrorism Assessment Centre created in 2004 to "centralize and facilitate the integration of intelligence into comprehensive assessments of potential threats to Canada, Canadians, and Canadian interests at home and abroad." It, too, brings together federal agencies to share information. Canadian security agents have always been protective of their turf, a problem that was blamed for the Air India bombing in 1985 that killed 329 people. After spending more than $100 million on fruitless prosecutions, the Canadian government asked John Major, a former justice of the Supreme Court of Canada, to look into the disaster. His 2010 report described a "cascading series of errors" caused by inter-service rivalry. Hopefully it won't take another mass murder to determine whether Canada's secret agents talk to each other.[3]

THE CANADIAN GOVERNMENT, ALONG WITH ITS ALLIES, has tried to counter the recruitment by ISIS and other jihadi groups with anti-terrorism laws that give security agencies the ability to snoop into the personal and online lives of everyone in the country. Prime Minister Harper's government, during its nine years in power (2006–2015), followed the lead of its Liberal predecessors by introducing ever-tougher anti-terrorism laws almost every time there was a high-profile attack in the West. Most of these laws were drafted to make it easier for police and domestic security agents to track and watch suspected terrorists, and to hold them for what have sometimes turned out to be long periods without trial. Some of the post-9/11 laws have given prosecutors the ability to present evidence in secret hearings, and to seal documents that may be important to national security. Sometimes, Ottawa's idea of national security can be perplexing. For instance, in 2015, federal lawyers demanded evidence in an employment lawsuit be sealed under the country's anti-terrorism laws, even though the information in the file was a collection of gossip about the prime minister's family.[4]

Bill C-51, the omnibus terrorism bill passed in 2015, contained provisions to outlaw what the law's drafters called "terrorist propaganda." Judges were given the power to delete such propaganda from the Internet, although it's still not clear how police could do so. Canada's terrorism laws also makes it a crime to advocate on behalf of terrorists, possibly extending the reach of the law to anyone who is part of ISIS's propaganda system. Critics of the bill said the law should have anchored offences of terrorist propaganda to existing laws that ban dangerous speech. That way, as University of Ottawa law professor Craig Forcese says, people could be prosecuted for actual or threatened violence, not for their beliefs. Forcese and Kent Roach, his colleague at the University of Toronto's law faculty, are experts on Canadian security law, and they worry that the law is far too broad.[5]

The same law allows customs agents to seize "terrorist propaganda" along with the usual obscene material and hate literature that they were already chasing. How do customs agents stop Twitter feeds and other online material that promotes ISIS and seduces people to join it? Again, the law uses a very wide net, but it doesn't really deal with the problem. Quite possibly, it fails to engage ISIS on the Internet because one government, especially that of a second-tier power like Canada, really has very little policing power on the World Wide Web. It also mirrors laws in France and other Western countries that make it illegal to promote or glorify terrorism. How can that be defined? What's the difference between peacefully agreeing with what ISIS does and glorifying ISIS's actions? Can suppressing freedom of expression that severely be justified under the Canadian Charter of Rights and Freedoms, which allows speech rights to be limited, if the law's provisions are justifiable and proportionate to the problem that's being addressed?

A similar law would never survive a court challenge in the United States. It would be struck down under the U.S. constitution's First Amendment, which has no escape hatch for justifiable muzzling of speech. Instead, the American government relies on social media to police itself (with the help of U.S. security agents who monitor the Internet), and it wages its own war on ISIS propagandists, attacking them personally with live ammunition carried by drones. Throughout 2015, the Americans located several of ISIS's top propagandists and killed them by remote control, and, in the summer of 2015, Britain used a drone to kill two of its citizens fighting for ISIS in Syria.[6] And in November 2015, the Americans targeted Jihad Johnny, the ISIS executioner who had shocked the West by his brutal beheadings of journalists and aid workers.

THE PRINTING PRESS CHANGED THE NATURE OF WAR. Almost as soon as movable type was attached to a wine press to make a machine to mass-produce words, people used the printed word to trash their enemies. So did governments. It came to be an expected part of warfare, although, because paper was expensive, many people couldn't read and distribution was difficult, very little propaganda reached its target. At most, it was good for homeland morale and to drum up recruits. Internal seditious propaganda was considered treason, while attacks on individuals in England were, starting in 1605, prosecuted as criminal libel.[7] By the time of the French Revolution, paper had become cheap to make and most people could read. The regime in France, which was eager to spread the revolution, printed tons of propaganda in the first months after the monarchy fell, trying to entice working-class people in the rest of Europe to join them. The printing presses stopped when the governments of the major powers of Europe complained.

Were those governments right? Is there some kind of natural rule or international law against governments attacking each other with words? There seems to be. Scholars have been tilling this field since the end of the First World War, when scientific propaganda was used by the British against Germany with devastating effect to undermine civilian morale and make U.S. support of the Kaiser's regime unthinkable.[8]

These laws have been enshrined in treaties, although a list of agreements that include anti-propaganda clauses would read like a bad joke. Countries affected by the Revolutions of 1848 agreed to try to stop the flow of propaganda between countries. Five years before the First World War broke out, the nations most responsible for starting it, Serbia and Austria, agreed to renounce the use of propaganda against each other, but Serbia broke that promise immediately. The ultimatum that the Austrians handed to the Serbs in the summer of 1914, after Serb-sponsored terrorists murdered the Austrian heir to the throne, Archduke Franz Ferdinand, demanded the end of the propaganda war the Serbs were waging. Once again, Serbia agreed, but its government, which was in the middle of its own election campaign during the crisis, had already dumped so much toxic propaganda celebrating the assassination of the Austrian heir that a peaceful solution to the Austro-Serb conflict was very unlikely. Serbia rejected other Austrian demands, and Vienna declared war.

The first treaty between the Soviet Union and the United States, signed during the Depression, promised that neither side would create or distribute propaganda aimed at the other. Both sides appear to have tried to keep their word. Nazi Germany made similar solemn vows to its neighbours in the years before it invaded them. The Nazis, however, used local fascist parties to get their message out.

Making lethal propaganda is now a war crime—or so it seems. It's clearly illegal to wage genocidal warfare and to plan it. International law, applied by war crimes tribunals, is supposed to hold people to account for the things they say, write and broadcast that incite other people to kill. Off and on since the Second World War, that legal concept has been enforced, but only rarely. In many ways, it has been, as the Nazis argued after the war, victors' justice, since existing regimes almost never hand over their own people to be tried for war crimes. War crimes tribunals demand solid proof that the propaganda resulted in murder, a much higher bar than prosecutors faced during the Nuremberg war crimes trials.

Julius Streicher was one of the most vicious Jew-baiters in the Third Reich. Streicher's propaganda was an incitement of hatred and violence against the Jews. Unlike the other major war criminals in the dock at the Nuremberg war crimes trials, the prosecutors could not tie Streicher to any of the planning of the war itself. Nor was Streicher guilty of anything resembling the waging of aggressive war, the charge that proved so lethal to senior Nazis, top generals in the German armed forces and leaders of Japan's militaristic clique. Even Hitler considered Streicher to be too crazy and stupid to be allowed near any real power. Since 1922, almost from the beginning of the Nazi movement, he had published the often pornographic tabloid *Der Stürmer*, which had run the very worst of the Nazis' anti-Semitic propaganda. As Nazi influence grew, so did circulation of Streicher's rag. What should have been, at most, a fringe publication took on a sinister importance when the Nazis became serious political contenders in the early years of the Depression, but once

Joseph Goebbels got control of the mainstream German media, Streicher and his paper lost their importance—although they still had a devoted following among the most vicious Nazis.

Nor could Streicher be directly tied to the Holocaust. He had never run a concentration camp, nor was it proven that he had even visited one. The International Military Tribunal convicted him of helping create the social and political environment that generated the Holocaust. Noting Streicher's reputation as "Jew-baiter number one," the tribunal ruled that Streicher's speeches and writings "infected the German mind with the virus of anti-Semitism and incited the German people to active persecution." Talk of the physical destruction of the Jews had started appearing in *Der Stürmer* in 1938, at a time when Jews were brutally persecuted in Nazi Germany but were not yet being murdered in large numbers. His propaganda was "poison [that] Streicher injected into the minds of thousands of Germans which caused them to follow the National Socialists' policy of Jewish persecution and extermination."

What sent Streicher to the gallows was Streicher's knowledge that his "propaganda of death" was inspiring the murders that he advocated. People in the Nazi leadership let Streicher know about the Final Solution. A person with some sense of morality might have stopped the hate campaign, but Streicher was inspired by the Holocaust to ramp up his vicious writings. In doing so, he had shown the *mens rea*—the guilty mind—needed to support a finding of guilt on charges of incitement of crimes against humanity. Many other Nazi propagandists and press hacks who had written anti-Semitic propaganda during the war escaped serious punishment because they, unlike Streicher, had not known how well it worked.[9]

Julius Streicher was the odd man out among the major war criminals. He was viewed by the court and his fellow defendants as a low-life. He was in the dock as a symbol of the rot of Nazi racial ideology. Short, ugly, bald and foul-smelling, Streicher was a man with no manners or social skills. When he went to trial at Nuremberg, he was quite insane. He was no leader and never had been. By the middle of the war, Hitler and most of his henchmen were sure Streicher had lost his mind. He had been removed from his lucrative job of Nazi leader in Franconia in 1940, after he had been caught cheating on his taxes.

His paranoia and other mental illnesses caused him to rage against the Jews, and his propaganda became more vicious and depraved as the war went on. At "Ashcan," the special jail that held the major German war criminals in the months before the trials, the other prisoners would not eat with Streicher, so he ate by himself at a small table. One field marshal told the Americans that Streicher washed his face and brushed his teeth in a toilet. Probably prisoners among the better class of Nazis were also bored by Streicher's rants against the Jews, which never stopped and became more obscene and ridiculous as the months of the war crimes trials dragged on. The lawyers offered to him were all Jewish, he said, and the judges were all Jews. (Neither was true.)

Streicher seemed so crazy that, at the recommendation of the Soviets, three psychiatrists were brought in to assess him. They found him strange, but sane enough to understand what was happening at his trial. Streicher was smart about one thing: he never stopped arguing that there was no connection between what he had written and the Holocaust. He had not planned the murder of Europe's Jews and other minorities. He had not taken part in the genocide. He had never visited the camps. While he advocated the destruction of the Jews after 1942, he claimed to have meant that in a metaphorical way. When he found out the Germans had built an entire industry of murder, he was as surprised as anyone.

The Holocaust would certainly have happened without Julius Streicher and his shabby newspaper. Yet he would die for the things he wrote.[10] Of all the major war criminals hanged at Nuremberg on October 16, 1946, Streicher was the only one who called out Adolf Hitler's name at the end. At 2:12 a.m., Julius Streicher was brought from his cell to the gallows. Kingsbury Smith, an American reporter, described the scene:

> *While his manacles were being removed and his hands bound, this ugly, dwarfish little man, wearing a threadbare suit and a well-worn bluish shirt buttoned to the neck bit without a tie (he was notorious during his days of power for his flashy dress), glanced at the three wooden scaffolds rising menacingly in front of him. Then he glared around the room, his eyes resting momentarily upon the small group of witnesses. By this time, his hands were tied securely behind his back. Two guards, one on each arm, directed him to Number One gallows on the left of the entrance. He walked steadily the six feet to the first wooden step but his face was twitching.*
>
> *As the guards stopped him at the bottom of the steps for identification, he uttered his piercing scream "Heil Hitler!"*
>
> *The scream sent a shiver down my back.*
>
> *As its echo died away an American colonel standing by the steps said sharply, "Ask the man his name." In response to the interpreter's query Streicher shouted, "You know my name well."*[11]

Some scholars believe that international law crafted by the United Nations General Assembly just after the Nuremberg war crimes trials made state-sponsored propaganda part of the acts involved in the waging of wars of aggression. In 1949, the UN General Assembly passed, by an overwhelming majority, a resolution called Essentials of Peace calling on all nations "to refrain from any acts, or threats of acts, direct or indirect, aimed at impairing the freedom, independence, or integrity of any state, or at fomenting civil strife and subverting the will of the people in any state."[12] In British, American and Canadian common law, the "principle of incitement" to violence has been entrenched since 1801.[13] That piece of court-made law found its way into most criminal codes in the West. Strangely, the British removed incitement when they amended their criminal law in 2008.

Prosecutors at the International Criminal Court have tried to use the Streicher precedent against Serb and Rwandan leaders accused of committing crimes against humanity. It has been a tough sell. The court insists that a clear link can be shown between hate propaganda and genocide. The court ruled that, in the case of the Serb leaders who ethnically cleansed parts of their country by slaughtering or forcibly moving the Croatian and Muslim minorities, hate speech, even propaganda aimed at inciting genocide, was not a crime under customary international law.

Too many attempts by the United Nations to make hate propaganda a crime against humanity had been thwarted by the superpowers during the Cold War. But the International Criminal Tribunal for Rwanda court could not ignore the vicious propaganda of that country's media, especially Radio Television of a Thousand Hills, or Radio Télévision Libre des Mille Collines (RTLM). It was a radio station that operated in Rwanda for a little over a year, from the beginning of July 1993 to the end of July 1994. During that time, it was partly responsible for the deaths of hundreds of thousands of people. The station waged a vicious propaganda war against the minority Tutsis, and against moderate Hutus and most foreigners within reach. The station was privately owned, but it received money from Rwanda's state-owned broadcaster, Radio Rwanda. It urged the mass murder of Tutsis. Once the slaughter began, it broadcast blow-by-blow accounts of the genocide. Witnesses to the genocide said the most common item they saw among the killers, next to machetes, was small radios tuned to the station.

The U.S. State Department, Reporters Without Borders and the Rwandan Ministry of Information made recordings of the station's call to violence. The new regime handed four of RTLM's executives over to the International Criminal Tribunal for Rwanda. They were tried for incitement to genocide, complicity in genocide, genocide and crimes against humanity. The tribunal found the station had "encouraged Tutsi civilians to come out of hiding and to return home or go to the roadblocks, where they were subsequently killed in accordance with the direction of subsequent RTLM broadcasts tracking their movements . . . RTLM broadcasts exploited the history of Tutsi privilege and Hutu disadvantage, and the fear of armed insurrection, to mobilize the population, whipping them into a frenzy of hatred and violence that was directed largely against the Tutsi ethnic group."[14] Georges Ruggiu, who had broadcast much of the anti-Tutsi propaganda, was sentenced to twelve years in prison. Hassan Ngeze, a major shareholder and editor of a magazine, *Kangura*, published by the station, was sentenced to life in prison. Two directors of the station, Ferdinand Nahimana and Jean-Bosco Barayagwiza, received the same sentence. It was reduced to thirty-six years on appeal.[15]

SENDING ONE LOW-RANKING NAZI THUG TO THE gallows and locking up a handful of Rwandan non-entities will not stop the flow of hate propaganda in this world, nor is it much of a deterrent to the people in ISIS who toil day in, day out, to recruit more cannon fodder and devise more wicked ways to kill people to make violence porn. Propaganda for war and genocide needs to be seen as a crime that sullies the reputation of a state. We're a long way from that. State broadcasters throughout the Middle East broadcast anti-Semitic television shows and radio rants that could easily have come from the twisted mind of Julius Streicher. Israel, too, is awash in anti-Arab propaganda.

Sometimes, the actors in the Middle East drama pretend to try to curb the torrent of publicly and privately made hate speech. Article 5 of a bilateral agreement between Israel and Lebanon (Israel-Lebanon Agreement on Withdrawal of Troops from Lebanon, 2 ILM 708 (1983)) was signed on May 17, 1983, after Israel invaded Lebanon to try to crush the Iranian-backed militant group Hezbollah. It contained a clause providing that "consistent with the termination of the state of war and within the framework of their constitutional provisions, the Parties will abstain from any kind of hostile propaganda against each other." The agreement didn't create much peace, but it was a baby step. No real, lasting peace will exist between Israel and its neighbours until the propaganda war stops.

Anti-propaganda clauses have turned up in other peace agreements. For example, Article 3(2)(f) of the Agreement on Non-aggression and Good Neighbourliness between South Africa and Mozambique, signed on March 16, 1984, obliged the parties to "eliminate and prohibit the installation in their respective territories of radio broadcasting stations, including unofficial or clandestine broadcasts, for the elements that carry out . . . violence, terrorism, or aggression against the territorial integrity or political independence of each other."[16] In Article II(10) of a 1988 treaty between Afghanistan and Pakistan, both countries promised "to abstain from intervening or interfering in the external affairs of the other High Contracting Party."[17]

In 1994, Israel and the Palestinian Authority signed a peace agreement. Article XII was aimed at ending the propaganda war between the two states and was supposed to prevent groups and individuals in the two jurisdictions from creating it. Each party was to "seek to foster mutual understanding and tolerance and shall accordingly abstain from incitement, including hostile propaganda, against each other, and without derogating from the principle of freedom of expression, shall take legal measures to prevent such incitement by any organizations, groups or individuals within their jurisdiction."[18]

For what it's worth, Article 20(1) of the United Nations International Covenant on Civil and Political Rights specifically prohibits propaganda for war, while Article 20(2) forbids hate speech advocating harm to people because of their race, religion or nationality.[19] The covenant limits the freedom of expression guaranteed in its own Article 19. Members of the United Nations had worked since the Second World War to develop some sort of framework outlawing propaganda aimed at inciting violence. Unfortunately, Cold War politics got in the way. And some countries like Canada had, eventually, passed laws against hate speech intended to incite violence against identifiable groups, although the laws were rarely enforced and charges were only laid when it seemed the propaganda was directed against people living in Canada. "Propaganda for war" international law (which forms part of the law in Canada and most other countries) has been very narrowly interpreted to mean "incitement to war." Propaganda aimed at undermining the values of other nations or challenging their right to even exist does not seem to be covered by international law, especially if that propaganda is created by individuals, rather than by governments. During the long negotiations over the wording of the International Bill of Rights, the Brazilian delegate came closest to advocating for laws to dial down international hate speech. He declared that it meant "the repeated and insistent expression of an opinion for the purpose of creating a climate of hatred and lack of understanding between the peoples of two or more countries, in order to bring them eventually to armed conflict."[20] Western countries opposed this interpretation.

UNTIL THE DEVELOPMENT OF THE INTERNET, ISIS-style propaganda wasn't seen to be much of a problem. No one tried to answer serious questions like, How would a law against it be enforced? Who would police it? Who would run a trial if charges were laid? And, in practical terms, how could the creation of such propaganda be stopped? Some governments, including Canada's, included anti-propaganda laws in anti-terrorism laws after 9/11. In doing so, they have run up against the freedom of expression pledges in democratic constitutions, leaving the courts to decide whether something that might be called "propaganda" by one ethnic group might actually be "free expression." In Canada, fostering hatred against a racial, ethnic or religious group is against the law, but charges have been laid only in cases involving incitement of hatred of other Canadians, not encouraging the killing of foreigners. And even then, charges are rarely laid, since they require the personal approval of each provincial justice minister or attorney general. And no one is going to charge a teenager who gets his thrills by watching men being locked into a cage and drowned.

Nor can Western governments seriously believe they can police the Internet or, if things got really bad, shut it down. Even in repressive states like China and North Korea, determined people still see what they want to. Rafal Rohozinski, senior fellow of the Ottawa-based SecDev Foundation, Ottawa, which refers to itself as an operational think tank working at the intersection of technology and social change, is studying conflict and radicalization in Syria, Iraq, Latin America and the Commonwealth of Independent States (made up of fragments of the former Soviet Union). His organization gets grants from Canadian government to study radicalization and populations at risk. He says that if the World Wide Web is shut down, people will create their own Internet the way Soviet scientists did. More than two-thirds of the people of the world have access to broadband, and there are more cell phones on earth than there are people. He testified at a parliamentary committee:

> *In our experience over the past 14 years, the one thing we can say is that most states that attempt to block sites fail miserably. Individuals invariably find a way around this. If they're determined, they'll find it. If they don't find it in the open Internet, they'll find it in the dark web. In fact, many of the forums used for the coordination of jihadi groups up till about three years ago existed in something called the "dark web," which means sites that are not actually visible on the public Internet, where you need to have special permission to be able to enter into it.*
>
> *The technical means for policing cyberspace are tremendously difficult . . . If, for example, we go to the government of the Russian Federation and say, "Please stop making it possible for Site X to be hosted out of a service provider within the terrain of the Russian Federation," they would say, "Great. We will, as soon as you start blocking these five Chechen web sites that we have been asking you to take offline that have been hosted in the United States for the past five years." There's a great deal of difficulty that way.*
>
> *At the same time, we've become quite sophisticated in the way we deal with child pornography online, creating non-government organizations requiring consent before people enter into particular sites, in other words creating speed bumps along the way that at least deter those who may sim-*

ply be casual viewers from necessarily entering into these particular web sites. To me, that kind of lightly, lightly, softly, softly approach is the best because it takes care of the 75 per cent problem of people that would casually go into these sites because there is no deterrence. It wouldn't really deal with the 25 per cent that will, but that is a separate challenge we need to look at.

He says the governments of Canada and other Western nations have never really come to grips with the changes created by new media.

I'm really surprised, given the importance that cyberspace now plays in this disjunction between the online and the offline worlds, that we haven't had a Royal Commission to discuss this in its fullest—not just its impact on radicalization or national security, but how it impacts on Canadians and their relationship as citizens to the state and other institutions. In my mind, that's almost the starting point before we can get into the nitty-gritty of such issues as whether or not we can establish norms for reporting radical content online.

Governments can't just pass tough laws and use sledgehammers to go at the troubles caused by the Internet. For one thing, the Internet is now ubiquitous. For another, people get a lot of good from the it and are suspicious whenever governments seek to limit what they can see and say. The Internet has turned readers into writers and publishers, and it's connected people to a vast wealth of facts and opinions that used to be available only to rich, urban people in the West. Any heavy-handed assault on it would fail, Rohozinski says.

One of the emerging lessons we have learned . . . is the need for restraint—to always default to a more conservative stance on privacy and to avoid seeing counter-narrative or counter-violent-extremism work exclusively through the lens of policing or national security law.

The marginalization of already marginalized populations runs the risk of a more systemic and intransigent adherence to violent ideologies. This is a lesson that has been learned by our community leaders and police forces in the province of Saskatchewan, for example, and others who have experimented with community approaches to violence reduction.[21]

And yet the flow of hate continues. Supreme Court of Canada Chief Justice Brian Dickson, writing in the decision of Ernst Zündel, warned of the dangers of hate speech:

"Hatred is predicated on destruction, and hatred against identifiable groups therefore thrives on insensitivity, bigotry and destruction of both the target group and the values of our society. Hatred in this sense is a most extreme emotion that belies reason; an emotion that, if exercised against members of an identifiable group, implies that those individuals are to be despised, scorned, denied respect and made subject to ill-treatment on the basis of group affiliation."

The hate still flows freely across borders, protected by the inability of governments to work together to stop it, harboured by social media companies and Internet providers without the resources to stop it and, sometimes, defended by people who believe the right to free expression extends to incitements to commit genocide and traffic in slaves.

CHAPTER 11

Mourning

Myth does not deny things, it purifies them, it makes them innocent, it gives them a natural and external justification, it gives them a clarity which is not that of an explanation but that of a statement of fact . . . it abolishes the complexity of human acts, it gives them the simplicity of essence . . . it organizes a world which is without contradictions because it is without depth, a world-wide open and wallowing in the evident, it establishes a blissful clarity: things appear to mean something by themselves.

—Roland Barthes, *Saturday Night* magazine, September 18, 1920[1]

PATRICIA EARL HEARD ABOUT THE DEATH OF HER SON John Maguire through the media. There had been allied air strikes in Kobani on December 13, 2014, and, at the beginning of the New Year, the Kurds renewed their attack to take all of the city back. The fighting caused 400,000 people to flee the Kobani area. As the winter deepened, half of Syria's population of twenty-two million had fled their homes, and nearly half of those refugees managed to get out of the country. John Maguire never left Syria. He was said to have been killed alongside another ISIS fighter. Reports of their deaths were tweeted by Abu Saman, an ISIS fighter in northern Syria and picked up by Amarnath Amarasingam. Soon afterward, the media had the news. Just a few weeks after she had been swamped by media wanting answers about her son's video, she was now fending off reporters who wanted her reaction to his death. Earl was angry. "Nobody gives a damn. They don't. They didn't know this kid as a child. This is not the kid I raised. I'm going to leave it at that, OK?"[2] She told reporters she had recently talked to her son by Skype. "I said 'John, how many people do you have to kill? It's wrong. Why?" Maguire had told his stepfather that he was in Syria "because [his] brothers have been mistreated."

Earl wasn't surprised by the news of Maguire's death.

"I've been kind of preparing for this moment since the day he left because I'm thinking: you're not going into a good situation.

"I've never had a problem with the faith, never dreaming in a million years that this is going to be the result of it. If that's what you're into and you're not harming anybody, fine. There wasn't anything concerning his behaviour."

She spread out family pictures for a reporter who visited her home. "That does not look like a terrorist. How does this beautiful kid end up on the dark side? It's beyond." Still, she had not abandoned him. They talked fairly frequently by Skype, and she would have gone to Syria for her son's wedding to a nineteen-year-old woman he had met while in ISIS, but it wasn't possible.[3]

Still, a tweet was not real confirmation that John Maguire was dead. In April 2015, Interpol issued a "red notice," a sort of worldwide warrant asking police to arrest John Maguire. One of the people he travelled to Syria with, Khadar Khalib, a twenty-three-year-old Algonquin College student, was also added to Interpol's wanted list.[4] The RCMP had already laid terrorism charges against Maguire and Khalib, and also charged Awso Peshdary, the former head of the Algonquin College Muslim Students Association, with recruiting Maguire. They said Peshdary was an ISIS talent scout in the national capital region. When he was arrested, Peshdary was working for an Ottawa community health centre, running a popular after-school program for children. Although he'd been caught up in an earlier terrorism investigation, Peshdary had no criminal record, and a standard records check showed nothing suspicious to his employers.[5]

CHRISTIANNE BOUDREAU IS A VICTIM OF JIHAD. HER son, Damian, is dead. She struggles to make a living and to keep the rest of her family together. Boudreau is the most public face of Canadian mothers who have lost their sons in the wars and insurrections in the Islamic world. It's not a role that she chose or wants.

Boudreau's son, Damian Clairmont, was born in Halifax in 1992. Boudreau and her son moved to Calgary five years later, without the boy's father. Damian was a somewhat withdrawn child. He was bullied in school and never seemed to be happy. When he was in his first year of high school, Damian fell into a deep depression and refused to go to classes. He became fearful and anxious and didn't want to leave the house. When he was seventeen, he decided suicide was the best way to end his suffering. He tried to kill himself by drinking car antifreeze.

Boudreau said her son was not expected to survive. The antifreeze attacks the brain and the vital organs. When he pulled through, he tried to find some meaning in his life. At the same time, Damian's psychologist suggested the boy move into his own apartment, rather than return home. "If he did come home, he would end up in the same ruts of agoraphobia and depression. I shouldn't have agreed. Every day, I regret that he was forced to confront the world alone," Boudreau said. Damian was able to rent a small apartment with money he got from a disability pension.

Damian began going to a mosque in downtown Calgary. His mother supported the decision to convert. For the first time in his life, Damian was calm and seemingly at peace with himself, at least in the beginning. But an online jihadi recruiter realized Damian was vulnerable. He was spending most of his waking hours in the mosque, reading and praying. Damian began pestering his mother and his friends with 9/11 conspiracy theories and listening on his computer to long, aggressive sermons by jihadi leaders. When he wasn't berating his mother for what he believed was the mistreatment of Muslims in the West, he stayed very quiet. (Boudreau said her son never talked about his dreams, but police later told her dreams were an important motivator of at least one of the people in Damian's circle of extremists.)

Boudreau says she believes the mosque draws a bad crowd. Because it's downtown, it attracts people passing through Calgary, including extremists who are heading to the oil fields nearby to make money before heading overseas. Police who try to gather information on extremists in Alberta have a hard time keeping track of the people who are coming and going. But CSIS had spotted Damian and was watching him as he became more radicalized.[6] Still, Damian was in a group of four or five extremists who eventually made their way to Syria.

"He met an individual (a recruiter with connections to the Calgary mosque) in early 2011 and went to Syria in late 2012," Boudreau said. "When he was recruited, he still had strong ties to his family, especially his younger brother. ISIS worked to break down those bonds. It was like a cult. Parents can't control who their kids talk to and what they see on the Internet. In my son's case, he lived on his own. I couldn't barge into his apartment and start unplugging everything.

"There was a group of them who reinforced each other's beliefs, and the Internet reinforced those beliefs. The recruiters look for people who are vulnerable, who are passionate, and who are intelligent."

Boudreau had no idea her son was planning to go to Syria. He had talked about studying Arabic in Egypt and work his way up to becoming an imam, but she had trouble taking the idea seriously. Except for some trips back to Nova Scotia, Damian had never travelled. He was still getting over agoraphobia and anxiety that had made him housebound.

Damian did leave. He flew from Calgary to Seattle, then to Amsterdam and Istanbul. Eventually, he called his mother, but he lied and said he was in Egypt. For a couple of months, Boudreau believed that, until CSIS agents came to the door. Then she phoned Damian, and he admitted he was in Syria, fighting under the names Mustafa al-Gharib and Abu Talha al-Kanadi with the al-Qaeda-affiliated group al-Nusra. Then, for weeks, she didn't hear from Damian. When she did, she would often hear artillery and small arms fire in the background.

Damian would decide when they talked. He would send his mother a text message, saying he was available. She bought an unlimited international calling plan for her cell phone.

> *A lot of time, they are not allowed to communicate. Once they arrive over there, they are sent to isolated training camps. They have to turn in their passports. People follow them around. They watch everything they do, everyone they talk to. They don't let them sleep. Then, after a couple of months, they get to talk to their families, but they are programmed to be argumentative and to put things in their communications that cause problems with their families.*
>
> *And eventually an argument did come up. . . .We had a terrible*

argument and we stopped talking. Weeks later, he reached out to me on Facebook. He said he was uncomfortable with me saying "I love you" and "I miss you." He said I was trying to guilt him into coming back.

It was the last time Damian spoke to his mother, and the fact that she and Damian fought during that conversation still troubles Boudreau.

Damian also tried to use social media to justify his decision to fight for al-Nusra. He told Stewart Bell of the *National Post*:

> *[Al-Qaeda] groups have been present a very long time but have just increased their numbers significantly. The infighting is minor and usually last a day or two if not hours. This usually consists of groups removing other groups that kill, rape, steal, use/sell drugs, and often even collaborate with the regime so few people are actually complaining here on the ground.*
>
> *As for those Al-Qaeda-types, they are clearly dominant everywhere you go but they do not steal or rape or sell drugs or murder or kidnap for ransom and so on. They are also the most effective fighting forces here and are in many cases single-handedly holding off the regime and their friends in many places while many others sit in the bases getting fat off crime and foreign money/aid. They do not bother me or my friends on top of all of this, and so I cannot bring myself to complain about them even if we have differences in opinion in several matters.... I'm here because I believe in something.*

Damian was captured near Aleppo by the Free Syrian Army in January 2014 and executed soon afterward. Al-Nusra sent out an email and social media posts saying Clairmont and the men who died with him should be remembered as martyrs.

Boudreau chooses to remember her son by advocating for help

for young people like him. She works part-time as an accountant and spends fifty to sixty hours a week as an unpaid volunteer for groups that are fighting radicalization. The work has taken her to Europe, the United States and across Canada. And, in the summer of 2015, she was angry, frustrated and worried that she wouldn't be able to do it much longer. She was especially troubled by the emphasis the Canadian government puts on investigations and arrests, rather than on prevention. Paying agents to follow Damian around hadn't stopped him from going to Syria. Boudreau says:

> *In Europe, families are starting to ask for help and get it from governments and from support groups. In North America, it's more of a blame game, and it's parents who get most of the blame.*
>
> *The reality is that we [the parents and other volunteers] have to do everything. Some people in the RCMP are trying to provide support for families. Certain individuals realize that throwing people in prison is not the best way to deal with the problem.*
>
> *But that's not the official policy. We get no help from the government. We are all volunteers. I have no funding, zero. The extra costs have left me close to bankruptcy. I work part-time as an accountant but I received an ultimatum from my employer to stop taking time off to travel for this work. And my income barely covers the mortgage.*
>
> *We need a lot more money invested at the front end for intervention. When Extreme Dialogue [an organization that used a website to combat jihadi recruitment] ran out of money, the government wouldn't put any more money into it. They're spending the money on CSIS and on implementing the new anti-terror laws, but they're not spending a penny on intervention. They think the solution is to put people in prison. But they're going to get out some day. Doesn't the government have any idea of the time bomb that they create when they lock these people up? They just interested in political sloganeering, but there's no room for politicking.*

The stress has caused fights with her present partner. "It's so hard with a blended family. The work that I do is causing unbearable stress on the family. I've been able to cope because of the strong support I've had in my life." But after almost two years of campaigning, researching and doing media interviews, she was broke, her car needed hundreds of dollars' worth of work and she was worried that her partner couldn't put up with the strain much longer. Still, she says, other families have not coped as well.

> *The worst is that the rest of society doesn't see the ripple effect. Parents in this situation are turning to drugs and alcohol. Some of them are living on the streets. Some of the kids, the siblings of the people joining ISIS, are shoplifting and acting out in other ways. And there are no services for families whatsoever.*
>
> *There are mornings when I wake up with the image of him in my mind. I think of him, and how he died.*[7]

AHMED HIRSI, WHOSE SON WAS KILLED IN SYRIA, SAID he had no idea his son was going to the Middle East. In an interview with CBC's *The National*, Hirsi said: "My son, they make brainwash. Who is Syria? I don't know. I have never been there. He called his brother Liban and he said, 'Listen, me and these three, my cousins, we're going to Syria. Bye bye. Bye mama, dad bye. Bye-bye.'"[8]

All four died in the fighting.

THERE WILL NEVER BE A PARADE FOR ISIS VETERANS, AT least not anywhere in the West. Nor will there be a monument. They won't be romanticized like the Spanish Civil War veterans have been in recent years (after decades of being ignored).

But they will live on as martyrs to ISIS's religious-political ideology. About one out of every five Canadians who went to Islamic countries—Syria, Iraq, Libya and Somalia—to fight have already ended up dead. Almost all of the rest are still overseas, leaving their families wondering if they have lost their sons and daughters forever.

The family of a twenty-three-year-old woman that CBC News calls Aisha to protect the identity of her family says they worry they will never see her again. In the summer of 2014, Aisha suddenly and secretly left Edmonton for Syria, along with one of her friends. Before joining ISIS, she had been taking an online course on the Qur'an that, her family said, radicalized Aisha.

"We all went to work, came home, all her stuff was gone. She had packed all her winter clothes, took her computer and left," her older sister said. "It was the most devastating, most scary, most shocking thing in the world."

Like Boudreau, they blame CSIS for allowing their child to leave Canada, although, arguably, a determined person with the support of a deep-pocketed multinational terror network will likely be able to find a way to get out of the country no matter what. CSIS agents talked to Aisha's family before the young woman bolted for Syria, but they were looking for information, not giving useful advice. They did warn the family that Aisha's Twitter account featured an ISIS flag. She was also part of ISIS's propaganda-spreading network.

"They told us she had been interacting with people they thought were dangerous and were influencing her in a negative way, but they didn't give us enough information and it was all very vague," her sister said. "If they had shown me the emails between my sister and this girl . . . If they had let me listen to the recordings of them planning on going places, I would have ripped her passport up. There's no way I would have let her leave if I knew now that she was going to the craziest war zone in the world."

Aisha's family says the recruiter in Edmonton who ran the online Qur'an course is still in the city. They're angry that the network that recruited Aisha, which appears to have members in Alberta and Quebec, still seems to be operating. Meanwhile, the family still keeps in touch with Aisha by text messages and social media, but they know they are losing to ISIS, which will probably never let her leave.

"Over time, reality's kind of showing her another light, and she's realizing it's not what she thought it was. And now her spirit is down. When we speak she sounds really sad and stressed," her sister said.[9]

Chapter 12

When Johnny Comes Skulking Home Again

Protection, therefore, against the tyranny of the magistrates is not enough; there needs protection also against the tyranny of the prevailing opinion and feeling.
—John Stuart Mill[1]

THE GOVERNMENT WAS GLAD TO SEE THE VOLUNTEERS leave for Spain. It didn't want them back, but the survivors returned home anyway. The government did try to hunt down the Communists who did the recruiting, but the recruits themselves found it quite easy to get to Spain and to come back. Rather than prosecute the returnees, the government had them followed—sometimes for fifty years. During the Spanish Civil War, politicians said they were worried that men trained to wage revolutionary war would be a danger to the Canadian state. Only a few of the Spanish veterans got into the Canadian army to fight in the Second World War, which began four months after the last holdouts of the Spanish Republic were snuffed out. Despite having fighting experience that the Canadian army desperately needed, many veterans—but not all—identified by the RCMP as "undesirables" were turned away from enlistment offices. Some, including very fine soldiers, were expelled from the army when their names showed up on the police blacklist.[2]

Things won't be that easy for ISIS veterans. They're fighting a dirty war, committing war crimes and threatening their home countries. If ISIS is beaten back from Iraq and Syria, those of its fighters who are not killed are likely to scatter to whatever country will have them, or to the next war zone. Since there are four other failed states where ISIS fighters can find work—Afghanistan, Yemen, Libya and Somalia—and likely more to come, ISIS fighters may not need a safe harbour soon. Some foreign fighters, however, already regret their decision to join ISIS and want to return home. Other members of ISIS might also want to come back to recruit new members or commit terrorism.

The first returning ISIS fighter to carry out an attack in the West was Mehdi Nemmouche. He was a French citizen who was radicalized in prison in France before travelling to Syria. He gunned down three people at the Jewish Museum in Brussels in 2014. The brothers who attacked the offices of Paris's satirical newspaper *Charlie Hebdo* had also been trained as jihadi fighters. The precision and lethality of their attack showed people in Canada what could be done by skilled, well-armed killers, compared with a poorly equipped and unskilled terrorist like Michael Zehaf-Bibeau.

In the early years of al-Qaeda in Iraq and ISIS, police weren't too worried about returning foreign fighters. Almost all of them were killed off quickly in suicide attacks. Even now, the death rate of foreign fighters in ISIS (especially from Western countries) is remarkably high. In the past few years, though, ISIS has taken better care of its Western recruits. It has replaced suicide bombers with real artillery, and it has improved its training to make ISIS fighters much better at house-to-house fighting. ISIS commanders have become better battlefield tacticians.

Now there are ISIS veterans who have the battle skills to take on the police and soldiers of Western countries. In May 2014, Nemmouche attacked the Jewish Museum in Brussels with an assault rifle. Police found a piece of cloth with "Islamic State of Iraq and the Levant" written on it among his possessions. A returned ISIS veteran killed himself in a car bomb in Stockholm in 2010. Participants in the 2007 Doctors Plot in the United Kingdom were caught with phone numbers for operatives of the Islamic State of Iraq, ISIS's predecessor.[3]

In 2012, Europol issued a Terrorism Situation and Trend Report warning that returning fighters "have the potential to utilize their training, combat experience, knowledge and contacts for terrorist activities inside the EU," and the Netherlands raised its terrorism threat level because of fears of radicalized Dutch foreign fighters returning from Syria. Germany's minister of the interior, Hans-Peter Friedrich, called returnees "ticking time bombs," while the president of Germany's domestic intelligence service, Hans-Georg Maaßen, said ISIS veterans would be seen as heroes by some Muslims. "In the worst case they are coming back with a direct fighting mission," he said.

Police aren't just worried about terrorism. ISIS has developed a large criminal fundraising operation, and its operatives have been selling loot from the five thousand or more archaeological sites in ISIS-held territories to brokers and distributors in Turkey and the West. These smuggling skills and criminal connections could be used to develop an even larger organized crime network, similar to the Taliban's large heroin-growing and export operations run out of Afghanistan and northern Pakistan.[4]

Not only do Western countries have to deal with their own damaged youth who return from the ISIS war, but likely they'll have to cope with the thousands of former (and possibly present)

ISIS adherents who might come to them as refugees. This is particularly true if ISIS is defeated and its fighters have to scatter to save their own lives. During the large migration of refugees that escalated in the summer of 2015, neo-fascist websites in Europe published photographs of ISIS soldiers and refugees who resembled them. Whether or not ISIS veterans are among them, many of the migrants are damaged people whose mental health only worsens in the face of hostility in parts of Europe. Very few countries are particularly good at dealing with PTSD cases among their own veterans. They are utterly inept and usually uninterested in treating civilians who have, without training and psychiatric support, waged war against civilians and soldiers, then tried to integrate themselves into the culture of another country. Most refugees really are fleeing from other people's wars and persecutions, but some are fleeing from their own.

Western soldiers who fought in Afghanistan and Iraq find it hard to adjust to civilian life. *They* have some government support and the respect of the people in their communities. What about the men who go overseas to fight for causes like ISIS and the Kurdish militias? Back home, there's public hatred of them, surveillance by security agencies and very little career opportunity. Survivors of the ISIS war who return to the West are individual disasters in waiting, even if they repudiate ISIS's rigid version of Islam and its violence.

RAFAL ROHOZINSKI, OF THE SECDEV FOUNDATION, SAYS:

> *The issue of foreign fighters represents a challenge, as crimes or acts of violence occurring outside of Canada raise the issue of whether individuals choosing to do so should retain the privilege of being Canadian citizens. In the global era of 24-7 access to information via the Internet and social*

> *media, the temptation, as well as the possibility, for young Canadians to act on emotion and join global causes carries a very low threshold. Several hundred have chosen to fight in foreign causes and foreign wars, including a young Canadian-Israeli woman currently fighting with the Kurdish forces in northern Syria.*
>
> *For many of these people, first contact with the realities of war will bring disillusionment. Many will want to come home. Many will also suffer from the same stresses and disorders that affect our fighting men and women in the armed forces. These people do need our help and consideration. Creating an environment that allows them to reintegrate back into Canadian society not only will allow us the opportunity to recover some of this youth but also may serve as a powerful beacon, a means and a mechanism to engage and possibly deter others from following the path to violence.*

He sees returnees as potentially valuable assets that can be used against ISIS recruiters.

> *A young person who has been incarcerated in the United Kingdom agreed to do a video and walk people through his journey. Then it becomes very evident where community and human service professionals could have actually intervened had they been aware or had they had a little bit of awareness about what radicalization to violence looks like and what the indicators are.*

But the British are closing that door. David Cameron's government will lay criminal charges against any fighters who are caught returning from Iraq and Syria.[5]

Richard Barrett, former head of counter-terrorism for MI5 and MI6, disagrees with that policy. He argues that repentant fighters should be allowed back into Britain for the kind of counter-propaganda described by Rohozinski and for the information they have on jihadi groups. The ones who are disillusioned by ISIS are the most valuable, he says. "You're denying yourself a fundamental tool of value in combating the narrative by preventing people from coming back just on the basis of being there rather than on the basis of why they want to come back, which is the key question."[6]

IN 2014, AS MANY AS ONE IN FIVE U.K. NATIONALS fighting with Islamist forces in Syria were said to be disillusioned and looking for a way to come home. Journalists have been coming across them in the fighting zone, including one unhappy fighter who knew John Maguire. Between three hundred and a thousand former ISIS fighters are back in the United Kingdom, and about sixty of them had publicly denounced ISIS's tactics by the fall of 2015.[7]

Unlike the British Muslims who had gone to Afghanistan after September 11, 2001, to fight alongside the Taliban, the ISIS recruits tend to be young and integrated into British society, and more capable of being deprogrammed and reintegrated. Many are leading normal lives, and several hundred are getting help from the government for reintegration.[8]

Since his surprise re-election in May 2015, Cameron has brought in laws and policies that undermine attempts to salvage ISIS recruits. Like Stephen Harper's government before it was defeated in the fall of 2015, Cameron has pushed through laws that allow police and security agents to go to court to get judicial permission to break the law. Britain, he said, is now engaged in a "battle of ideas" with extremists. Organizations that "promote hatred" can be targeted with "extremism disruption orders." Cameron also imposed tighter restrictions on foreign broadcasters. Cameron's idea of extremism, expressed in one of his 2015 speeches to Parliament, casts a very wide net, and includes forced marriage, female genital mutilation and the oppression of women in general. "No more turning a blind eye on the false basis of cultural sensitivities," he told the British House of Commons.[9] Britain will, however, let ISIS veterans return if they are willing to go through a deradicalization program.

Most European countries have taken a different tack. When ISIS began recruiting from Germany's four million Muslims and from ethnic Germans, the local and national governments had already developed family support programs to deal with neo-Nazi skinheads and other homegrown extremists. They realized families of young people at risk of radicalization need support to stay together and maintain a supportive family environment, if there's to be any hope of proving positive alternatives to jihad. The German government encourages families of foreign fighters to keep in touch with them. Germany wants the fighters to know they will be welcomed back by their families and won't be packed off to jail if they return to Germany. If a person does commit a crime in Germany and is imprisoned, governments provide support to families to help them reintegrate and rehabilitate the prisoner when he or she is released. Convicts aren't simply released, as they are in Canada. They get support to find a job or go back to school.

At the same time, the support system helps families identify and dissuade other members from being radicalized by a member who has joined an extremist group. Families who have a member fighting with ISIS and similar groups also get help coping with that situation, and to maintain their ability to function in society.[10]

Germany's Federal Office for Migration and Refugees launched a national help line in 2012 to take calls from people who are worried that a family member has become radicalized. The hotline steers people to four non-government service agencies. Hayat ("life" in Arabic) was built on the foundations of EXIT-Germany, formed three decades ago to deprogram right-wing extremists. Hayat provides a service that exists only sporadically in Canada. It tries to dissuade would-be fighters from leaving Germany. It also contacts fighters who have already joined jihadi groups and tries to talk them into returning to Germany and reintegrating into society. This may be difficult for many fighters, since ISIS might consider them apostates, which is a capital crime. Hayat also helps strengthen the resolve of family members to help them get through the crisis that they've found themselves in, and gives them information to help counter ISIS recruitment propaganda.

The Violence Prevention Network helps young people who have been arrested in Germany for ideologically motivated acts of violence. The network supports the families of imprisoned jihadis. Within five months of being jailed, ideologically motivated criminals are offered training in civics as well as educational upgrading. The organization continues to work with them after they get out of jail. The Violence Prevention Network also began as an outreach program for neo-Nazis, some of whom had gone to the Balkans in the 1990s to fight in that region's civil wars.

VAJA Kitab offers support for young people who struggle with Islamic identity questions. It is an offshoot of an older, respected youth organization, which was also originally set up to help young people drawn into neo-Nazi culture, especially in the tough city of Bremen. IFAK, the Association for Multicultural Child and Youth Services—Migration Work runs an advisory network to support parents, school associations and educational institutions that are challenged by children, parents or clients who are insecure in their identities and turn to Islamist values, traditions and structures.

France, too, has a national help line, but callers are referred to the police. Belgium has a phone line that offers support from the Muslim community's group Les Parents Concernés. Denmark, which has seen hundreds of its nationals leave to join ISIS, has a reintegration program for returning ISIS fighters. Steffen Nielsen, a Danish crime prevention adviser, told Al Jazeera, "We are actually embracing them when they come home. Unlike in England, where maybe you're interned for a week while they figure out who you are, we say, 'Do you need any help?'"[11] Denmark also operates a help line. This one connects people to Somali clerics who counsel Somali-Danish fighters and their families. In the city of Aarhus, the community council created a support network to help families who have a member in Syria. Parents are invited to its meetings by the police or the city administration, but no police are allowed into the meetings unless the parents ask for briefings from the Danish foreign ministry or intelligence services.

In the Netherlands, a Moroccan-Dutch non-government organization launched a community hotline as a resource for parents and relatives of people who seem to be drifting toward radical Islam. The hotline connects families to social service agencies and to Muslim clerics who can advise them on ways to convince the person being targeted for ISIS recruitment that its claims to be a caliphate and the true voice of Islam are wrong.

It's hard to know how well these services work. No one keeps records of the number of people who have been persuaded to abandon ISIS's version of Islam. European Muslims are often isolated from mainstream society and suspicious of anything to do with the government and the police. They may try—and succeed—in dealing with ISIS propaganda inside their own families and communities. But people do come forward to ask for help dealing with the fighting in their homes or with demands from a son, daughter or sibling in ISIS-held territory that they make *hijrah* by moving to the war zones in Iraq and Syria.

Saudi Arabia, surprisingly, has a deradicalization program to try to rehabilitate the more than three thousand supporters of Osama bin Laden who have returned to the kingdom. At most, 10 per cent have returned to violent militancy. Saudi Arabia has included clerics who formerly supported bin Laden on the teams of professionals who work to deprogram the young men. The Saudis throw a lot of money into this program, setting returning, penitent jihadis up with jobs, apartments and wives.[12]

What about Canada? We have the toughest rules of all, and offer almost no support to anyone connected to ISIS fighters. As Christianne Boudreau, whose son died fighting in a jihadi army in Syria, says, Canadian authorities seem much more concerned with gathering information about potential terrorists than with helping troubled veterans of the jihadi war in Syria and Iraq readjust to life in Canada or aiding their families. This country has a law against going to ISIS-held territory, so any veterans will be arrested if they're caught returning. The Canadian government will also revoke the citizenship of any dual citizen fighting for ISIS, and can revoke the passport of any Canadian posing a threat to security—they had done the latter to John Maguire before he was killed. Those are not particularly good ways to deal with the problem.

Stripping people of their citizenship simply exports the problem. It may protect Canadians, but someone else will pay the price. Arresting returnees may give police the chance to sort through them to determine which ones are dangerous and damaged. But then what? They can't be locked up forever, and if there's no deprogramming, including intervention by articulate Muslim clergy who can go head-to-head with ISIS ideologues, we'll simply have dangerous ex-convicts on the streets. They'll be under expensive surveillance, and no amount of money can guarantee that every ISIS veteran will be identified, assessed and tracked.

The RCMP High Risk Travel Case Management Group watches potential and known jihadis. Only one returning Canadian fighter has been charged under the 2013 anti-terrorism law. "It's very difficult sometimes to extract information from an overseas jurisdiction, especially one that is in the midst of a war, and then deploy that evidence in a court . . . and satisfy standard of proof beyond a reasonable doubt," law professor Craig Forcese told a television reporter in 2014. "In instances where someone who has boasted so publicly of their participation with ISIS [such as Maguire], evidence probably isn't an overwhelming difficulty, if you happen to bring a prosecution," he said. "In other instances it may be more complex, if their overseas track record isn't quite as transparent."[13]

All of that enforcement is dependent on police and security forces actually knowing who's fighting for ISIS. Do they have a complete list? Does ISIS have the technology and expertise to create believable fake identities and documents? The fact remains that hundreds, if not thousands, of battle-toughened ISIS fighters may be able to get back into Canada, the United States and Western Europe simply on the passports they carry.

CHAPTER 13

The Unsolvable Puzzle

IN THE NINETEENTH CENTURY, TERRORISTS CHAMPIONING A wide range of causes were able to up the ante by using dynamite to shake up the powers that they hated. Then came Semtex, giving murderers even more explosive energy in a much smaller package. In the 1980s, fighters' rifles and shotguns were replaced by automatic rifles selling for $50 or less and the world was flooded with surplus Soviet AK-47 assault rifles. At the same time, shoulder-held rocket launchers, cheap and relatively easy to ship, gave terrorists and insurgents the ability to take on tanks and even warplanes. Now, complicated timers in car bombs have been replaced with parts from cheap cell phones. And, of course, the Internet and cellular technology has made planning and communication so much easier.

But recruitment was always the toughest nut to crack. Unless cornered, few people want to die or kill for their country, let alone the lands of strangers. Modern new media helps recruiters get into the homes of the troubled, the damaged and the needy. ISIS and its ilk compete with Western consumer culture using its own media and manages to find thousands of people, born Muslims and converts, who believe dying in the deserts of Iraq and Syria is a good alternative to the lives they live now. ISIS has not been a spectacularly successful recruiter. At most, it has nibbled at the very edges of the great mass of unhappy and disaffected people, especially in the West. But when it is able to recruit, it has shown the ability to condition its followers—whether in the Middle East or in the West—to engage in acts of extreme violence and cruelty. It isn't even the most lethal terrorist group in the world—Boko Haram, the Islamist separatists in Nigeria, were far more lethal in 2014, ISIS's break-out year—but ISIS is much more media-savvy.[1] ISIS has cast a very wide net to catch very few fish, yet it has been able to use the tools at hand to create the world's best-financed, most formidable and most feared terrorist organization and change the political climate of the Middle East, Europe and North America.

One U.S. Homeland Security report summed it up well: the future of terrorism "will depend, in large part, on the use and accessibility of technology. Increasingly destructive weaponry makes terrorism more lethal; advances in transportation increase the reach of terrorists; and cheaper and more secure means of communication make terrorism harder to detect. As these technologies advance, proliferate and become available to a wider range of actors, more and more potential enemies may use terrorism as a strategy and tactic."[2]

Jonathan Powell, author of the book *Talking to Terrorists*, says, "Terrorism is the ugly twin of democracy. The threat grew up alongside modern democracy, and is a manifestation of the vulnerabilities of a democratic system. If democratic governments resort to extra-legal measures to suppress terrorist movements in the way autocracies can, they risk doing irreparable harm to the very essence of their democracy. While there clearly needs to be a strong security component to the solution, we are fooling ourselves if we think it will provide a complete answer in itself."[3]

Most countries and popular movements are unconquerable. At most, tough security—and war—give democratic governments the possibility of negotiating from a stronger position. You can have temporary "victory" in a war between states—as George W. Bush claimed to have in Iraq—but it is almost impossible to maintain the level of control and, to be blunt, oppression, needed to keep urban terrorism and popular resistance down in the long term. And even if an area is "pacified" by the use of overwhelming force and repression, terrorists and resistance fighters can, and do, simply find a less hostile place to establish themselves.

Radical Islam is vulnerable to several counterattacks. The most potent comes from persuasive, learned Muslims who can argue back against ISIS's simplistic and violent interpretation of Islam. This is already happening, but more Muslims have to get involved, and they need the media skills to be able to face ISIS on the Internet. Moderate Muslims also need to ensure that their mosques and social groups aren't dominated or hijacked by radicals. At the same time, authorities in Canada and other Western countries should back these people up and do more than just arrest terror suspects. They need to look at the way European states work with the families of extremists and develop a Canadian system that provides effective intervention and support for the relatives of people drawn to extremism. Right now, some Muslims feel intimidated by the extremists. They need protection so they can speak out.

The companies that run social media platforms have already improved their policing. They have faced resistance from people who believe the new media should be wide open for any kind of publishing, and from jihadis who work full-time to thwart attempts to shut down their recruitment and communications networks. They need to be given the resources to stay ahead of ISIS. Whether the self-styled Islamic State succeeds in setting up a permanent regime in Iraq and Syria is still an open question, but even if it's crushed, its propagandists can easily set up shop anywhere with Internet connections.

There needs to be even more international co-operation to share information and fight jihadi recruitment. United Nations Resolution 2178 on Foreign Terrorist Fighters, which outlaws the recruitment and transportation of people across borders to wage terrorism, is a good start. It shows countries can at least talk about solutions. Whether UN resolutions can be translated into effective action is a question that can only be answered by the countries that are members of that organization.

We're going to have to spend some money. We've been pushed into a war, or at least onto the fringes of one, and we have to accept that modern war and policing involve much more than handing guns to young men. We need dedicated programs to address the needs of young people—immigrants and non-immigrants—in Western countries for meaningful work, decent housing, a meaningful say in how their country is run and optimism for the future. Our changing economy leaves a lot of young people with little reason to put much faith in our system, and most political talk about opportunities for young people is just pap. Our political system, dominated by lobbyists, fundraisers and advertising copywriters, unconvincingly calls itself a democracy. By refusing to get involved or even show up to vote, many young people clearly communicate their lack of interest in that game.

Lines of communications must be kept open between all regimes and factions, whether through the UN or through secret diplomacy. We need to negotiate with terrorists, not to pay ransoms and hear demands that are really just propaganda, but to determine what really motivates them. ISIS's leaders must know that they will be held to account for crimes against humanity, whether those are attacks on people or the destruction of world heritage sites. The rest of the world is legally and morally right when it uses force to stop ISIS atrocities. At the same time, people who belong to ISIS have the same right to self-determination as anyone else. If the Sunnis of Iraq and Syria want to establish a caliphate that operates within international norms of behaviour, and if people born into Islam or converts want to live in this caliphate, more power to them. The factions in that region may fight their way to a settlement, but the rest of the world should force them to observe the laws of war in regard to treatment of prisoners and civilians, weapons used and the protection of cultural heritage.

These disputes can be settled. The Wars of Religion in Europe ended with people learning to live with each other's differences of belief and with the separation of church from state. The English and Irish were able to make peace after more than seven hundred years of bloodshed and hatred. Basques have also worked out something of an agreement with the government of Spain. These people may not like each other, but at least the cycle of violence has stopped. It takes international co-operation and goodwill.

It's my view that we're seeing the beginning of a general war in the Islamic world. It may be fought simultaneously, or the fighting may move from one country to another. Internal forces will tear apart Saudi Arabia and continue to threaten the regime in Iran. Shiites, backed by Tehran, push against Sunnis backed by the Saudis. The regime in Egypt, the most populous country in the region, survives because the army still has the ability to suppress Islamism, but time may be running out for Egypt's generals.

And there's always the threat the fighting will spill into Israel, as yet the only real nuclear power in the region.

Somehow, we've managed to use propaganda—or advertising—to sell cars and Marilyn Manson albums and to redefine the hamburger. We have developed the greatest communication systems the world has ever seen and hooked almost everyone in the world to them. In many ways, we've built an entire civilization on salesmanship. We should be able to handle ISIS and its ilk, but we might also want to spend a moment wondering whether we are reaping what we've sown, and to ask ourselves how much value we place upon the truth.

Acknowledgements

THIS BOOK EXISTS BECAUSE MY PUBLISHER, PATRICK Crean, believed I could analyze the complex communication and propaganda system of ISIS and its attraction to young people. This book is as much his work as it is mine. My friends in the Canadian military have given valuable advice. I can't name all of them, but I should single out my lifelong friend Maj. James McKillip, who served in the UN contingent in Iraq after the Iran-Iraq War, and later was deployed to Afghanistan. Propaganda theorist Prof. Randall Marlin of Carleton University gave me invaluable advice. I'm indebted, too, to Dillon Hillier, Christianne Boudreau, Asma Bala, Amarnath Amarasingam, Prof. Iain Edgar of Durham University, and Profs. Craig Forcese, Adam Dodek, Marina Pavlovic, Adam Daimsis and Constance Backhouse of the University of Ottawa law school, my amazing editor Tilman Lewis and the staff at HarperCollins Canada, and to several people whose help was very important but who asked for anonymity. I also want to acknowledge the work of the scholars and journalists whose academic work and reportage is cited in this book. Without bold scholars and smart journalists, we'd live in a world of ad hominem and prejudice. Hopefully, academia and journalism will overcome the dreadful problems they've faced in the past few decades.

I want to thank my wife, Marion, whose advice and support made this book possible; my three kids, who think I actually like Twitter; friends who helped with the project or gave moral support; and my sisters and mom, who have said they'll detour from their voracious reading of fiction to read this.

Appendix

Canadians Known to Have Joined ISIS

Calgary Cluster

Damian Clairmont, convert, suffered from bipolar disorder, dropped out of high school and was homeless for a time. A close friend of Salman Ashrafi, whom he tended to dominate. Fought in an al-Nusra unit until January 2014, when he was captured and killed by the Free Syrian Army.

Salman Ashrafi, born Muslim, quit a good job at Talisman Energy, was married and had a child when he left. Died in a 2013 suicide attack in Iraq that killed forty people.

Gregory and Collin Gordon.

Ahmed Waseem lived in Windsor, Ontario, but had close links to the Calgary cluster. Returned to Canada to have an injury or wound treated in 2013. His passport was suspended but he was able to get a forged passport and returned to Syria to fight in ISIS forces. He was a prominent presence on Twitter but his account was suspended in 2015 and he hasn't returned.

Farah Shirdon, also known as Abu Usamah, was shown in early 2014 in an ISIS video burning his passport and threatening Western countries. For a while, he was believed to be dead, but he resurfaced in a Skype video with a *Vice* reporter in September 2014, in which he says Canadian streets would run with blood because the Harper government had sent planes to bomb ISIS.

Plus others.

EDMONTON CLUSTER

Hamsa and Hirsi Kariye, Somali-Canadian brothers.

Mahad Hersi, cousin of the Kariye brothers.

All three were killed in Syria, along with a cousin from Minnesota.

Approximately ten more are believed to be part of this group.

MONTREAL-LAVAL CLUSTER

Bilel Zouaidia, Shayma Senouci, Mohamed Rifaat, Imad Eddine Rafai, Ourdia Kadem, Yahia Alaoui Ismaili. All left the city to join ISIS.

Others from Montreal

Tarek Ben-Kura, a student who went to fight Muammar Gaddafi and returned severely injured, with a gunshot wound to the spine.

ONTARIO CLUSTER

Andre Poulin (Omar Abu Muslim) from Timmins, Ontario. Born in 1989, he converted to Islam when he was twenty. In 2011, he moved to Toronto, where he met Muhammad Ali, whom he had got to know online years before.

Muhammad Ali, from Mississauga, a frequent contributor to jihadi and Islamic online forums, where he met Andre Poulin. He studied aerospace engineering at Ryerson but flunked out. Ali left for Syria in April 2014, after Poulin's death.

Tabiruil Islam, Abdul Malik, "Noor," "Adib." Friends of Poulin who left Canada at about the same time. At least two of them returned to Canada in February 2013, then left Canada again in July 2014.

Mohamud Mohamed Mohamus, twenty, from Hamilton, a professional dancer who loved modelling and fashion.

Ottawa Cluster

John Maguire, Khadar Khalib (both joined ISIS), Suliman Mohamed (twenty-one), twin brothers Ashton and Carlos Larmond, Awso Peshdary (arrested and charged in Canada).

Others from Ontario.

Mahad Ali Dhore crossed into Somalia while visiting Kenya to join an al-Shabab training camp. He is believed to have been killed in a 2013 terrorist attack in Mogadishu.

Hassan El Hajj Hassan, wanted by Bulgaria for a bus bomb attack that killed six people and injured twenty-three. Believed to be with Hezbollah.

Ali Mohamed Dirie, one of the Toronto 18 who had been imprisoned for planning terrorist attacks in Ontario. Within a year of his release in 2014, he travelled to Syria to fight with ISIS and is believed to have been killed there.[1]

Endnotes

A Note on Terminology

1. Paul Wilkinson, *Terrorism Versus Democracy: The Liberal State Response*, 3rd edition (Oxford: Routledge, 2011), 4.

2. Adapted from Paul R. Pillat, "Jihadi Terrorism: A Global Assessment of the Threat," in Rik Coolsaet, ed., *Jihadi Terrorism and the Radicalisation Challenge: European and American Experiences* (Farnham, UK: Ashgate Publishing, 2013).

3. Adam Withnall, "Iraq Crisis: What Is a Caliphate?," *The Independent*, June 30, 2014.

Chapter 1

1. Quoted in Jytte Klausen, "Tweeting the Jihad: Social Media Networks of Western Foreign Fighters in Syria and Iraq," *Studies in Conflict and Terrorism* 38, no. 1 (2015).

2. Sarah Boesveld, "Ottawa Student Believed to Be Fighting for ISIS Was Smart, Funny and Loved Punk Rock: Classmates," *National Post*, August 14, 2014.

3. Chris Cobb, "Report Fellow Students on the Road to Terrorism, Local Imam Urges," *Ottawa Citizen*, December 8, 2014.

4. Jessica Hume, "Extremist Had Passport Cancelled," *London Free Press*, December 8, 2014.

5. Stewart Bell, "Extremists Trained to Hit West, Report Says," *National Post*, August 30, 2014.

6. Stuart Bell, "Al-Qaida Calls for Attacks on Canada: 'Lone Wolf' Jihadis; Security Agencies Monitoring, Have 'Measures in Place,'" *National Post*, January 21, 2015.

7. Terry Glavin, "Family of Children Found on Turkish Beach Were Trying to Come to Canada," *Ottawa Citizen*, September 3, 2015.

8. Michelle Shephard, "Flight or Fight on the Jihadi Highway," *Toronto Star*, January 26, 2015.

9. Andrew Duffy and Meghan Hurley, "From JMag to Jihad John: The Radicalization of John Maguire," *Ottawa Citizen*, February 7, 2015. This is, by far, the best biographical article on John Maguire, and I've drawn on it for this chapter.

Chapter 2

1. The Jesuit novitiate lasted two years and was so tough that a German Jesuit named Rudolf Mayer could write that the Jesuit initiation prepared him for his days in a Nazi prison: "The routine of life inside reminds me of the days I spent as a novice at Feldkirch." Manfred Barthel, *The Jesuits: History and the Legend of the Society of Jesus* (New York: William Morrow, 1982).

2. Joseph Goebbels, *The Journal of Joseph Goebbels from 1925 to 1926*, edited by Helmut Heiber (London: Weidenfeld and Nicolson, 1962).

3. Jay Baird, "Goebbels, Horst Wessel, and the Myth of Resurrection and Return," *Journal of Contemporary History* 17, no. 4 (October 1982): 633–50.

4. Frederic Spotts, *Hitler and the Power of Aesthetics* (New York: Overlook Press, 2009), 69.

5. For a fine examination of Arcand's movement, see *Lita-Rose Betcherman, The Swastika and the Maple Leaf: Fascist Movements in Canada in the Thirties* (Toronto: Fitzhenry and Whiteside, 1975). For a detailed examination of the various shades of fascistic and non-fascistic Quebec nationalism during the Depression, see Donald J. Horton and Andre Laurendeau, *French Canadian Nationalist 1912–1968* (Toronto: Oxford University Press, 1992), chapters 2 and 3.

6. Graham S. Mount, *Canada's Enemies: Spies and Spying in the Peaceable Kingdom* (Toronto: Dundurn Press, 1993), chapter 4.

7. Michael Petrou, *Renegades: Canadians in the Spanish Civil War* (Vancouver: UBC Press, 2008), chapter 1.

8. Ibid., 33.

9. Interview, August 15, 2015.

10. Stewart Bell, "Canadians Who Travel Abroad to Fight ISIL Get Little Scrutiny upon Return, Suggesting Canada Isn't Keen on Stopping Them," *National Post*, June 1, 2015.

11. Elhanan Miller, "IS Rape and Torture of Yazidi Women Pushed Me to Fight with Kurds, says Gill Rosenberg," *Times of Israel*, July 17, 2015.

12. Kate Pickles and Gill Rosenberg, "Canadian Woman Who Fought Alongside Kurds against ISIS after Being Released from Prison Returns to Hero's Welcome in Israel and an Investigation over Broken Probation," *Daily Mail*, July 25, 2015.

Chapter 3

1. Klausen, "Tweeting the Jihad."

2. "Army Targets Video Gamers," *Blacklocks Reporter*, July 14, 2015.

3. The crowd wanted to free John Wilkes, a popular pamphleteer, who was jailed for a year for seditious libel.

4. Perceval is the only British prime minister to be assassinated. In 1843, a mentally ill man killed the principal secretary to Prime Minister Robert Peel, mistakenly believing his victim was the prime minister. There were plots by the Nazis during the Second World War to kill Sir Winston Churchill, but none of these seem to have been serious. The IRA did blow up part of the Grand Hotel in Brighton in 1984 to try to kill Margaret Thatcher, and in 1991 the IRA fired mortar rounds at 10 Downing Street, hoping to hit Prime Minister John Major.

5. "2014 Public Report on the Terrorism Threat in Canada," Public Safety Canada, Minister Stephen Blaney.

6. I tried this experiment. I failed Unplugged: 24 Hours without Media, and I am not inclined to try again. There were so many similarities between giving up a habit/chemical addiction like smoking and giving up the Internet: the moodiness, the sense of disruption, the need for stimulation to replace what's lost (in my case, the candy). When I quit smoking, I kept a cigarette around for months, just to feel secure. I kept my iPhone with me during the time I was trying to be unplugged and made it to within an hour of succeeding before convincing myself I *had* to check my email. I haven't smoked a cigarette in more than twenty-eight years. I've never had a puff. I've never accepted a good cigar. I still have dreams in which I'm smoking, and once in a while I have the slightest cravings. Quitting the Internet—for many of us who have let ourselves be hard-wired into it—is harder than quitting smoking. I had every advantage the day I tried Unplugged: 24 Hours without Media. I got

myself away from computers, had a supportive partner, had experience beating an addiction, and still failed.

7. Amanda Lenhart, Kristen Purcell, Aaron Smith and Kathryn Zickuhr, "Social Media and Mobile Internet Use Among Teens and Young Adults," Pew Research Center (February 3, 2010); Roman Gerodimos, *Going "Unplugged": Exploring Students' Relationships and Its Pedagogic Implications* (The Media School, Bournemouth University, March 2011).

8. Bill Davidow, "Exploring the Neuroscience of Internet Addiction," *The Atlantic*, July 18, 2013.

9. Frances E. Jensen and Amy Ellis Nutt, *The Teenage Brain: A Neuroscientist's Survival Guide to Raising Adolescents and Young Adults* (Toronto: HarperCollins, 2015), 105–110.

10. Ibid., chapter 13.

11. Dave Mosher, "High Wired: Does Addictive Internet Use Restructure the Brain?" *Scientific American*, June 17, 2011.

12. The author would likely have been diagnosed with this affliction as a child and would certainly be so now.

13. Joel Weinberger, *What Kind of Citizen? Educating Our Children for the Common Good* (New York: Teachers College Press, 2015), 85–86.

14. See Howard Rheingold, "Mobile Media and Political Collective Action," *Handbook of Mobile Communication Studies*, 2008: 225.

15. Klausen, "Tweeting the Jihad."

16. For an excellent analysis of terrorist bidding wars, see Justin Conrad and Kevin Green, "Competition, Differentiation, and the Severity of Terrorist Attacks," *Journal of Politics* 4, no. 22 (published online February 6, 2015).

17. Ben Rich and Dara Conduit, "The Impact of Jihadist Foreign Fighters on Indigenous Secular-Nationalist Causes: Contrasting Chechnya and Syria," *Studies in Conflict & Terrorism* 28, no. 2 (2015).

18. Scott Gates and Sukanya Podder, "Social Media, Recruitment, Allegiance and the Islamic State," *Perspectives on Terrorism* 9, no. 4 (2015).

19. Conrad and Greene, "Competition, Differentiation, and the Severity of Terrorist Attacks."

20. Klausen, "Tweeting the Jihad."

21. I discuss the reasons for this in my book *Fighting Words*, published by Dundurn Press in 2013.

22. A similar trend is occurring in political, business and entertainment reporting.

23. Tarek Fatah, founder of the Muslim Canadian Congress, "Proceedings of the Standing Senate Committee on National Security and Defence," April 28, 2014.

24. Meghan Hurley, "Spike in Converts 'a Big Concern,'" *National Post*, January 16, 2015.

25. "Chief Imam in Ottawa Responds to John Maguire, the Ottawa Man Who Has Called Out to Canadian Muslims to Join ISIS or to Attack Canadians," The Iranian Atheist (iranian-atheist.tumblr.com), December 15, 2014.

Chapter 4

1. Guglielmo Ferrero, *The Principles of Power: The Great Political Crises of History* (New York: G.P. Putnam's Sons, 1942), 199–200.

2. Scott Atran, Hammed Sheikh, and Angel Gomez, "Devoted Actors Sacrifice for Close Comrades and Sacred Cause," *Proceedings of the National Academy of Sciences of the United States of America* 111, no. 5 (December 16, 2014).

3. William Manchester, *Goodbye, Darkness: A Memoir of the Pacific War* (New York: Little, Brown, 1979), 451.

4. R. Spector, *After Tet* (New York: Vintage, 1994).

5. Arrequin-Toft, "How the Weak Win Wars," *International Security* 26, no. 15 (2001).

6. Prem Mahadevan, "The Neo-Caliphate of the 'Islamic State,'" Center for Security Studies *Analyses in Security Policy* (2014).

7. All figures in this book are in U.S. dollars.

8. Jack Moore, "ISIS Forces Christians to Live Under Its Rules in Syrian Town after Release," *Newsweek*, September 4, 2015.

9. Center for Security Studies (CSS) ETH Zurich, Paper No. 166, December 2014. See also Aymenn Jawad al-Tamimi, "The Dawn of the Islamic State of Iraq and al-Sham," *Current Trends in Islamist Ideology*, 16.

10. Canadian Andre Poulin was killed in this battle.

11. Al-Tamimi, "The Dawn of the Islamic State of Iraq and al-Sham."

12. Marek Pruszevicz, "The 1920s British Bombing Campaign in Iraq," BBC.com, October 7, 2014.

13. Barry Rubin and Wolfgang G. Schwanitz, *Nazis, Islamists, and the Making of the Modern Middle East* (New Haven, CT: Yale University Press, 2014), 2.

14. Ibid., 3.

15. Ibid., 156.

16. Ibid., 199.

17. Ibid., 218.

18. Ibid., 225.

19. Ibid., 290. Brunner is supposed to have died in Damascus in 2010.

20. Paul Rutherford, *Endless Propaganda: The Advertising of Public Goods* (Toronto: University of Toronto Press, 2000), 24.

21. Ibid., 30

22. Ibid., 30–31.

Chapter 5

1. It's actually a misquote, but, like many time-edited catchy lines, it's more concise than what was actually said. In this case, Edward was walking about his son, Edward, the Black Prince, who was caught in the thick of the battle. See "Misquotation: 'Let the Boy Win His Spurs,'" Oxford Academic (http://oupacademic.tumblr.com), August 15, 2013.

2. Peter Vronsky, *Ridgeway: The American Fenian Invasion and the 1866 Battle That Made Canada* (Toronto: Allen Lane, 2011). See chapter 7.

3. Ibid., 127.

4. Ibid., 131.

5. Ibid., 3.

6. Jake Bilardi, a troubled fourteen-year-old Australian, was one of the foreigners used by ISIS as a suicide bomber. Like many ISIS recruits, he had been brought up with almost no knowledge of Islam and showed no interest in religion. When family life deteriorated during Bilardi's adolescence, he converted to Islam, became a heavy follower of ISIS posts on social media and went to the Middle East to join the group. John Lichfield and Ben Lynfield, "Australian Boy Is Suicide Bomber in Iraq," *The Independent*, March 11, 2015.

7. The author's paternal grandfather shot his brother's eye out with a homemade bow and arrow.

8. Dave Grossman, *On Killing: The Psychological Cost of Learning to Kill in War and Society* (New York: Little, Brown, 1996), 320.

9. Ibid., xviii–xix.

10. Ibid., 329.

11. Manchester, *Goodbye, Darkness*, 391.

12. Ibid., 358.

13. Ibid., 6–7.

14. J.C. Cochrane, "Confession," in *Priceville and Its Roots (Routes)*, ed. Katie Harrison (Owen Sound, ON: Priceville and District Historical Society, 1992), 176. Quoted in Jonathan F. Vance, *Death So Noble* (Vancouver: UBC Press, 1997), 220.

15. Sara Almukhtar, "The Strategy behind the Islamic State's Destruction of Ancient Sites," *New York Times*, August 24, 2015.

16. Grossman, *On Killing*, 212.

17. Rutherford, *Endless Propaganda*, 20.

18. Ibid., 21.

19. Ibid., 166.

20. Michael Strangelove, *Watching YouTube: Extraordinary Videos by Ordinary People* (Toronto: University of Toronto Press, 2010), 154.

21. Evolution of Jihad Videos 6–8, IntelCenter (Alexandria, VA: Tempest, 2005), quoted in ibid., 151.

22. Strangelove, *Watching YouTube*, 152.

23. Hsinchun Chen, Sven Thoms and T.J. Fu, "Cyber Extremism in Web 2.0: An Exploratory Study of International Jihadist Groups," paper presented to the IEEE International Conference on Intelligence and Security Informatics, Taiwan, June 17–20, 2008. Quoted in ibid., 151.

24. Strangelove, *Watching YouTube*, 153.

25. One of the ways the Israelis have tried to tighten the screws during negotiations with Palestinians is by threatening their access to wireless. See Ben White (compiler), "Update on Conflict and Diplomacy, 16 February–15 May 2014," *Journal of Palestinian Studies* 42, no. 4: 123.

26. Peter Chambers, "Abu Mussab al Zarqawi: The Making and Unmaking of an American Monster (in Baghdad)," *Alternatives: Global, Local, Political* 37, no. 1 (2012).

27. Strangelove, *Watching YouTube*, 111.

28. Richard Barrett and Joanne J. Myers, "Foreign Fighters in Syria," *Carnegie Council for Ethics in International Affairs* (March 11, 2014).

29. Brian Michael Jenkins, "The Lure of Violent Jihad," Rand Corporation. Testimony presented before the House Homeland Security Committee on March 24, 2015.

30. Most of the material on ISIS sex slavery came from Rukmini Callimachi, "ISIS Enshrines a Theology of Rape," *New York Times*, August 13, 2013.

31. "The Revival of Slavery before the Hour," *Dabiq* (May 2015). Made available at www.danielpipes.org.

32. Chris Hughes, "ISIS Sex Slaves: Captured Iraqi Women Strangling Each Other and Killing Themselves to Escape Rape," *Daily Mirror*, December 22, 2014.

33. Rachel Vorona Cote, "Iraqi Woman Forced into Sex Slavery Kills ISIS Commander," Jezebel.com, September 8, 2015.

34. Ashley Collman, "ISIS Leader 'Repeatedly Raped and Kept 26-Year-Old American Aid Worker Hostage Kayla Mueller as His Personal Sex Slave' before She Was 'Killed by US Air Strike,'" *Daily Mail*, August 14, 2015.

35. For a fascinating account of how a street thug was turned into one of the most important heroes of the Nazi regime, see Daniel Siemens, *The Making of a Nazi Hero: The Murder and Myth of Horst Wessel* (London: I.B. Tauris, 2013). Wessel, a Nazi street fighter, was killed by a gang of Communists in what may well have been a dispute

over rent. The Nazis remade Wessel into a national hero, and one of his marching songs became the unofficial anthem of Nazi Germany.

36. Jessica Stern and J.M. Berger, *ISIS: The State of Terror* (New York: HarperCollins, 2015), 87–88.

37. Amarnath Amarasingam and Rory Dickson, "How ISIS Gets Its Western Recruits," *National Post*, October 3, 2014.

Chapter 6

1. Stewart Bell, "You'll Never Kill the Love of Jihad," *National Post*, December 9, 2014.

2. Michelle Shephard, "Islamic State Canadian Fighter Reported Dead," *Toronto Star*, March 20, 2015.

3. Michael Weiss and Hassan, *ISIS: Inside the Army of Terror* (New York: Regan Arts, 2015), 161.

4. Klausen, "Tweeting the Jihad."

5. James P. Farwell, "The Media Strategy of ISIS," *Survival: Global Politics and Strategy* 56, no. 6: 49–55. Published online November 25, 2014.

6. For a detailed and riveting account of ISIS's preparations for the End Times and an analysis of ISIS within Islam, see Graeme Wood, "What ISIS Really Wants," *The Atlantic*, March 2015.

7. Stern and Berger, *ISIS: The State of Terror*, 63–64.

8. Anthony N. Celso, "The Islamic State and Boko Haram: *Fifth Wave* Jihadist Terror Groups," *Orbis* 59, no. 2 (2015): 249–68.

9. Klausen, "Tweeting the Jihad."

10. Andrew Griffith, "'Operation ISIS' Anonymous Activists Begin Leaking Details of Suspected Extremist Twitter Accounts," *The Independent*, November 17, 2015.

11. Cory Bennett, "ISIS Calls Anonymous 'Idiots,' Offers Tips to Evade Hackers," TheHill.com, November 17, 2015.

12. Weiss and Hassan, *ISIS*, 172.

13. Hugues Sampasa-Kanyinga and Rosamund F. Lewis, "Frequent Use of Social Networking Sites Is Associated with Poor Psychological Functioning among Children and Adolescents," *Cyberpsychology, Behavior, and Social Networking* 18, no. 7 (July 2015): 380–85.

14. "Government Is 'Struggling' with How to Stop the Spread of Extremist Propaganda," *Ottawa Citizen*, December 9, 2014.

15. "Kurdish Rebels Use Facebook to Recruit Young Autistic Briton to Fight ISIS," RT.com, June 19, 2015.

16. Heather Saul, "'Attractive' Jihadists Used as 'Eye Candy to Recruit British Girls into Extremist Groups,'" *The Independent*, March 3, 2015.

17. Vassy Kapelos, "How ISIS Recruits Women in Canada," *Global News*, March 12, 2015.

18. Vikram Dodd and Sharmeena Begum, "British Girl Left to Join ISIS after Upheavals at Home," *The Guardian*, March 13, 2015.

19. Shaykh Abu Qatada al-Filistini, "Importance of Jihadi Media," trans. Al Muwahideen, Al Muwahideen Media (almuwahideenmedia.wordpress.com), September 9, 2015.

Chapter 7

1. "Sheikh bin Laden's Dream," Ummah.com, August 27, 2014.

2. Iain Edgar, "The Inspirational Night Dream in the Motivation and Justification of Jihad," *Nova Religio: The Journal of Alternative and Emergent Religions* 11, no. 2 (2007).

3. The phenomenon of *Ishtakara* is discussed at length in Iain Edgar and David Henig, "Istikhara: The Guidance and Practice of Islamic Dream Incubation through Ethnographic Comparison," *History and Anthropology* 21, no. 3 (2010): 251–62. The author has also relied on Iain Edgar's articles "The Inspirational Night Dream" *in Nova Religio* and "The Dreams of Islamic State," *Perspectives on Terrorism* 9, no. 4 (August 2015). See also Iain Edgar, *The Dream in Islam: From Qur'anic tradition to Jihadist Inspiration* (Oxford: Berghahn Books, 2011). Prof. Edgar also gave the author advice by email and an interview on August 14, 2015.

4. For a thoughtful analysis of the evolution of Simpson's faith, see Amarnath Amarasingam, "Elton 'Ibrahim' Simpson's Path to Jihad in Garland, Texas," Warontherocks.com, May 2015.

5. Rita Katz, "Texas Attack: The Chain of Terror Tweets That Led to Elton Simpson Rampage at Draw Mohammed Contest," *International Business Times*, May 6, 2015.

6. "Texas Shooting: FBI Had Monitored Gunman Elton Simpson since 2006," theguardian.com, May 5, 2015.

7. Fisk's personal reaction to bin Laden's dream is from Robert Fisk, "ISIS Using 'Dreamology' to Justify Its Nightmarish Vision of the World," *The Independent*, August 16, 2015. The rest of the story is Edgar, "The Dreams of Islamic State."

8. Charles Cameron, "A 'Big Dream' Attributed to Osama bin Laden," zenpundit.com, December 13, 2011.

9. See "Dream of Bird in Islam," Interpretation of Dream in Islam (dream-islam-interpretation.blogspot.ca), October 23, 2013, for various interpretations of the appearance of birds in dreams. See www.islam.org.uk/dreams.php for one very comprehensive set of dream interpretations.

10. Rahimulla Yusufzai, "A Recollection of Mohammad Omar, the Taliban Leader Whose Death Two Years Ago Was Only Recently Revealed," Al Jazeera (america.aljazeera.com), August 6, 2015.

11. Edgar, "The Inspirational Night Dream."

12. Email conversation with Prof. Flagg Miller, August 20, 2015.

13. "Reports: ISIS Jihadist Converts to Christ after Dream," CBN News (cbn.com), June 12, 2015.

14. www.ummah.com.

15. Rachel Aspden, "*Circling the Square* by Wendell Steavenson Review—the Egyptian Revolution, up Close and Personal," *The Guardian*, August 6, 2015.

16. For instance, in my book *Ninety Fathoms Down* (Toronto: Hownslow, 1995), I tell the story of a woman passenger of the *Waubuno*, a steamship that disappeared on Georgian Bay in 1979, who wanted to cancel her ticket on the ship before it sailed from Collingwood because she had a dream the ship would be lost. Her husband, who was travelling to Parry Sound to open a medical practice, talked her into staying on the ship. The story of the prophetic dream was published in local papers when the *Waubuno* was torn apart in a storm.

17. As of the fall of 2015, there were more than twelve hundred books on dream interpretation listed on Amazon.com.

18. Edgar, *The Dream in Islam*. Also personal interview, August 14, 2015.

19. David Cook, *Martyrdom in Islam* (Cambridge: Cambridge University Press, 2007), 121.

20. Edgar, "The Inspirational Night Dream."

21. Stewart Bell, *The Martyr's Oath: The Making of a Homegrown Terrorist* (Toronto: Wiley, 2009), 196.

Chapter 8

1. Royal Canadian Mounted Police media release, March 6, 2015.

2. Stern and Berger, *The State of ISIS*, 97.

3. See Evan Solomon, "Ottawa Shooting: Stroller Mom Who Alerted RCMP to Zehaf-Bibeau Threat Speaks Out," CBC News (CBC.ca), June 5, 2015; Bruce Campion-Smith, "Parliament Attacker's Hand Wound Hindered Reloading, Source Says," *Toronto Star*, June 12, 2015; Ian MacLeod, "Six Minutes of Terror: OPP Report Details Hill Shooter's Rampage," *Ottawa Citizen*, June 3, 2015.

4. *National Post* (news.nationalpost.com), October 25, 2014.

5. Much of the biographical material is from Michael Friscolanti, "How Michael Zehaf-Bibeau's Life Spiraled from Privilege to Petty Crime and Drugs to, Eventually, Deadly Extremism—the Story of a Desperate Madman," *Maclean's*, October 30, 2014.

6. Stern and Berger, *The State of ISIS*, 97.

7. Stewart Bell, "ISIS Urges Jihadists to Attack Canadians: 'You Will Not Feel Secure in Your Bedrooms,'" *National Post*, September 21, 2014.

8. Ian Mulgrew, "Accused B.C. Terrorists Guilty of Murder Conspiracy in Bomb Plot," *Vancouver Sun*, June 2, 2015.

9. Ryan Maloney, "Tories' Latest Anti-Trudeau Ad Uses Images from ISIS Videos," Huffingtonpost.ca, June 25, 2015.

10. Alex Boutillier, "CSIS Highlights White Supremacist Threat ahead of Radical Islam," *Toronto Star*, March 15, 2015.

Chapter 9

1. Nahla Ayed and Xristos Katsiroubas, "Canadian in Algeria Gas Plant Attack, Attempted Suicide Bombing," CBC News (CBC.ca), January 16, 2014; Randy Richmond, "Homegrown London Terrorists' Final Hours Revealed," *London Free Press*, February 26, 2015.

2. Amanda Connolly, "Canada Lacks Data and Desire to Confront Radicalization, Senate Committee Told," *iPolitics*, February 23, 2015.

3. Brian Fishman, Prepared Testimony to the House Armed Services Committee, July 29, 2014. Full text available at http://docs.house.gov.

4. "Ottawa Imams 'Categorically' Denounce Local ISIL Member's Call for Violence in Canada," *Ottawa Citizen*, December 10, 2014.

5. Chris Cobb, "Report Fellow Students on the Road to Terrorism, Ottawa Imam Urges," *Ottawa Citizen*, December 8, 2015.

6. Syad Sohail Raza, Testimony, The Standing Senate Committee on National Security and Defence, November 24, 2014.

7. Dylan Robertson, "Ottawa ISIS Recruit Likely Had Identity Crisis: Psychologist," *National Post*, December 9, 2014.

8. Dr. Chris Kilford, "Canada's First De-radicalization Program: Work with Nazi Prisoners in the 1940s Taught Us Lessons," *Ottawa Citizen*, December 23, 2014.

9. Joel Westheimer, *What Kind of Citizen? Educating Our Children for the Common Good* (New York: Teachers College Press, 2015), 13.

10. Joel Westheimer, ed., *Pledging Allegiance: The Politics of Patriotism in America's Schools* (New York: Teachers College Press, 2007),15.

11. Ibid., 16.

12. Ibid., 17.

13. Ibid., 29.

14. Ibid., 31.

15. Kent Roach and Craig Forces, "Legislating in Fearful and Politicized Times," in Edward M. Iocobucci and Stephen J. Toope, *After the Paris Attacks: Responses in Canada, Europe, and around the Globe* (Toronto: University of Toronto Press, 2015), 45.

16. Craig Forcese, Testimony, The Standing Senate Committee on National Security and Defence, December 8, 2014.

17. Shirley Cuillierrier, Testimony, The Standing Senate Committee on National Security and Defence, November 17, 2014.

18. Reid Southwick, "Imam Wants Inquiry into Recruitment of Radicals," *Calgary Herald*, December 9, 2014.

19. Kanishka Project, Public Safety Canada (publicsafety.gc.ca).

20. "Ottawa's De-radicalization Focus Much Too Narrow, Reformed Skinhead Says," CBC.ca, March 5, 2015.

CHAPTER 10

1. "Canada to Tighten Borders, Aims to Disrupt 'Jihadist' Financing," Reuters, June 5, 2015.

2. Bill Graveland, "Damian Clairmont's Mother Says Harper Pushing 'Quick Fix' on Terrorism," Canadian Press, August 10, 2015.

3. "Air India Case Marred by 'Inexcusable' Errors," CBC.ca, June 17, 2010. The original page has been removed but a copy can be found at web.archive.org.

4. Stephen Maher, "Media Seeks Access to Sealed Documents Alleging Leaks in RCMP Security Unit That Protects Stephen Harper," *National Post*, December 9, 2014.

5. Craig Forcese, Bill C-51: Backgrounder no. 4: The Terrorism Propaganda Provisions, craigforcese.squarespace.com, February 27, 2015.

6. Ewen McAskill, "Drone Killing of British Citizens Marks Major Departure for UK," *The Guardian*, September 7, 2015.

7. De Libellis Famosis 5 Co. Rep. 125a, 77 Eng. Reports 250 (K.B. 1605).

8. Britain not only undermined Germany and its allies, but it also was able to maintain British morale and recruitment in the face of horrendous losses. British propaganda was directed at the United States to sway public opinion against Germany and toward the Allies. After the war, psychologists and political scientists wrote extensively about Britain's huge leap in propaganda science. I discuss this in my 2012 book *The Fog of War: Censorship of Canada's Media in World War II* (Vancouver: Douglas and McIntyre).

9. Richard Overy, *Interrogations: The Nazi Elite in Allied Hands, 1945* (New York: Viking, 2001); International Military Tribunal (Nuremberg), Judgment and Sentences, October 1, 1946.

10. Overy, *Interrogations*, 185–87.

11. Kingsbury Smith, *It Happened in 1946, 1947*, ed. Clark Kinnaird. Quoted in John Carey, *Eyewitness to History* (Cambridge, MA: Harvard University Press, 1987), 645–47.

12. UN Yearbook 344, Res. 290 (IV) (UN Pub. Sales No. 1951.I.24).

13. Rex v Higgins, 2 East 5, 102 Eng. Rep 269 (K.B. 1801).

14. Prosecutor v Ferdinand Nahimana, Jean-Bosco Barayagwiza, Hassan Ngeze, Case no. ICTR-99-52-T, Judgment and Sentence, Dec. 3, 2003, para 969 (Kearney 223).

15. For a description of the radio station's role in the genocide and translations of transcripts of its broadcasts before and during the genocide, see www.rwandafile.com/rtlm.

16. "Agreement on Non-Aggression and Good Neighbourliness between Mozambique and South Africa (Nkomati Talks)," United Nations Peacemaker (http://peacemaker.un.org), March 16, 1984.

17. Bilateral Agreement between the Republic of Afghanistan and the Islamic Republic of Pakistan on the Principle of Mutual Relations, in Particular on Non-interference and Non-intervention, 27 ILM 581 (1988).

18. Israel-Palestine Liberation Organization Agreement on the Gaza Strip and Jericho area, 33 ILM 622 (1994).

19. The provisions are quite blunt: "1. Any propaganda for war shall be prohibited by law. 2. Any advocacy of national, racial or religious hatred that constitutes incitement to discrimination, hostility or violence shall be prohibited by law." The full text can be found at www.ohchr.org.

20. A/C.3/SR.1079, para 2 (Mr Mello), at Kearney 132.

21. Rafal Rohozinski, Testimony, The Standing Senate Committee on National Security and Defence, November 24, 2014.

Chapter 11

1. Quoted in Vance, *Death So Noble*, 9.

2. Meghan Hurley, "'That Does Not Look Like a Terrorist': Maguire's Mother, Reportedly Dead in Syria," *National Post*, January 16, 2015.

3. Stuart Bell and Adrian Humphreys, "Death Toll of Canadian Jihadis Grows; Killed in Syria," *National Post*, January 15, 2015.

4. Stewart Bell, "Interpol Issues 'Red Notice' for John Maguire, the Ottawa Student Who Joined ISIL," *National Post*, April 21, 2015.

5. Aeden Helmer, "Terror Suspect Worked Closely with Ottawa Youth," *Ottawa Sun*, February 10, 2015.

6. "Damian Clairmont's Grandfather Blames CSIS for Inaction: Mustafa al-Gharib, Born Damian Clairmont, Left Calgary to Fight in Syria in November 2012," CBC News, January 16, 2014.

7. Interview with Christianne Boudreau, September 2, 2015. Background information from Stewart Bell, "Canadian Killed in Syria: Calgary Man, 22, Joined Fight after Converting to Islam," *National Post*, January 15, 2014.

8. Interview with Ahmed Hiris, *The National* (CBC), January 14, 2015.

9. Natalie Clancy, "ISIS Recruited Canadian Woman to Join Fight in Syria: 'We All Went to Work, Came Home, All Her Stuff Was Gone,' Sister Says," CBC News, February 25, 2015.

Chapter 12

1. Randall Marlin, *Propaganda and the Ethics of Persuasion*, 2nd edition (Peterborough, ON: Broadview Press, 2012), 224.

2. Michael Petrou, *Renegades: Canadians in the Spanish Civil War* (Vancouver: UBC Press, 2008), 176–77.

3. Brian Fishman, Prepared Testimony to the House Armed Services Committee July 29, 2014.

4. Prem Mahadevan, "Analyses in Security Policy," *The Neo-Caliphate of the "Islamic State,"* Centre for Security Studies (CSS) ETH Zurich no. 166, December 2014.

5. Testimony, The Standing Senate Committee on National Security and Defence, November 24, 2014.

6. Richard Barrett and Joanne J. Myers, "Foreign Fighters in Syria," Carnegie Council for Ethics in International Affairs, March 11, 2014.

7. Kimiko De Freytas-Tamura, "ISIS Defectors Reveal Disillusionment," *New York Times*, September 20, 2015.

8. Chris Greenwood, "Returning Islamist Fighters Offered 'Jihadi Rehab' Instead of Prosecution for Supporting Blood Thirsty Terrorist Groups despite May's Pledges," *Daily Mail*, November 10, 2014.

9. "The Battle of Ideas: Britain Is Struggling to Deal with a New Breed of Fundamentalist," *The Economist*, August 15, 2015.

10. Amy-Jane Gielen, "Supporting Families of Foreign Fighters: A Realistic Approach for Measuring the Effectiveness," *Journal for Deradicalization* 2 (Spring 2015).

11. Henry Oppenheimer, "Returning ISIS Fighters: Forgiveness or Punishment?" *Newsweek*, December 25, 2014.

12. Farish A. Noor and James M. Dorsey, "Responding to the Islamic State's Foreign Fighters: Retribution or Rehabilitation?," *RSIS Commentaries* no. 176 (Singapore: Nanyang Technological University, 2014). See also Edwin Bakker, Christopher Paulussen and Eva Entenmann, *Dealing with European Foreign Fighters in Syria: Governance Challenges & Legal Implications* (The Hague: International Centre for Counter-Terrorism, 2015), and Akil N. Awan, "What Happens When ISIS Comes Home?" *The National Interest* (www.thenationalinterest.org), September 19, 2014.

13. Nick Logan, "The Problem with Charging Canadian ISIS Fighters," Global TV (www.Globalnews.ca), December 12, 2014.

Chapter 13

1. Mark Anderson, "Terrorist Killings up by 80% in 2014, Report Says," *The Guardian*, November 18, 2015.

2. Jonathan Powell, *Talking to Terrorists* (London: The Bodley Head, 2014), 359.

3. Ibid., 320.

Appendix

1. See especially Amarnath Amarasingam, "The Clear Banner: Canadian Fighters in Syria: An Overview," Jihadology.net, March 4, 2015.

Index